¡VIVA MEXICO! ¡VIVA La INDEPENDENCIA!

D1040724

¡VIVA MEXICO! ¡VIVA LA INDEPENDENCIA!

CELEBRATIONS OF SEPTEMBER 16

Edited by

William H. Beezley • David E. Lorey

A Scholarly Resources Inc. Imprint
Wilmington, Delaware

Scholarly Resources Inc.
104 Greenhill Avenue
Wilmington, DE 19805-1897
www.scholarly.com

Library of Congress Cataloging-in-Publication Data

¡Viva México! ¡Viva la independencia! : celebrations of
    September 16 / edited by William H. Beezley and David E.
    Lorey
        p.   cm. — (Latin American silhouettes : studies in history
    and culture)
    Includes bibliographical references and index.
    ISBN 0-8420-2914-1 (alk. paper) — ISBN 0-8420-2915-X
(pbk. : alk. paper)
    1. Mexico—Social life and customs. 2. Independence Day
(Mexico). 3. Mexico—History—Wars of Independence, 1810–
1821—Centennial celebrations, etc. 4. Mexico—History—19th
century. 5. Mexico—History—20th century. I. Beezley, William H.
II. Lorey, David E. III. Latin American silhouettes.

F1210.V58   2000
972—dc21   00-041325

∞ The paper used in this publication meets the minimum requirements of the American National Standard for permanence of paper
for printed library materials, Z39.48, 1984.

We dedicate this book to our mothers-

and fathers-in-law: Page and Ned Champion,

Dawn and Ed Marges, Melinda Woodward, and Frank Meyer

We acknowledge the professional support cheerfully

given by the staff at Scholarly Resources,

especially Rick Hopper, Michelle Slavin,

and our crackerjack copy editor, Ann M. Aydelotte

Contents

Introduction
The Functions of Patriotic Ceremony in Mexico

On September 21, 1821, Agustín de Iturbide led his army into Mexico City, proclaiming an end to the rule of the armies of the Spanish king, Fernando VII, after a ten-year struggle. Iturbide's victory made Mexico independent, but it did not create a Mexican nation or make the residents of the independent country loyal to a new, Mexican nationality. Constructing a nation and a national identity remained problematic for decades after 1821 as the people went about the business of defining both what Mexico meant and what it meant to be Mexican. Heated debates over these issues and others resulted in civil and foreign wars, which overturned governments and unleashed political and cultural polemics that affected Mexicans from all walks of life.

During the early decades of Independence, government officials authorized such public constructions as fountains adorned with the new national symbols; they renamed streets, erected statues, and transformed even the calendar, with its holidays.[1] Critical questions arose: How and when should Independence be celebrated? Should the holiday commemorate the birth of the struggle (September 16) or its conclusion (September 21)? The questions betrayed political positions and revealed deeply held assumptions and practices. From its beginnings in the 1820s, the anniversary of Independence from Spain on either date has constituted one of the primary ritual occasions for debating the meaning of Mexico, discussing the form and orientation of the new nation, and stimulating patriotic sentiments. Independence Day (now celebrated on September 15 and 16) has long been the most important public festival in the civic ritual calendar and has bequeathed to Mexicans a rich tradition that is part creation myth, part official pomp, and part popular merrymaking. Of course, political leaders have attempted to mold the holiday in ways to cement loyalty both to the nation and to the regime in power. Of these efforts, the first has generally succeeded and the second has had only desultory success.

Today, Independence Day celebrations intrigue historians for several reasons. Such rituals constitute one of the few means accessible to the historian for viewing public expressions of private experience. This novel vantage point offers invaluable information about social, political, and cultural change: the evolving social structures, shifting political forces, and the gradual construction and codification of views about the past that characterize a period and reveal its unique ambience and flavor.

Celebrations in public places constituted a central part of the social environment of contending official and popular ideologies after Independence. Commemoration of patriotic dates served as a component of political consolidation as well as a vehicle for the institution of new political cultures.[2] Because both grand and small public celebrations provided one of the prime means for the construction of social meaning, they offer a window on the central preoccupation of the nineteenth and early twentieth centuries: Mexican efforts at forging a new nation. Public rituals involved large numbers of people who planned them, acted in them, witnessed them, reacted to them, and remembered them. A careful analysis of these rituals contributes to our understanding of the nineteenth and early twentieth centuries. Public festivities reveal how individuals participated in the activities conducted in the public sphere. Celebrations also demonstrate changing perceptions of social relations and cultural processes on the part of the people who flocked to these patriotic commemorations. The historical analysis of public discourse made evident in symbols, performances, music, and speeches allows access to otherwise inaccessible aspects of historical change.

Our attention to Independence Day celebrations in the present volume rests on two fundamental premises about Mexico after 1821. First, public spaces were extraordinarily important in the years before the 1940s, influencing and reflecting all aspects of daily life. What Juan Pablo Viqueira Albán discovered about the late eighteenth century also held true for the nineteenth and the early twentieth centuries: streets served not only for the circulation of goods and merchandise but also as the center of social life: "In the streets the inhabitants of the city worked, shopped, ate, took part in civil and religious ceremonies, strolled, played, and got drunk. In the streets one saw sex and death on a daily basis. The street made its way into all other kinds of activities: into shops, bars, artisans' workshops, government buildings and even into private houses."[3] Privacy, as we know it today, did not exist. Second, parades and other commemorative events on patriotic anniversaries involved large numbers of Mexicans and attracted massive crowds year after year; most people voluntarily and enthusiastically attended several gatherings each year. Moreover, the participants represented all segments of society, as contemporary drawings, photographs, and newspaper reports make clear. For Independence Day, regularly one quarter of Mexico City's population turned out to hear or to view the *grito* delivered by the president in the central plaza, the Zócalo, on the night of September 15. On the next day, tens of thousands of people attended, took part in, and discussed the parades in a spirited fashion.[4]

The studies gathered here demonstrate that the public celebrations of September 15–16 had three interrelated functions in the nineteenth and early twentieth centuries. Because we are so far removed from these functions in the late twentieth century, it is useful to underline their central importance in the social and political milieu of the period before 1940. First, in a country where perhaps no more than one-half of the urban population could read at the end of the nineteenth century, parades and other public spectacles filled the roles now dominated by newspapers, radio, television, magazines, comic books, and, increasingly, the Internet. Like these later communications media, rituals on the anniversary of Independence and other holidays informed the people of the most pressing national issues of the day: the milestones of state building, the evolution and resolution of social conflicts, and the emergence of new national heroes and villains. (In examining the creation of a national community, theorists have identified print media in early modern Europe and national theater in Renaissance England as critical instruments.[5]) Mexico's Independence Day and other holiday celebrations combined both print and performance to create an imagined community comprised of those who were taking part in the holiday everywhere in the nation. The major difference between these events and their present-day mass-media counterparts comes in location: the former took place in public spaces, whereas now media information is generally received by individuals or small groups in private spaces.

Second, Independence Day parades served as public theater. In this capacity, they reflected the social structure and presented appropriate norms of social interaction, proper behavior in the public arena, and the relationship of individuals to the government. The manner in which the organizers chose to observe Independence Day reveals the period's "dramaturgical kit, [its] 'settings,' 'props,' costumes, roles, script formulas, and . . . 'styles' of action and gesture."[6] Through these celebrations, the organizers enhanced the development of two new points of reference and two new actors on the Mexican stage: the individual possessed of a national identity, and the state expressed in national institutions.

Third, and finally, Independence Day festivities provided a medium for informal education, sketching on the canvas of the public sphere national values, glorifying specific historical events and individuals, and celebrating government plans and achievements. During the colonial period, the Roman Catholic clergy organized festivals to reinforce their didactic aims, and then nineteenth- and early twentieth-century government leaders used civil festivals to convert the people to national ideals and ends.[7] Celebrations of September 16, in their educational role, were a "textbook" of national history, with two advantages over formal education: the participants did not need to be literate to understand and evaluate the messages offered to them; and celebrations had a dramatic quality—the excitement, the crowds, the smells, the food and drinks, and the holiday atmosphere—not possible in formal education.[8] Moreover, these public festivities were usually inexpensive and reached far out into the countryside from the urban centers in which they most often were created. As in formal education, the most important effect of Independence Day observances was to teach values, particularly encouraging patriotism and legitimating new governments.[9]

In outlining these functions, we should not forget that the explicit purpose of Independence Day parades was entertainment. Just as we are far removed from the functioning of public celebrations as media, as theater, and as informal education, we are also far removed from their fun. Nowadays, holidays are generally commemorated in private homes and in small groups; their character has been overwhelmed by the two-day weekend, a rather recent introduction that has largely obviated or at least undermined the need for frequent religious or civic holidays. How different was the period from the 1820s to the 1840s, when public festivities marked the calendar with episodes of pleasure-taking by communities small and large! For thousands of participants and onlookers, Independence Day events were an annual high point of leisure and excitement.

Because they performed the functions outlined here, public patriotic celebrations merit close examination. Just as the mass media or public education are at the center of economic and social processes and now receive serious study, the parallel social process of previous times must be carefully analyzed. As we attempt to understand the different historical world of Mexico in the nineteenth and early twentieth centuries, we must shift our focus to respect the conventions of that world and examine it on its own terms. Celebrations in the public sphere demand a prominent place in this historical inquiry.

In the ten chapters that follow, historians from Mexico, Great Britain, and the United States approach patriotic commemorations as primary texts. The records of these celebrations—painted images of Independence themes, engravings of floats, photographs of parades, paper trails of official plans, ephemeral arches of branches and flowers, banners and placards, and reports of popular participation—undergo the familiar processes of evaluation and exegesis. Although the sources are sometimes distinct from the customary archives and statistics, the methodology remains the same as the classic techniques of historical investigation. These historians go about the business of disentangling the various strands of the ritual fabric of past celebrations and of highlighting interconnections among the threads. They interpret the constituent parts in the historical context, often adding a new dimension or contributing rich subtleties to general interpretations.

The first essays in the volume examine early celebrations of Independence and the debates about the holiday. In the opening chapter, Isabel Fernández and Carmen Nava reveal in their essay the rich possibilities of combining both source materials and analytical methods of history and art history. In doing so, the authors underline the importance of the formation of abstract values, rather than just concrete symbolic formulations, through public ritual and national icons. Moreover, their essay examines the events surrounding Independence that would become the stuff of later celebrations. Michael Costeloe discusses the earliest celebrations of Independence after its momentous achievement. His research reveals the fierce debate over the significance of various dates in the long struggle against Spain and the conflict to establish the appropriate date to celebrate. Sergio Cañedo Gamboa and Verónica Zárate Toscano add regional dimensions to the discussion launched by Costeloe's contribution. In his examination of the September 16 commemorations in the city of San Luis Potosí, Cañedo Gamboa offers relief from the facile conclusion that events in Mexico City represent the entire nation. Obviously they did not, and Cañedo Gamboa highlights clear differences in the meaning of Independence to people in the northern part of the nation. The suburban town of San Angel, located within the Federal District, is the location for Verónica Zárate Toscano's examination of Independence celebrations during the troubled times of the 1860s. Her essay establishes continuities with the patterns of celebration in the national capital and illustrates local variations. In an intriguing discussion, Zárate shows how Independence Day offered an opportunity to express opposition to Emperor Maximilian, who held power only as a result of the French occupation of central Mexico from 1862 to 1867. (Readers who want to compare the discussion of suburban celebrations with those sponsored by the imperial government in the national capital should consult the article in *Mexican Studies* by Robert H. Duncan.[10])

Javier Rodríguez Piña, in Chapter Five, demonstrates how interpretations of Independence structured the classic nineteenth-century political rivalry among Liberals and Conservatives. His essay shows the ways in which the competing centralist and federalist, and national and regional, ideas of the nation found expression. William Beezley offers a brief examination of the Independence holiday directed by the president but celebrated locally in Puebla in 1867, and he compares it to the capital city's celebrations in 1883. These festivals dramatically revealed the underlying political principles promoted by Benito Juárez, and the nature of the Liberalism he represented; Beezley then offers a look at the changing emphasis during the early years of the Porfirian era.

With the greater centralization of political and economic authority beginning with Porfirio Díaz in 1876 and later as the revolutionaries reconstructed Mexican society, the government took a more active part in creating national patterns of patriotic celebrations. The essay by Nora Pérez-Rayón E. places the celebration of Independence Day in 1900 within the context of other civic festivals of the time. Her choice of year is particularly well suited to the themes addressed by the other authors: an awareness of the turning of the century moved commentators to reflect on the overall significance of Mexican events and personages of the nineteenth century and the future of the nation. Observances of Independence Day in 1900 give us an unusually direct view of evolving nationalism. A decade later, Mauricio Tenorio examines the elaborate, costly, and monumental celebrations of the centennial of Padre Miguel Hidalgo's 1810 appeal to the people to sever their colonial relationship with Spain. The *Centenario* took place before guests from across the globe and displayed Mexico's history and culture to this attentive audience. However, within months of the national fiesta, the Díaz regime had been forced into exile as revolutionaries took power. In his essay, Tenorio captures the art, architec-

ture, and performances of the celebrations and also identifies the iro-
nies of honoring an Aztec past while ordering contemporary indigenous peoples to dress in the European style or be excluded from the
major events.

Elaine Lacy, in Chapter Nine, skillfully describes the events of
the 1921 Centennial of the completion of Independence. Because this
celebration took place as the leaders of the Revolution were attempting to reconstruct society, they seized on the occasion to relate the
struggle for independence with the struggle for revolutionary justice.
Many of the Revolution's themes—the recognition of the indigenous
peoples, for example—found expression in the celebration, in this
case with the crowning of La India Bonita. In the final chapter, David
Lorey focuses on the relationship between two national festivals in
the decades following the hostilities of the Revolution of 1910. Lorey,
like Pérez-Rayón in her essay, places the celebration of September 16
into the larger ritual context of the evolving festival calendar. In a
case study of the commemoration of November 20 (Revolution Day)
between 1920 and 1940, he argues that this new festival was counter-
poised to traditional celebrations of September 16. Try as they might,
officials could not bring the century-old ritual of the *grito* under their
control as traditional disorder continued to reign. New rituals became
the locus of official attempts to demarcate the pre- and postrevolutionary worlds, distinguishing between traditional and modern ways of
celebrating in public spaces. The imposition of order in the public
sphere on Revolution Day served in particular to create the notion of
an orderly, official revolutionary process, presenting to the public
mind a nation very different from that of the chaotic, contradictory
period from 1910 to 1920.

This volume ends with the outbreak in 1937 of World War II,
which involved the Western Hemisphere by the end of 1941. The world
war era marked the golden age of radio, movies, comic books, and
recorded music in Mexico. In the capital city, President Lázaro
Cárdenas spoke his Independence Day message into a radio micro-
phone on September 15, 1938. For the first time, Mexicans who were
not present in the Zócalo could hear the message. From this time
forward, celebrations took second place to these new forms of communication. Judging by the numbers of participants and spectators,
the popular enthusiasm for public celebrations waned. Additionally,
Mexicans increasingly began to commemorate their holidays away
from the public areas, preferring to celebrate in private homes and in
the new tourist resorts.

The selections gathered in this volume reveal several general find-ings about the celebrations of September 16. In sketching these con-clusions, we want to answer the following question: What do historians learn from this attention to patriotic commemoration that they did not know before about Mexico? In applying this litmus test for any new historical focus, we hope to be informative, even provocative, and to suggest some new topics of research. First, examining people from many different walks of life as they celebrate national holidays provides us with a snapshot of daily life unparalleled in its richness and social complexity. Debates over holiday meanings and metaphors add to our picture of the issues that informed daily political discus-sions across the civic spectrum and throughout social sectors. This snapshot gives us a view of both the main currents and the lesser eddies of life in the nineteenth and early twentieth centuries.

Second, the themes of everyday life as revealed in the Septem-ber 16 celebrations were significant issues—in fact, the major issues of the period. The September 16 celebrations address tensions that plagued society for a century after the break with Spain: the instabil-ity of politics, especially the problem of legitimate succession; the weakness of civil authority compared to the military and the Church; the conflict of central versus regional power, usually defined as the Liberal-Conservative struggle, which emerged for the first time dur-ing the Independence period;[11] the role of the government in every-day life; and the creation of both a nation and a national identity after three hundred years of identification with Spain. How striking and significant it is that ordinary people were conversant with the issues of the day.[12] The lessons of parades and other commemorative events show that the people, even though most of them could not read, were remarkably well informed about pressing political and social mat-ters. The conclusions of the contributors to this volume comprise a vivid commentary on the self-conscious and articulate views of the general population that, taken together, represent in many ways the common knowledge of nineteenth-century Mexico.

Third, Independence Day celebrations not only suggested how society should look but also actually shaped the nineteenth-century and early twentieth-century worlds. They actively contributed to the creation of Mexico and Mexicans by crafting dominant visual im-ages, creating rhetorical conventions and conceits, serving as one is-sue of debate among Liberals and Conservatives, providing a milieu for ideological consolidations, and presenting a new national history. Patriotic rituals performed in public, in other words, did not form the superstructure of Marxian terminology. Rather, they provided the symbolic context and performance habits that encompassed other activities, such as political and economic ones. This finding sheds light on the reflecting-shaping dichotomy that sometimes troubles historians of informal institutions. Cultural historians in particular have confronted the issues of whether the cultural phenomena they seek to understand are "mere reflections" of more profound infrastructural relationships, or whether in fact such phenomena play an active, determining role in historical change. The evidence brought to bear in the following chapters suggests that the counterpoising of the two concepts-—reflecting and shaping—-is unnecessary. In fact, holiday parades, images, floats, speeches, and contestation all functioned as mirrors that, because of their ability to reflect social reconfigurations, shaped behavior, historical understandings, and identity.[13]

Scholars who have assessed the implications of public symbolic usages have gradually transformed our understanding not only of nineteenth-century Mexico but also of historical processes in general. In particular, studies of public ritual reconsider models of historical change that assigned primacy to economic forces. Increasingly, they suggest a more elaborate multicausal model that assigns to cultural transformation a central role, even in such apparently self-referential realms as economic policymaking, judicial reform, and human rights issues. The essays in this volume advance the view of the centrality of cultural issues in history and enhance our understanding by providing concrete evidence and thorough analysis to a broad audience.

Celebrations of Independence continue today, almost two hundred years after the struggle began. Even though modified by the mass media, September 15–16 remains the most important civic celebration in Mexico. Now, in the capital city, the president steps onto the balcony at the National Palace on September 15 and at 11 P.M. rings the parish bell brought from the town of Dolores Hidalgo, Guanajuato. He then repeats the speech of Padre Hidalgo calling for independence to television and radio audiences throughout Mexico. Once during his six-year term, he travels to Dolores Hidalgo to perform this ritual. We do not know with certainty that he rings the same bell that Padre Hidalgo rang, and we certainly do not know if he repeats the same words that Hidalgo spoke. But, in a real sense, it no longer matters, because Mexicans across the nation repeat with him words that express their sense of national identity, ending with: "¡Viva México! ¡Viva la Independencia!"

Notes

1. See Shannon L. Baker, "Santa Anna's Legacy: *Caudillismo* in Early Republican Mexico" (Ph.D. diss., Texas Christian University, 1999), esp. chapter 2, for a discussion of these early campaigns to foster Mexican nationalism.

2. Eric Hobsbawm and Terence Ranger, eds., *The Invention of Tradition* (New York: Cambridge University Press, 1983), 12, 13.

3. Juan Pedro Viqueira Albán, *¿Relajados o reprimidos? Diversiones publicas y vida social en la ciudad de México durante el Siglo de las Luces* (Mexico City: Fondo de Cultura Económica, 1987), 133. See the English translation of this volume, *Propriety and Permissiveness in Bourbon Mexico* (Wilmington, DE: Scholarly Resources, 1999).

4. For a discussion of different types of celebrations, see Hobsbawm and Ranger, *Invention of Tradition*, 9.

5. Benedict Anderson, *Imagined Communities: Reflections on the Origin and Spread of Nationalism* (London: Verso, 1991); Joseph Roach, *Cities of the Dead: Circum-Atlantic Performance* (New York: Columbia University Press, 1996).

6. Rhys Isaac, *The Transformation of Virginia, 1740–1790* (Chapel Hill: University of North Carolina Press, 1982), 350.

7. See, for example, William E. French, *"Progreso Forzado*: Workers and the Inculcation of the Capitalist Work Ethic in the Parral Mining District," in William H. Beezley, Cheryl English Martin, and William E. French, eds., *Rituals of Rule, Rituals of Resistance: Public Celebrations and Popular Culture in Mexico* (Wilmington, DE: Scholarly Resources, 1994), 191–212.

8. Christopher Lane, *The Rights of Rulers: Ritual in Industrial Societies: The Soviet Case* (Cambridge: Cambridge University Press, 1981), 61 and passim; Beezley et al., *Rituals of Rule*, 2.

9. Eugen Weber, *Peasants into Frenchmen: The Modernization of Rural France* (Stanford: Stanford University Press, 1976), 332.

10. "Political Legitimation and Maximilian's Second Empire in Mexico, 1864–1867," *Mexican Studies/Estudios Mexicanos* 12, no. 1 (Winter 1996): 27–66.

11. Guy P. C. Thomson discusses popular strains of Liberalism and Conservatism in the Mexican countryside in the nineteenth century. See *Patriotism, Politics, and Popular Liberalism in Nineteenth-Century Mexico: Juan Francisco Lucas and the Puebla Sierra* (Wilmington, DE: Scholarly Resources, 1999).

12. See Peter F. Guardino, *Peasants, Politics, and the Formation of Mexico's National State: Guerrero, 1800–1857* (Stanford: Stanford University Press, 1996).

13. See Steven Haber's comments on historians' approaches to culture in *Mexican Studies/Estudios Mexicanos* 13, no. 2 (Summer 1997): 18. Haber emphasizes that informal institutions establish "the implicit rules of behavior and interaction" . . . [and] "permit and bound economic and political activity."

CHAPTER ONE

Images of Independence in the Nineteenth Century
The *Grito de Dolores*, History and Myth

ISABEL FERNÁNDEZ TEJEDO
*CARMEN NAVA NAVA**

What historical events substantiate the imaginary fabric of the celebrations known as El Grito? How should we approach this complex system of ceremonies, rites, symbols, and theatrical reenactments that establish the *grito* as the foundational myth of our nation, of our homeland? In its present form, the *grito* ceremony stems from the reinterpretation and redefinition process involving a historical episode that took place at daybreak in the village of Dolores on September 16, 1810. Successive generations have fused history[1] and myth,[2] thus giving this event the status of "primordial revelation" or "exemplary model." This circumstance has gradually transformed the *grito* into the unifying, restructuring nucleus of other historical events also commemorated during the *fiestas patrias*, or Independence celebrations.

*The authors are deeply indebted to Patricia Ayala and her family for their encouragement in our efforts, through making available to us Lic. Roberto Ayala Gastelúm's treasured collection of books on the Mexican Independence wars. We gratefully acknowledge the assistance and suggestions of Ricardo and Carlos Alday of the Archivo General de la Nación, Mexico City, in locating the iconographic material for this essay. We also thank Isabel Guerrero, Saúl Moreno, and Gerardo León as well as the members of the Area de Investigaciones Históricas y Sociales (AIHS) for their valuable technical support.

This text was translated from the Spanish by Margarita González Aredondo and Elena Murray de Parodi.

We do not regard history and myth as antinomic terms. To be sure, during the past two centuries, as Mircea Eliade so masterfully documented, the myth has come to "denote everything that cannot actually exist."[3] However, despite the differences that distinguish history from myth, they are both representations of the society that forges them, and "in their forms and themes, they maintain a relationship with the fundamental structures which, at a given moment and place, organize and distinguish the distribution of power, the organization of society, and the economy of personality."[4]

As to the infiltration of mystifying elements into historical works, we need only mention the use of concepts such as progress and evolution or categories such as scientific revolution. Historiography is rife with examples of methodological resources used to reconstruct and shape historical events in order to either magnify or minimize the importance of a given historical figure or social group.[5] Furthermore, it is common knowledge that in order for a myth to be captured by the collective imagination, its fabric must necessarily exhibit certain identifiable, discernable historical facts. Every archetypical personage, every "primordial action," and every exemplary model encompass distinctive and contextual aspects that enable whoever appropriates or espouses them to either endow them with significance or to redefine them. As Alfredo López Austin has pointed out:

> myth is also a synthesized expression of man's occupations and preoccupations in his daily contact with his fellow men and with nature. As an instrument, the myth teaches, imposes, or supports certain arguments and justifies certain forms of behavior. It is, in brief, much more than a mere anecdote. It is an institution imbued with tremendous vitality, capable of combining conjectures with practical knowledge.[6]

It is our purpose here to illustrate how, throughout the process of structuralization, stratification, and redefinition, the *grito de Dolores* was gradually transformed into the unifying nucleus of the series of ceremonies, rites, symbols, and images comprising the national Independence celebrations. The *fiestas patrias* as a whole condense two significant events in the War of Independence: its beginning and its culmination. The first episode, which took place at daybreak on September 16, 1810, was Father Miguel Hidalgo y Costilla's exhortation to a general insurrection in pursuit of liberty, justice, and social equality. The second, which occurred on September 27, 1821, was the arrival in Mexico City of the victorious Trigarante Army (the Insurgents'

Three Guarantees), led by Agustín de Iturbide and symbolizing the end of the Independence wars and the consummation of political separation from Spain.

Despite its cohesive attributes, the *grito* symbolically evokes the subversion of the political status quo, the social upheaval and the first step taken toward eradicating the colonialist order. Thus, the *grito* represents a regenerative "primordial chaos" whose mise-en-scène demands the appropriate surroundings and conditions. Consequently, the *grito* is a celebration with its own distinctive characteristics and contents far removed from the official ceremonies.

During the official ceremony there appears to be a sense of harmony between the officiant in charge of the *grito* and the celebrants—the multitude who responds. However, an unmistakable tension erupts as soon as the official part of the ceremony is over and the *verbena* begins—the real fiesta of and for the people.[7] The public takes advantage of this revelry to re-create the regenerating "primordial chaos" that the official rites and ceremonies strive to exorcise and control.[8] Upon celebrating freedom, Mexicans display their creativity in a complex mix of physical, visual, and acoustical symbolism, easily perceived in the gestures, attire, and objects devised by them to flaunt their patriotism. Hence, during the *grito* festivities, the popular collective memory clearly expresses its delight in portents, in the unique, in extravagance, in the exalted nature of the event itself, in irreverence, in its glorified solemnity, in its impassioned spontaneity, and in the comic and the grotesque.[9]

The analysis of the *grito* festivities, then, provides infinite possibilities for understanding the different ways in which Mexicans symbolically represent their idea of freedom. This still holds true, despite the fact that for the past century the official ceremony has remained virtually unchanged, thus giving the impression that year after year the crowd mechanically repeats "the same coded gestures, the same verbal pronouncements, and the exchange of key roles in perfect reciprocity."[10]

Together, but Separate

In the secular calendar, the 16th of September officially marks the anniversary of Mexico's Independence. At present, on this date, the chief representatives of the Executive Power at every governmental level initiate the ceremonies by placing funeral wreaths at the monuments dedicated to the heroes of Independence. They then preside over a solemn ceremony, complete with guest speakers, choral music, and the presentation of awards to the winners of contests pertaining to these particular holidays. Depending on the locale, this event culminates in a colorful parade made up mostly of schoolchildren and adolescents and occasionally complemented by a procession of colorful floats or by military units.[11] However, the *grito* itself, the genuine popular celebration, takes place on the previous night, starting at eleven o'clock. At that precise moment, the president rings the bell that usually hangs from the main balcony of the National Palace and immediately gives a series of cheers extolling a select group of national heroes (who vary according to the current circumstances in Mexico) and Independence.[12] The cheers uttered by the corresponding authorities are resoundingly echoed by the masses. This histrionic show, at once dramatic and joyful, is the re-creation of the "primordial act" that serves as the framework for the foundational myth of the nation's Independence.

The echoes of the *grito* have barely died down when suddenly an ear-splitting racket fills the air. Armed with noisemakers, whistles, horns, and firecrackers, the multitude marks the transition between the official ceremony and the beginning of the popular fiesta itself. In some places, shooting pistols into the air (as still occurs in Querétaro's Sierra Gorda) attests to the violation of the limits that authorities attempt to impose on the festivities, dating back to at least 1825. It was then that the Citizens' Council who organized the first post-Independence era celebrations in Mexico City banned the sale of liquor and begged the revelers to avoid at all costs any kind of "disturbance or incident that could disrupt public peace and order," despite the fact that its main objective was purportedly to allow for "the population's free expression of their patriotic feelings."[13]

The boisterous enthusiasm marking the transition between the official part of the ceremony and the public celebration is followed by the *verbena*, the popular fiesta, with the traditional participation of musical groups and *ranchero* (folk) singers who tirelessly perform until daybreak. In small villages and remote cities, the municipal governments provide free rum punch, *atole*, and tamales.

The official *grito* ceremony has remained virtually unmodified since 1896, when the Independence bell was placed above the National Palace's main entrance, over the presidential balcony. It can be safely said that this event is the boundary line dividing the period before and after the celebrations of the *grito*. We will subsequently discuss this aspect at length. For the time being, we will begin by describing the events constituting the historical undertones of the festivities themselves.

"The Three of Us Agreed to Give the *Grito*"

The word *grito* (shout, cry) as used by the Insurgents was a rallying cry, an exhortation to rebellion and sedition. At first, it was a literary metaphor, probably employed to preserve the clandestine nature of the conspiracy. Its permanence and perpetuation in the designation of the patriotic celebration have been endorsed by historiography, literary images, and commemorative works of art, but above all, it is because the word *grito* was precisely the term used by Father Miguel Hidalgo to describe his call to arms in search of freedom and justice.

During the fabrication process of the *grito* as a foundational myth, the personalities of the precursors of the freedom movement and the events that took place that early morning of September 16, 1810, have undergone so many restructuralizations, stratifications, and redefinitions that, at this point in time, it is practically impossible to reconstruct these events with a reasonable degree of accuracy. By adhering to eyewitness accounts and testimonies, we will proceed by prioritizing those elements of this episode that have been consolidated into the dramatized representation of the celebration[14]—that is, the *grito* as an inducement to sedition, its protagonists, the watchwords uttered during the course of the harangue, and the place where it occurred.

Let us now reconstruct the event itself. In the documents pertaining to the court-martial proceedings dated May 7, 1811, in Chihuahua, Father Hidalgo's reply to the question concerning the initial acts of insurrection and the identity of its originators is recorded in the third person:

> Three or four days prior to the 16th [of September], [Hidalgo] received word that [Captain Ignacio] Allende had been betrayed, for which reason he [Hidalgo] summoned him [Allende] to the [village of] Dolores in order to resolve the matter, but nothing was accomplished on the 14th and the 15th, until, at 2:00 A.M. on the 16th, Juan Aldama arrived, informing him [Hidalgo] that his confederates had been captured in Querétaro, in view of which the *three of them immediately agreed to give the* grito, summoning for this purpose, about ten of their subordinates.[15]

There is no doubt that to "give the *grito*" is used in this testimony as the proclamation or initiation of the rebellion. Upon establishing the betrayals and the capture of his confederates as precedents to the events of the 16th of September, Father Hidalgo presents the case as an act of self-defense. Furthermore, the inclusion of Captain Ignacio Allende, a professional soldier, and Juan Aldama, councilman for the village of San Miguel el Grande, in the "agreement" or pact prior to the call to arms, reveals Hidalgo's plan to clearly establish that the leadership of the movement fell to the criollos,* representatives of the three principal institutions in New Spain: the clergy, the militia, and the local city councils.

This statement, when linked to the section of his deposition dated May 7—"and joined by the Indians and farmers who, since it was Sunday had attended Mass, the Insurgents attempted to head for San Miguel el Grande to pursue their project"—implies that the agreement undertaken by Hidalgo, Allende, and Aldama to take up arms against an unpopular and unjust order was also part of a popular plan supported by an extensive network of followers who, sooner or later, would continue the struggle that had begun in Dolores. He declares that he "attempted" to reach San Miguel el Grande with his troops, as if it were not common knowledge that Allende's supporters there, some of whom were extremely wealthy, were legion.[16] In any case, the repercussions of the *grito* were obvious, since the trial involving the "*principales* of the insurrection" was taking place in Chihuahua. Thus, Hidalgo contradicted the Spanish authorities' accusation regarding the criollos' inability to handle government matters and plan their own future.

On his part, Ignacio Allende sought to imbue his own actions, and those of his co-defendants, with political overtones by establishing a sequence of events indicative of their respect and loyalty vis-à-vis the Spanish monarchical traditions, customs, and legal procedures. His statement regarding what occurred in Father Hidalgo's home is specific and concise: "*the three [of us], Aldama, Hidalgo, and the deponent, who is under interrogation*, held consultations . . . and it was resolved, and also accepted by don Mariano Hidalgo and don Santos Villa, to summon, that same night, all those denizens who were, or who appeared to be, prepared to follow them."

Upon including Father Mariano Hidalgo and don Santos Villa in the pact made in Hidalgo's home, Allende implies that the consensus

---

*Persons born in Spanish America but of Spanish descent. [Translators' note]

of opinion among the prominent criollos, both civilians and military men, consisted in an actual convocation rather than a mere proclamation. He clearly states his intention to summon the "denizens"—people from the rural and urban middle class—in order to disassociate himself from the "rabble" who, despite his reservations, adhered to the cause. Thus, he justified his decision to take up arms as a last resort, since it had been impossible to convince the Spanish authorities by any other means that they should undertake reforms aimed at a just and equitable treatment of New Spain's criollos.[17]

Juan Aldama, who at 34 was the youngest of the rebellion's leaders and surely inspired by one of Father Hidalgo's favorite sayings— "Holding your tongue may save your neck"—interjected certain misleading details in his description of the events and tried to convince the court that the fear of losing his life drove him away from the law:

> while the deponent [Aldama] was drinking chocolate . . . the priest addressed everyone: "Gentlemen, we are lost, there is no alternative but to go after the gachupines* . . . to which the defendant asked: "Sir, what are you going to do?" Everyone [all those present in Hidalgo's house] gradually rose to their feet. . . . the priest and Allende urged the defendant: "Quickly, Aldama!" And for fear of being killed he also rose and went with them.

Aldama, anxious to obtain a light sentence, omitted his role in the agreement but neither denied it nor provided an alternative version; he merely tried to convey the impression that he, too, was a victim of the "heroic resolution," as José María Lafragua was to state years later, in reference to that night's events. In short, Allende's and Hidalgo's testimonies demonstrate that the expression, "to give the *grito*," refers to a concerted decision to convoke an armed struggle.[18]

The Voice of Freedom

Two additional testimonies describe the manner in which the actions following the *grito de Dolores*—the "primordial act"—were gradually adopted by popular tradition. In his memoirs, Pedro José Sotelo

---

*Now regarded as a pejorative term for Spaniards, gachupines originally was used to describe people born in Spain. The word is believed to derive from the Nahuatl *cactli* (shoe) and *txopini* (something that pierces), which resulted in *catzopini* (men with spurs), to describe the conquistadors. It was during the struggle for Independence that gachupines took on the derogatory connotations that it has today. [Translators' note]

reports that since 1809, Father Hidalgo had apprised him and other artisans "of a very important venture . . . extremely secret."[19] It involved taking up arms in order to implement the plan to abolish the gachupín government, to obtain greater freedoms, "and to enjoy the fruits of our soil." For several months the preparations for the rebellion were conducted in complete secrecy until midnight on September 15, when Allende notified the parish priest (Hidalgo) that the "venture was on the verge of collapse, and that in one instant all their efforts would be futile." In the face of this revelation, Sotelo adds that Hidalgo immediately notified the artisans, musicians, and farmers who had already been contacted, and that while they were on their way, Hidalgo rapped out to Allende: "We have no choice, *we must give the rallying cry for freedom right now.*"[20] In Sotelo's view, the likelihood that "the venture" would fail was the spark that prompted Hidalgo, at that moment, to take matters into his own hands and to proclaim the purposes and objectives of the armed struggle.

Sotelo recollects how and where Hidalgo made public his determination to declare war on the Spanish regime while addressing his congregation. According to this witness, the worshippers who were arriving for Sunday Mass were surprised at the commotion caused by the mobilization. Therefore, several parishioners gathered around Hidalgo's house, and

> *were harangued* by the parish priest through his sitting-room window exhorting them to embark upon the struggle for our independence, and, *courageously raising his voice, he said*: "Long live Our Lady of Guadalupe, Long live Independence!" . . . There was a tremendous clamor from the people, who kept cheering the priest and shouting, "Down with the gachupines!"[21]

In his memoirs, Pedro García, a resident of San Miguel el Grande, recollects other details already consigned to popular tradition.[22] In his writings, García transforms the meeting mentioned by Allende into a select coterie at Hidalgo's house and views the consensus to launch the insurrection as a courageous act on Hidalgo's part. According to García, the latter proposed his idea of capturing the Spaniards and locking them up in prison so that they would be forced to renounce their privileged status. In view of the objections and misgivings voiced by his confederates, who feared dreadful reprisals from the Spanish authorities, Hidalgo countered:

> That's exactly how children behave; they never weigh the circumstances of a given situation nor consider the most insignificant de-

tails. Possessing the ability to consolidate them, they can transform them into a formidable whole. At the rallying cry: "Down with the gachupines!" tomorrow everything will be in our favor. Now, let's get down to business without losing any more time, for now, we must pocket our fear.[23]

From García's perspective, as Sotelo's, the *grito* was a willful, calculated plan of Hidalgo's to capitalize on the popular animosity against the Spaniards as leverage to provoke social and political changes. In order to enhance Hidalgo's audacity and courage, García has Hidalgo addressing his confederates as a mentor who reprimands a group of children terrified at the consequences of their temerity. García, on the other hand, depicts Hidalgo's harangue as a means of informing and explaining the motives and objectives of his cause to the masses. Therefore, amid the flurry of activity surrounding the insurrectionists,

> it seemed to that respectable parish priest that it was the right time to address the multitude *informing them of his reasons for embarking upon such a new and unfamiliar movement.* He stepped out into the gallery and explained: "Neither the king nor tribute exists for us any longer. . . . In a few hours you will see me marching in front of men who pride themselves on being free . . . the cause is Holy and God will protect it. . . . Long live, then, the Virgin of Guadalupe! Long live the America for which we are going to fight!"
> To this, the multitude enthusiastically responded in kind. . . . That spirit of freedom spread through that meeting with lightning speed.[24]

Despite the discrepancies between José Sotelo's and Pedro García's versions, it is clear that both men viewed the *grito de Dolores* as a decision exclusively conceived and executed by Father Hidalgo, outwardly expressed in the form of a harangue. For Sotelo, its purpose was to urge the people to join the struggle in defense of religion and independence. The people's thunderous response and cheers to Hidalgo's proclamation denote a tacit agreement between the leader of the insurrection and his grounds for popular support. Sotelo exonerates Father Hidalgo from any intentions of fomenting racial hatred upon attributing the phrase, "Death to the gachupines!" to "the tremendous clamor" stemming from an anonymous source. In García's case, the harangue was a brief summary of the aims—indeed, the program—of the armed struggle. According to García, the sheer force of the "spirit of freedom" embodied by Hidalgo had an electrifying effect on the multitude, who, upon enthusiastically approving the watchwords uttered by the priest of Dolores, also envisioned a new horizon in this "unfamiliar movement" that was beginning to take shape and to gain momentum before their very eyes.

To this day, there is controversy regarding the watchwords and rallying cries uttered by Hidalgo during his initial tirade. A detailed analysis would require a separate paper. Suffice it to say that the vice-regal authorities themselves made it their business to record the political slogans relative to the insurrection and therefore accorded special attention to the inscriptions printed on a banner confiscated from the Insurgents.[25] To the image of Our Lady of Guadalupe were added: "Long live religion! Long live Our Most Holy Mother of Guadalupe! Long live Fernando VII! Long live America and down with bad government!"[26] On the other hand, Ernesto Lemoine's well-documented research suggests with solid arguments that during its initial phase, the *grito*'s political watchwords were literally: "Long live the Catholic religion! Long live Fernando VII! Long live our homeland! May our holy patroness, the Holy Virgin of Guadalupe, live and reign forever in this American continent! Down with bad government!"[27]

Popular tradition has transformed the harangue and the mass response to its slogans into virtual synonyms of the *grito*, since they involve the anonymous multitudes in the quest for their freedom and in the construction of their own destiny. Therefore, the exhortation has remained implicit in the harangue, which, in turn, seems to have become the predominant ritual in the official ceremony, despite the circumstantial slogans uttered by the corresponding authorities.

There is also a long debate on whether the bells actually rang for Mass on the dawn of September 16, or not. A detailed description of this particular chapter in the *grito*'s history would be lengthy indeed. In fact, it was Lucas Alamán, probably in order to reinforce his thesis that Father Hidalgo lacked any religious scruples, who was one of the principal propagators of the version that the original harangue leading up to the 1810 revolt took place in the parish church's atrium.[28] Other sources repeat it without question; and when it was immortalized in the monumental work, *México a través de los siglos*,[29] it has, to this day, been regarded as incontrovertible fact. In view of the prestigious nature of this authority, little consideration has been granted to the emphatic assertion by General Pedro García, a witness of that time, who maintained in writing that on the 16th of September "there was no pealing of bells, nor much less, plundering of Spaniards."[30]

After noon on September 16, Hidalgo, Allende, and Aldama left the village of Dolores, leading an army largely made up of Indians and mestizos armed with lances, machetes, rakes, slings, and sticks. This improvised militia was headed for San Miguel el Grande to swell its ranks and obtain greater financial resources. Hidalgo, thoroughly versed in the eloquence of symbols and the persuasive power of signs and portents, was at the head of the insurrectionists astride a dark, short-legged horse.[31] The priest was bedecked in outlandish attire:

> ankle boots; purple trousers; blue sash; scarlet waistcoat; a green coat; a black ruffle and collar; a straw-colored kerchief around his neck; a turban with plumes of every color except white; on his chest, the emblem of the Eagle rampant ready to destroy the Lion; a Moorish scimitar at his waist; and in his right hand [he held] a pike four meters long.[32]

It seemed as if by wearing the insignia on his chest, Hidalgo wanted to convey the message that the Eagle of New Spain was embarking upon a second conquest that would completely eradicate the damage and the offenses arising from the Conquest led by Hernán Cortés and his successors, pawns of the Castilian Lion in its subjugation of the Americas.

Excoriations against the Sweet Voice of Freedom

In an attempt to counteract the Insurgent leaders' use of certain symbols, Loyalist writers employed a circumstantial literary form—dialogues—to ridicule them. In a conversation allegedly held between two women, one of them declares, in verse:

> Have you ever heard
> in the manner most absurd
> the madmen boast
> that one is a general, the other El Cid,
> the other Scipio . . . or his ghost?[33]

The learned Loyalists could make fun of the "rabble-rousers" as much as they pleased, but their pompous references betrayed their fear that the struggle for Independence would attain epic proportions, similar to the Spanish Reconquest or to the Punic Wars. It is extremely symptomatic, for example, that the viceregal authorities put a price on the heads of Hidalgo, Allende, and Aldama of 10,000 pesos.

As they passed through the parish of Atotonilco, the Insurgents took a canvas painting bearing the image of the Virgin of Guadalupe and adopted it as their banner, the principal emblem of their cause. The significance attributed to this symbolic act can be inferred by the fact that the ecclesiastical authorities lost no time in excoriating and excommunicating the Insurgent leaders.[34] By December 1810, on the orders of Brigadier Félix María Calleja, the king's honorary chaplain preached a sermon in Guanajuato portraying Hidalgo as the "rabid, deranged progenitor of the abominable fetus of Independence," which he had "instigated with the fetid breath of his errors." Therefore, September 16 should be "marked with the darkest color"; the priest from Dolores "deserved to be judged as a prisoner, guilty of high treason or infidelity to America, Spain, and the Church."[35] The high clergy's increasing concern over the rebels' appropriation of the Virgin of Guadalupe as their symbol, protectress, and *generala* (appointed general) can be deduced from the sermon preached in May 1811 by Father Antonio Camacho in the Cathedral of Morelia, purportedly in order to atone for the outrages committed by the rebels against the image of the Virgin of Guadalupe:

> No, it was not religion nor love for the Holy Virgin Mary that compelled them to clamor in this manner. *The first . . . those who gave this* grito, *had other motives at work: their intention was to incite the people to rebellion, and they [used] this invocation [to the Virgin of Guadalupe] as the most suitable means to attain it.* What more powerful incentive to action than to invoke the sweet name of the Virgin whom they had always worshipped? At the rallying cry, "Long live our Holy Virgin of Guadalupe!" the masses rise up and, repeating other such echoes, sedition spreads rapidly like wildfire in every direction. Poor, wretched Indians, miserable laborers, unfortunate masses! Oh, how they take advantage of your credulity![36]

In the struggle for control of the symbolic capital, Hidalgo and his troops seem to have made considerable progress in vindicating the Virgin of Guadalupe and the insignia of the Eagle on the cactus as the emblematic representations of the insurrection. In his defense against the vilifying edict issued by the Inquisition, Hidalgo professes his Catholic faith and refutes the Inquisitors' accusations by asking them to explain what dogma or article of faith prevents one from being a true Catholic "if one is not subject to the Spanish despot." Hidalgo reproaches the Inquisitors "who are Catholic only for political reasons: their God is money, and oppression the sole purpose behind their condemnations." Excommunication and excoriation are only ploys used by the clergy to conceal an undeniable reality, since, as Hidalgo maintains, "the nation that lay dormant for so long *suddenly awakens from its slumber to the sweet voice of freedom*; the people rush to arms, so as to uphold it at all costs."[37]

It is no wonder that the members of the Inquisition, undisputed experts in the command of images and symbols, uttered the most offensive epithets against Hidalgo: "deluder of Indians," "deceiver of the riffraff," "rabble-rouser," "seducer of the unwary," "Calvinist," and "sacrilegious blasphemer." Furthermore, the Inquisition had Hidalgo unfrocked prior to his death and justified his execution and the desecration of his corpse on the grounds that he had committed "crimes against the state."

Fiery Revolutionary Tongues Devour the People

Twelve days after the onset of the rebellion, Brigadier Félix María Calleja, who was in San Luis Potosí, informed Viceroy Francisco Javier Venegas of the "apprehension of two [of the] people who instigated the insurrection." Calleja recommended extraordinary measures "to prevent the fire of rebellion from spreading, which apparently is not restricted to the people whom it is devouring up to now."[38] Calleja warned the viceroy that for the time being, he could not guarantee the effective defense of the territory under his jurisdiction because the Loyalist troops, most of whom were criollos, were unsympathetic to the king's cause.

In late September the news of the execrations and abuses committed by the Insurgent militia against the Spaniards and several criollos after the raid on the Alhóndiga de Granaditas (the Corn Exchange Building) and the occupation of Guanajuato both shocked and horrified the population. These incidents detracted from the popularity of the rebel cause. However, the Loyalist troops' brutal reprisals against the Insurgents, their families, and entire villages suspected of supporting them rekindled the spirit of the pro-Independence sector.

For three and one-half months when triumphant entries into villages and cities alternated between summary executions of Spaniards (at Guanajuato, Valladolid, and Guadalajara), Pyrrhic victories (Monte de las Cruces), and bitter defeats (Aculco, Guanajuato, and Puente de

Calderón), the Insurgent troops, considerably depleted and virtually disbanded, headed north to seek support from their adherents in the Interior Provinces. By that time, there was considerable infighting among the Insurgents' high command. At the end of January 1811 a military council in Zacatecas relieved don Miguel Hidalgo y Costilla, commander in chief of the Forces of New Spain, of all military responsibility. This same council conferred upon Ignacio Allende the supreme command of the troops. As of that date, although Hidalgo ostensibly preserved his executive functions, he, in fact, ceased to fulfill them altogether. In late March, when the Insurgent high command was ambushed and captured in Norias de Baján, Coahuila, Hidalgo, in his own words, was with them "more as a prisoner than through his own free will."[39]

Brought to trial and then sentenced to death by a Loyalist court-martial, Hidalgo, Allende, and Mariano Abasolo, together with other Insurgent leaders, were executed between June and July. Prior to his death, Hidalgo had been subjected to the degradation imposed by the Inquisition. Hidalgo, who was by then 58, munched on some candy while he calmly awaited his death and confronted the volley of bullets from the firing squad with his hand over his heart.[40]

On Félix María Calleja's recommendation, the Insurgent leaders responsible for the political and military aspects of the movement were decapitated. Their heads were transported to Guanajuato and hung on each corner of the Alhóndiga de Granaditas.[41] Calleja's macabre humor assumed that a public display would act as a permanent reminder of the decapitation of the Insurrection movement itself and would serve to quench the "raging flames of revolutionary fire," thus sealing the lips of anyone on the continent who dared to raise his voice against Spanish rule. The bishop of Durango, more prudently, granted permission to the commander in chief of the Interior Provinces to keep a watchful eye on the clergy because he had received word that the sparks of rebellion had even reached New Mexico.[42]

The shattering blow to the Insurgency was not enough to annihilate New Spain's aspirations to autonomy. To the south, the troops led by Father José María Morelos y Pavón were gaining ground; and Ignacio López Rayón, a lawyer, the "official replacement" for the fallen Insurgent leaders, surmounted countless obstacles in order to pursue the political projects that they had charted.[43] However, it was obvious that it would be some time before the Insurgents could catch their breath and get back on their feet.

One year after the tragic events in Chihuahua, Fray Servando Teresa de Mier, who was in London at the time, clamored:

> *Shall we fail to seek reparations for the souls of Hidalgo and his generals who inspired us with their first cry of freedom* and who were brought to the infamous scaffold by treachery? Will not the flames that consumed Irapuato and Zitácuaro ignite our spirits? Shall we, like women, be content to weep sterile tears over the slaughter of Guanajuato and Quito? For the first [atrocity] the Spanish government has awarded Venegas the Cross of Carlos III and for the second [massacre] it has presented Abascal with the Embroidered Cross. It has handed out staffs of office to the Callejas, Cruces, Goyenecheas, and other barbarian murderers. Shall we let these scandals go unpunished? No! Mankind, who was horrified at the butchery of innocent people, will be even more horrified at our ignominious indolence. To arms![44]

"The Anniversary of Our Joyful Independence Shall be Duly Solemnized"

In March 1811, after a perilous march that had started off in Saltillo, López Rayón succeeded in installing a government council in Zitácuaro whose main objective was to convene a Constituent Congress. As president of the Supreme Governmental Council, López Rayón proposed in Item 33 of his "Elementos constitucionales" (April 1812) that "among the civic festivities that must be solemnized as the most august of our Nation, [are] the 16th of September, since it is the day proclaiming our joyful independence; the 12th of December, devoted to our most genteel protectress Our Lady of Guadalupe; the 29th of September and the 31st of July, the birthdays of our supreme Commanders Hidalgo and Allende."[45] Items 34 and 35 of this same constitutional draft propose the establishment of four military orders: Our Lady of Guadalupe, Hidalgo, Allende, and the Eagle, each to be presided over by a Knight of the Grand Cross.

On September 16, 1812, in support of his own proposal, López Rayón issued a manifesto in Huichapan whose essence summarizes the significance of the *grito de Dolores*:

> *A sudden call to freedom was uttered in Dolores*; it resounds throughout the length and breadth of the realm, like the echo expelled from the depths of a jungle, stirring the soul, joining together in huge numbers to assert the authority of their grievances.

The people realize the danger of their situation; they feel the need to remedy it; an army is created.[46]

On that same day, with a series of simple military, religious, and civic ceremonies, the custom of officially commemorating the *grito* was initiated. Don J. Ignacio Oyarzábal, López Rayón's secretary, gives a brief account of this first celebration: "With a volley of artillery and pealing bells the glorious memory of the call to freedom uttered two years ago in the congregation of Dolores by the illustrious heroes Hidalgo and Allende was first solemnized at daybreak."[47]

A Mass was celebrated on the morning of the 16th, attended by the members of the Governmental Council's executive power, along with the officers and the troops under their command. Blasts of gunfire could be heard during the religious services. On the previous day, so as to include the civilian population in the celebration, an official edict asked the inhabitants to decorate and illuminate their streets. At noon on the 16th, military bands competed among themselves by playing a series of favorite melodies, much to the amusement of the president of the Governmental Council and the general public.[48]

The precariousness with which the authorities of the Governmental Council performed their functions and their constant mobility did not foresee, in the short term, any plans for legislating the commemoration of the *grito* with any special festivities honoring the memory of those men who had uttered it, although, barely a year after his death, the figure of Juan Aldama gradually faded into the background. Perhaps his confederates never forgave his fainthearted attempts to save his neck by denying his role in the consensus to give the *grito*.

A year later, the anniversary of the birth of the Independence movement was celebrated with ceremonies endowed with considerable political and juridical significance. On the 14th of September the Congress convened by the Insurgents to draft the basic legislation for the budding nation was installed in Chilpancingo. That same day, José María Morelos y Pavón, commander of the Ejércitos Americanos (Forces of the Americas), read before the Congress the "Sentimientos de la nación." Item 19 of this document proposed that the future constitution regard December 12 as a national holiday devoted to the "patroness of our Freedom, Our Holy Virgin of Guadalupe." The last article, Item 24, stipulated

That the 16th of September be similarly solemnized every year, as the anniversary in which the voice of independence was raised and our blessed freedom began, since it was on that very day when the Nation's silence was finally shattered in order to demand, sword in hand, the right to be heard, always evoking the virtues of the great hero don Miguel Hidalgo and his confederate don Ignacio Allende.[49]

On the 15th the Congress elected Morelos y Pavón supreme commander of the Forces of New Spain and chief of the Insurgents' executive power. When several officious constituents attempted to saddle him with the title of His Serene Highness, he requested instead the status of Servant of the Nation. With the installation of the Constituent Congress in Chilpancingo and the organization of the Insurgent Government, the Insurgent patriots had every reason to hope that the end of the war was near. One of them, writing under the pseudonym of Juan en el Desierto (John in the desert), confided to the *Correo del Sur* his enthusiasm at the prospect of being a free citizen of a sovereign nation:

Abundant mountains of Guanajuato, repeat the sweet echo of FREE-DOM, whose first voice has just emerged from the village of Dolores. You merry, playful genies, pay court to Our Mother America who, with a majestic air, strides forward toward the hallowed abode of the great HIDALGO and the gallant ALLENDE, singing to the sounds of the melodious Teponaxtli, the harmonious Tlapahuéhuetl and the simple marimba, swelling with pride. . . . My chains are broken forever, the day of my long-awaited freedom has dawned.[50]

By that time, the image of the *grito*, like a voice exhorting its hearers to freedom, had remained indelibly impressed in the Insurgents' imagination. This fact is clearly demonstrated in the Declaration of Independence of New Spain promulgated by the Anáhuac Congress on September 28, 1813. In its preamble, the image of the *grito* is used to link the different struggles for Independence throughout the continent as stemming from "primordial acts" born of one and the same root:

Caracas, who, before any other province [in America] cried out against these injustices [of the Spanish empire], acknowledged its rights and armed itself to defend them. It created a Council, a paragon of moderation and wisdom; and when the insurrection, like a new plant in fertile soil, began to produce the fruits of freedom and life in that part of America, a tiny corner of our provinces was stirred by the voice of its parish priest, and our immense continent prepared to imitate the example of Venezuela.[51]

With the passage of time, the literary and artistic images of the *grito* and its protagonists were transformed into an indispensable point of departure for every foundational event associated with Freedom and Independence. Insurgent promoters, orators, and artists would ensure that the collective imagination was permeated with various and sundry redefinitions of the *grito*, both on the historical and on the mythical plane.

The Common Well-being Is Founded on Unity?

After eleven years of strife and public unrest, the society of New Spain yearned for peace. The political turmoil in Spain and the Crown's neglect of the situation in its dominions made it highly unlikely that the solution would come from the other side of the Atlantic. Both these circumstances transformed the Plan de Iguala into a lifeline and Agustín de Iturbide, its author, into the nation's savior.

On February 24, Iturbide officially expounded his Plan before his own troops and Vicente Guerrero's militia when they met in the city of Iguala.[52] In the manifesto that preceded the Plan, Iturbide presented his proposal as the logical outcome of the *grito de Dolores*.[53] Although he could not conceal the fact that he regarded these precedents as disastrous and that he, unlike his predecessors, was offering to act as an instrument of peace and reconciliation,

> Public opinion and that of every country favors absolute Independence from Spain and every other Nation. . . . That same voice that resounded in the village of Dolores in the year 1810, provoking endless misfortune to this beautiful country of delights due to the ensuing chaos, neglect, and a multitude of other vices, also established among public opinion that the union among Americans and Europeans, Indians and indigenous peoples [*sic*] is the only solid foundation for our common well-being. Let us astound the cultured nations of Europe; let us let them see that North America has become emancipated without shedding one drop of blood.
>
> Long live the holy religion we profess! Long live New Spain, independent of all the nations in the world! Long live the union that forged our happiness![54]

One week later, the Army of the Three Guarantees—Union, Independence, and Religion—swore to uphold the Plan de Iguala. The overwhelming support of the Plan from Insurgents and Loyalists alike, and the signing of the Treaties of Córdoba (August 24, 1821) between Viceroy O'Donojú and Iturbide, paved the way for the dissolution of the viceregal government and the remaining Loyalist troops' return to Spain.

Early in September, entire villages and cities took great pains to show their gratitude to the different divisions of the Trigarante Army on its way to Mexico City. Meanwhile, in Mexico City, the municipal authorities were deeply distressed over the lack of funds required to accord them the reception they deserved. To solve this embarrassing problem, a troupe of actors donated three days' worth of box office receipts, humble artisans handed over their day's wages, merchants offered part of their merchandise, the general population contributed either cash or gifts in kind, and a wealthy mayor provided a 20,000-peso loan without interest.[55] With the funds collected, the mayor and councilmen ordered the construction of a magnificent triumphal arch, commissioned a series of tricolored flags (green, white, and red), and contracted catering services and whatever else was required to celebrate on a grand scale.

On the 26th of September, troops of the line, volunteers, and partisans began arriving in Chapultepec, where they were instructed to observe "order and composure" during their triumphal entry into the city. The residents of Tacubaya, noting the deplorable condition of the soldiers' uniforms and boots, sought contributions. Store owners answered their plea by supplying clothing and fabric; seamstresses worked hard, free of charge, to mend the frayed uniforms or to sew new ones. The City Council obtained some rather shabby uniforms from the Commerce regiment to cover the half-naked volunteer units.[56]

The residents of the capital decorated their homes without sparing any expense or effort. Everyone was determined to "display their finest, their most splendid, possessions." The women's hairstyles and dresses exhibited the colors of the flag representing the Three Guarantees, while the men proudly flaunted tricolored ribbons, bows, and rosettes on their clothing and hats.[57]

At last, at ten o'clock in the morning on the 27th, when the first contingent of the "Liberators of the Nation" reached the La Piedad sentry box, thousands of voices welcomed them with shouts of joy. Agustín de Iturbide, commander in chief of the Trigarante Army, accompanied by his military staff, led the column. The hero of Iguala was decked out in "riding boots, white wool breeches, a waistcoat of the same material, a cutaway hazel-colored frock coat, a hat set with three beautiful plumes [corresponding] to the colors of the national flag; he was riding a spirited black horse, whose harness and saddle were studded with gold and diamonds."[58]

His proud bearing and grave expression made Iturbide seem as "arrogant as a statue."[59] The column, comprised of 16,000 soldiers, advanced along the Paseo Nuevo (Bucareli) and the Avenida Corpus Christi. Iturbide dismounted in front of the imposing triumphal arch erected next to the Monastery of San Francisco. The members of the City Council were already awaiting him in order to pay their respects to the Trigarantes and presented their Supreme Leader with the keys to the city. He once again mounted his steed and crossed under the arch, followed on foot by the City Council and the Indian factions from San Juan and Santiago. The heroes of Independence and the "gallant champions of our freedom" were pelted with garlands, jewels, kerchiefs, and blessings from the balconies. Several decades later, Vicente Riva Palacio, grandson of Vicente Guerrero, observed that never before had the people in the city been so carried away by the "blessed vertigo of patriotism."

Upon reaching the main plaza, Iturbide entered the Viceregal Palace only to reemerge on the central balcony with Viceroy Juan O'Donojú. Both men presided over the military parade. In the afternoon, the high clergy celebrated a Mass of Thanksgiving in the Cathedral as a stamp of approval for the arrival of peace and the birth of the new nation. When the religious services were over, a speech was delivered by Dr. Guridi y Alcocer, a "silver-tongued orator who had been a member of the Cortes de Cádiz" and who, in a few hours, would form part of the Provisional Government Council.[60]

Iturbide concluded the official ceremonies by addressing the nation. In his proclamation, he took it for granted that the transition period stipulated in the Plan de Iguala had ended; he acknowledged the "expressive cheers" showered on the Trigarante Army and the "prayers of gratitude" to Divine Providence on his behalf. He declared his satisfaction at having contributed to the emergence of the independent nation and ended with a resounding phrase: "You know the path to freedom; now it is your turn to indicate the [path] to happiness."[61]

The festivities began in the afternoon. The new authorities offered a banquet for two hundred people in honor of the "Consummator of Independence," who observed his 38th birthday that same day. In the evening, when riding with his wife through the heart of the city, Iturbide was cheered and applauded by the crowds. Finally, the long day ended, for them, with the performance of a play dedicated to the man of the hour. Meanwhile, serenades, parties, drinking sprees, and bonfires in the barrios and plazas induced merrymakers to keep their spirits up until dawn the following day.

On the next day the Mexican Empire's government was installed. The executive power was entrusted to a Regency composed of five members, among them Agustín de Iturbide; the legislative power, to the Provisional Government Council. The latter consisted of thirty-eight members, selected by Iturbide, to represent the main social concerns and the predominant political sectors in the country. There was not one former Insurgent among the Council members. After formally assuming their functions, the new government representatives proceeded to sign the Declaration of Independence, which proclaimed the establishment of the Mexican Empire and "a new sovereign nation, Independent from Spain." In this document the members of the Provisional Government Council identified the Plan de Iguala as the consummation of Independence's foundational act, which they defined as that "eternally memorable enterprise which an incomparable genius [Iturbide] with all [our] admiration and praise, love, and glory of his country, began in Iguala, continued and carried out by overcoming insurmountable obstacles."[62] It was highly revealing that the members of the Provisional Government Council omitted any mention of the *grito de Dolores* and that they adhered to the proclamation of the Plan de Iguala and the signing of the Treaties of Córdoba as the fundamental acts of Independence.

Mexico Swears Allegiance to Independence

Since the reception for the Trigarante Army in Mexico City had been a spontaneous celebration, forced by the circumstances, so to speak, the City Council assumed complete responsibility for organizing the ceremonies as well as for covering part of the expenses. This situation had given the celebrations a certain air of improvisation, whose rowdy carnival-like atmosphere considerably annoyed the city's most prominent citizens. Furthermore, the fact that the festivities had been concentrated in the new nation's capital had contributed little toward reinforcing the sense of nationality in the Mexican Empire's provinces, in view of the country's huge territorial expanse. Consequently, the Provisional Government Council and the Regency contemplated the reinstatement of certain pre-existing traditions and symbols in order to forge the new national images and models. The Council revived the ancient tradition of the Oath of Allegiance[63] as the ideal vehicle for instilling the principles of the new Imperial government—Union, Religion, and Independence—in the populace throughout the country while at the same time creating a sense of continuity between the old order and the one about to begin. Thus, the Council scheduled the Oath of Allegiance to the Mexican Empire's Declaration of Independence for October 26, 1821.

The organization of these particular ceremonies scrupulously adhered to the old usages and customs. On October 13 in Mexico City the first poster bearing the full text of the Declaration and the official ordinances pertaining to the Oath of Allegiance ceremony were affixed next to the National Palace's main entrance, during the signal announcing an edict. A pavilion was erected in the middle of the main plaza, surrounding the statue of Carlos IV: "The center was the pedestal of a monument covered with sixteen allegorical paintings, as was the statue that disappeared under the cone-shaped finial; at one end, one could detect a cactus over which rested an Eagle, symbolizing the Nation's freedom."[64]

Unlike the previous month's festivities, when popular enthusiasm and ingenuity made up for the Council's straitened circumstances, the wealthy citizens provided the Council members with substantial donations to ensure that the ceremonies would be conducted according to protocol and the rules of etiquette. The decorations on public buildings and commercial establishments gave the city an impressive appearance indeed. On the great day, at ten o'clock at the City Council's headquarters, after a reading of the Declaration of Independence, the Plan de Iguala, and the Treaties of Córdoba, the entire City Council and two representatives from each existing political sector swore the Oath of Allegiance.

At noon a general pardon was granted to all prisoners sentenced to death. According to Luis González Obregón, this measure implied that the nation's children were embarking on a new life. Perhaps we should recall here that one of the first insurrectional acts that took place on the 16th of September of 1810 was the release of prisoners from the Dolores jail. However, it is possible that the Council had in mind either the Loyalist concept of magnanimity or the Christian virtue of clemency.

In the afternoon the Provincial Delegation[65] and a committee from the City Council went to the Imperial Palace to pay their respects to the Regency and to the Provisional Council. The mayor presented each representative with a commemorative gold coin. Then, while the Cathedral bells rang incessantly, the Provincial Delegation and the members of the City Council mounted the platform and presided over the standard-bearing ceremony.[66] The flag now bore the colors of the national emblem: white symbolized Religion, red stood for Union, and green represented Independence. Except for slight variations, the procession that followed the standard complied with the same hierarchical order corresponding to the principal sectors in New Spain: civil authorities, dignitaries from the clergy, university staff, members of guilds, friars, public officials, and the military high command.

On his return from the ceremony, the mayor ordered from the platform that the three documents submitted to the Oath of Allegiance that morning in the City Council Building should be read aloud throughout the country; and when it was over, he grasped the tricolored standard,

> and facing West, he proclaimed: "Mexico, Mexico, Mexico swears the Oath of Allegiance to the Independence of the Mexican Empire under the fundamental principles of Iguala and Córdoba." The people, as if they were one person and one voice, shouted fervently, "We swear!" The authorities flung proclamation medals, the artillery fired its cannons, and the bells rang at full peal, announcing to the City that the proclamation had been uttered toward the East. Immediately that same ceremony was held toward the South, West, and North of the Metropolis.[67]

The Oath of Allegiance festivities continued for three more days. For the public's amusement, the main plaza was kept illuminated while dances, bullfights, and theatrical performances were held in the Coliseum. At whatever time of night or day "the gallant leaders of the emancipation" were acclaimed in the streets, although it was Agustín de Iturbide who was the main target of attention and affection from his compatriots.[68]

The Provisional Government Council and the Regency could now rest easy because the Oath of Allegiance to the Declaration of Independence had been extremely successful as a bridge between the old conquerors and the new emancipators. The pledge of fidelity to the Mexican Empire, with its strong colonial and Loyalist undertones, had served its purpose as a self-congratulatory rite for a group of members who firmly and perhaps sincerely believed in the virtues of a moderate constitutional monarchy and who had a superb command over its symbols and images in order to further their own cause. In the midst of this overwhelming adulation, only one poetic writer,

Andrés Quintana Roo, was inspired to pay tribute to Father Hidalgo
in the manner befitting the times:

> To what end did that valiant priest
> in Dolores utter his freedom cry,
> echoed by the mob so nigh
> with monotonous zeal at least?[69]

The Empire's Last Gasp

Once the spirit of war had waned, it was not long before the under-
handed struggle to gain official recognition for services rendered to
the country was unleashed. The race for filling the gallery of heroes
was on. The Liberator of Mexico lost no opportunity in adopting an
air of aristocracy and grandeur by commissioning for posterity a series of paintings, sculptures, engravings, and gilded objects extolling
the highlights of his campaigns. From its rather depleted resources
the City Council authorized "whatever is needed to defray the expenses for the portraits of His Serene Highness Mr. Iturbide and His
Excellency Mr. O'Donojú."[70] Iturbide's likeness, initials, and the
events aimed at glorifying his image were reproduced in oil paintings, in lithographs, on Sèvres china, and on Baccarat goblets. This
rich visual testimony is in itself well worth a detailed description.
Suffice it to say that the principal national symbols (still in use today) were either officially instituted or designed during the brief period when Iturbide guided the destiny of the nation.

In January 1822 the Regency issued a decree on the components
of the Imperial coat of arms, "to be represented by a rock jutting out
of the lagoon and on it a cactus over which rests a crowned Eagle
standing on its left leg."[71] This emblem was to appear in the center of
the flag. Iturbide was also the first to wear the tricolored sash across
his chest as a symbol of his investiture to the executive power. The
Provisional Council approved the establishment of the Order of
Guadalupe, proposed by the "Christian hero" when he presided over
the Regency.[72] This order would be an honorary body, whose purpose
was to acknowledge the special merits of divers public figures and
give an aristocratic air to the Imperial court without resorting to titles
of nobility. The Order of Guadalupe sought to emulate, in peacetime,
the prestige of the Virgin of Guadalupe whose standard had been bran-
dished by Hidalgo. Lucas Alamán called this standard "the holy banner of the army" because, for the Insurgent troops, it was imbued

with a mysterious power capable of ensuring victory on the battle-field. There are also several versions of the story that Iturbide made off with the Guadalupe banner captured by the Loyalists in the battle of Monte de las Cruces and that he was seen on the Mezquital plains flourishing it like a war trophy.[73] At the height of his fame, Iturbide ordered that an image of the Virgin of Guadalupe be placed under a damask canopy as the honored witness to the Oath of Allegiance ceremony.

Although Iturbide's contrived brand of patriotism was enveloped in the symbols of the Insurgents, he was, in fact, intolerant with them. Whenever he could, he excluded the Insurgents from public life and carefully rationed out to the veterans the distinctions and rewards they deserved. A conflict was imminent and finally erupted in the Congress. One of the bitterest disputes between the Insurgent repre-sentatives and Iturbide's supporters revolved around the national fes-tivities. The debates took so much time from the regular deliberations that Iturbide suggested a transaction that resulted in the forcible in-clusion of the 16th of September among his numerous commemora-tions. Consequently, a degree issued in March 1822 stipulated the following as general festivities: the proclamation of the Plan de Iguala (February 24), the Oath of Allegiance to the Plan de Iguala (March 2), the *grito de Dolores* (September 16), and the triumphal entry into Mexico City of the Trigarante Army (September 27). These dates would be celebrated with a volley of artillery fire, a Thanksgiving Mass, and a receiving line made up of the corresponding authori-ties.[74] And, in retaliation for Iturbide's grudging acceptance of incor-porating the 16th of September into the Imperial civic calendar, the Insurgent representatives compensated for the blatant disregard of this highly symbolic date by describing it as "the anniversary of the glorious exhortation to Independence in New Spain."[75] In exchange for his consent, Iturbide, now Agustín I, succeeded in including the day of his ascent to the Imperial throne (May 19) and his own birth-day (September 27) among the official national holidays.[76] No won-der that Edmundo O'Gorman sarcastically observed: "While Iturbide was in power, the Insurgents' only great accomplishment was the in-clusion of the 16th of September in two decrees regarding the na-tional holidays."[77]

Due to the last-minute rush, since the official edict had been pub-lished in late August 1822, the brand-new Patriotic Council in charge of organizing the festivities scarcely had the chance to commemorate the 16th of September, keeping it to the bare minimum.[78] A Spanish monarchist commented on the shabbiness of the festivities: "There was a Thanksgiving Mass, cannon fire, a reception with a performance in the Coliseum to honor the souls of Hidalgo, Allende, . . . although it was all very impersonal, the Emperor was not in the receiving line and no one was in full dress."[79] This apparently understandable omission initiated a long dispute over the use of the civic calendar's fundamental symbols, which still remains. In 1996, for example, Felipe Calderón, president of the National Action Party (PAN), cheered Agustín de Iturbide during the *grito* festivities at the foot of the Independence Monument where the PAN members habitually celebrate at this particular time.[80]

Iturbide had fabricated a meteoric career for himself, claiming all the honors derived from Independence, pacification, the union of the races, and the preservation of religion by obtaining the title of emperor through his ascent to Mexico's Imperial throne. The brilliance and glory of his feats were the loftiest expression of the characteristicly convoluted nature of the Mexicans, only to evaporate and perish with lightning speed and to leave behind the specter of his image.

The conspiracy organized by several congressional representatives and then a rebellion from the Republican faction led by Antonio López de Santa Anna in Veracruz finally ousted Iturbide from the Imperial throne. A provisional government annulled the legal fabric of Iturbide's regime and declared him a traitor. The Plan de Iguala and the Treaties of Córdoba were pronounced ineffective and were revoked. A few days later, in Mexico City, the City Council published a notice to the public:

> We agreed that the effigies of Iturbide and his wife, who had established themselves as Emperors of these provinces, be removed and erased from the public places where they had been placed with this title, effective in three days under penalty of a fine of 10 to 50 pesos.
> God and Freedom![81]

"Make the Most of This Joyful Occasion," but Behave Yourselves

Once the Republic was instated, the disdain for the celebration of the *grito de Dolores* abated as well. In 1823 the Patriotic League in charge of raising the funds required for the festive protocol drew up a full-scale program:

1) At 11:00 o'clock on the 15th, the pealing bells and fire-crackers will announce to the people the hour when the heroic *grito de Dolores* marked the period of its Independence.

2) The following day, at 12:30, the solemn procession will take place. It will proceed from the City Council Building to a platform erected between the National Palace's two main entrances. The entire route of this procession will be accompanied by a military band which will play its finest tunes.

3) After arriving at the platform, the orator will deliver a fervent speech reminding all Mexicans of the glorious period of our emancipation.

4) In behalf of the nation, the President will free those slaves capable of redeeming themselves, by uttering the following words: "Slaves: On this day that commemorates the anniversary of your freedom, receive it in the name of our homeland and remember that because you are free now you can honor and defend freedom."

5) The ceremony will conclude without further ado.

6) In the afternoon, orchestras, dances, and allegorical tableaux of Independence will take place in the Alameda. Patriotic songs will be sung.

7) In the evening there will be general illumination (of the square), with fireworks and bands playing in front of the Council Building in the National Palace's main square as well as opposite the Chamber of Deputies.[82]

Thus, the basic elements for the reenactment of the Independence struggle were instituted with the very first celebration. Variations, omissions, and alterations would come later, hand in hand with the (ensuing) political conflicts, social change, ideological struggles, and transformations in the Mexicans' sentimental education.

In September 1825, during the City Council meetings, there were new attempts to defer the 16th of September holiday by linking it to the commemoration of the triumphal entry into Mexico City of the Trigarante Army on the 7th. This debate once again brought up the problem of which event should take precedence: on the one hand, the *grito de Dolores* as the "primordial act" generating all the other events stemming from Independence as well as the moral and political legitimacy of the institutions characteristic of an independent and republican Mexico; while on the other hand, the repudiation of the violence and failures corresponding to the earliest phase of the Independence movement whereby the Plan de Iguala and the consummation of Independence were identified with a triumphant, auspicious era founded on the concept of royalism, the law, and the privileges of the old regime.

Amid this stormy political climate, so susceptible to disturbances, the insults and the attacks on monarchists and Hispanophiles were a common occurrence. In 1823 an angry mob, aroused by anti-Spanish orators and journalists, declared their intention of exhuming the bones of Hernán Cortés from their crypt in the Hospital de Jesús and hurling them into the mud.[83] Although, in fact, this desecration never occurred, these reactions prompted the authorities to control the behavior of the crowds during the patriotic celebrations and, if possible, to restrict them within the bounds of the official ceremonies. A special committee called on President Guadalupe Victoria requesting that he prevent the disturbances generated by the nocturnal street festivities.[84] The president agreed to suppress the nighttime functions from the calendar of events.[85] The *grito* celebrations tapered off considerably over the following years, and only the joy over a failed attempt to recapture Mexico by the Spaniard Isidro Barradas in 1829 prompted the authorities to proclaim in an edict:

> During the commemoration of the day when General Hidalgo pronounced the heroic *grito* of "Freedom or Death," the government urges all Mexicans to make the most of this joyful occasion, . . . especially now that the execrable Spaniards have once again profaned Mexican soil.[86]

The Patriotic Leagues, sometimes also known as the Civic Leagues, or *civicos*, had been established since 1822. In some cases, they were composed of enthusiastic citizens well disposed to organizing the festivities. This initially good idea eventually came up against the indifference of the authorities, who frequently washed their hands of any financial responsibility, which had a definitive impact on the dreariness of the celebrations. In other cases, the Patriotic League surmounted the difficulties and managed to overcome all the obstacles in their way.[87] In 1832, while deploring the obvious reduction in public and private cooperation, the *civicos* in Mexico City were determined that the program would not fall short of those held in previous years. Therefore, they announced the ascension of a hot-air balloon, much to the surprise and delight of the population. Finally, the Patriotic League let it be known that any surplus funds would be used either to assist the Insurgents' widows and orphans or be turned over to the neediest veterans.[88]

The precarious political situation had direct repercussions on the celebrations. One such example is Anastasio Bustamante's attitude toward national heroes and celebrations. In 1832, eager to curry favor with both republicans and monarchists, this self-appointed conciliator went to the village of Dolores to celebrate the *grito* while at the same time also setting out to revive the splendor of the festivities commemorating the Trigarante Army's triumphal entry on the 27th of September.[89] Six years later he enforced an old decree of Santa Anna's regarding the retrieval and transfer of Iturbide's mortal remains from Padilla, Tamaulipas, to the Cathedral in Mexico City. However, Bustamante decided that Iturbide's remains should be consigned to a place separate from that already occupied by the Insurgent heroes in the former crypt of the viceroys as of 1823.[90]

Until about 1870, the nighttime patriotic celebrations, especially the street festivities, were regarded with considerable apprehension. Political tensions and the constant uprisings found fertile ground in the heat of the revelry stimulated by all-night binges. Firearms, alcohol, and any nocturnal gatherings of a festive nature were strictly forbidden. This measure, however, did not discourage President Ignacio Comonfort in 1855 from offering a banquet for more than two thousand artisans on La Piedad boulevard on the 16th of September as proof that the Liberals were not afraid to mingle with the people. The feast included a roast bull, four pigs, two lambs, and portions of ham and fowl, accompanied by *pulque* and beer. A prominent member of the aristocracy noted that "at four o'clock in the afternoon, the president of the Republic put in an appearance to have a drink with the people. Evidently he is in complete contradiction with Napoleon, who said, Everything for the people and nothing for him."[91]

A Call to Arms

The authorities gradually transferred the nocturnal festivities from the main squares and public parks to theaters and circus tents. The latter, which were covered and therefore easier to control, were ideal for regulating excesses. In 1850 on the 5th of September, at seven o'clock, the Patriotic League welcomed President Santa Anna at the Gran Teatro Nacional. The ceremony began with a group of little girls presenting him with several flags once belonging to the Insurgent heroes and which several patriotic women had saved as relics. Then the Manifesto de Valladolid and the Decree Abolishing Slavery, both written by Hidalgo, were read, followed by the Declaration of Independence of 1813, the Declaration of Independence of 1821, and the Chilpancingo Congress Manifesto. Finally, an opera company and students from the San Gregorio School sang a series of beautiful melodies and operatic arias. At eleven o'clock the bursts of gunfire, the pealing bells, and the strains of the military bands spread throughout the city to commemorate the *grito* of Independence.[92]

By the second half of the nineteenth century the *grito de Dolores* celebrations were gradually transformed into a succession of formal, monotonous ceremonies that the Patriotic Leagues of this period had placed at the service of the authorities in an attempt to regain the credibility lost by the government some time ago. Nevertheless, several innovations were introduced into the formal rites: the reading of Hidalgo's Manifesto and the Decree Abolishing Slavery, which usually took place the next day, on the 16th of September, was now held behind closed doors, thus removing one of the most dramatic symbolic elements from the popular festivities.[93] The reading of the Declaration of Independence of 1821 was the only document to evoke the loyalist concepts dating back to the consummation of Independence. However, the substitution of the Plan de Iguala for the Chilpancingo Congress Manifesto reinforced the republicans' principles and those of a representative democracy.

Antonio López de Santa Anna's constant attempts to strengthen his political position and exalt his own personality were duly noted by Lucas Alamán and other distinguished members of the Conservative party, who proved invaluable to him by improving and popularizing his image. One of their ideas was to establish a competition, summoning musicians and poets to write the words and music of an anthem that could be adopted on a nationwide level. The announcement of the contest was made in November 1853. Three months later a young poet, Francisco González Bocanegra, was declared the winner. A great many of his stanzas were aimed at flattering Santa Anna, while there were none dedicated to the heroes of Independence. However, as the anthem gained in popularity, the first line of the first stanza's martial air, "Mexicanos al grito de guerra," was interpreted as a poetic, though somewhat distant, allusion to the *grito* as a call to freedom. It was not until August 1854 that the winner of the contest for the best musical composition was announced: it turned out to be a well-known Spanish composer, Jaime Nunó. González Bocanegra and Nunó's anthem was introduced on September 15, in the Santa Anna Theater; and since His Serene Highness did not attend because of illness, he was represented by the governor of the Federal District, accompanied by Mrs. Dolores Tosta, wife of the president. González Bocanegra was accorded the honor of giving the customary harangue.

Since Santa Anna was ousted by the Liberals adhering to the Plan de Ayutla, it would be some time before González Bocanegra and Nunó's composition was widely accepted by Mexicans as their national anthem.[94] When the 1857 Constitution was promulgated, the 16th of September was finally recognized as the official national Independence holiday. The 1861 program listing the civic festivities stipulated that the Declaration of Independence to be read on the 15th of September was the version promulgated by the Chilpancingo Congress in 1813. The program also stated that at eleven o'clock the corresponding authorities present in various theaters and at the main plaza would lead the Independence cheers. As to the popular festivities, it was announced that the bands would stroll through the streets, all playing together, and, if possible, would accompany the official commission assigned to the *grito* ceremony. At the same time a volley of artillery and a general ringing of bells at full peal would announce "the anniversary of the moment when the immortal Hidalgo proclaimed the independence of Mexico."[95]

During Maximilian of Hapsburg's short reign as emperor, the battle over symbols can be safely described as an all-out war. The head of the so-called Second Empire was surrounded by a group of experts devoted to creating his corporate image (if we may be allowed a literary license)—heraldists, historians, artists, protocol officers, et al. He himself was well versed in the implementation and the significance of certain gestures and images. The Imperial emblem was designed to legitimize his aspirations to the grandeur of pre-Hispanic civilization. His attire, for example, was in keeping with the current fashion as well as with the local taste. His saddle featured a Mexican emblem, while paintings of the Virgin of Guadalupe hung in the empress's bedroom and in the throne room at Chapultepec Castle.

Shortly after his arrival, Maximilian expressed his admiration for Father Hidalgo; but to the great displeasure of those who had invited him to rule the country, in 1864 he suppressed the 27th of September celebration on the official calendar.[96] He did, on the other hand, adopt a descendant of Agustín de Iturbide's as his dynastic heir. In that same year, Maximilian visited the city of Dolores to conduct the *grito* ceremony in situ. Perhaps heeding the suggestion of his advisers, he stood at the very window from where, according to the oral tradition upheld by Pedro José Sotelo, Father Hidalgo had exhorted the villagers to join in the struggle for freedom. From that same window, Maximilian read a speech and immediately cheered Independence, Napoleon III, Empress Carlota, and his father-in-law, King Leopold of Belgium. As a final touch in his endeavor to figuratively cover himself with the mantle of patriotism, the emperor sat down in the chair once occupied by Father Hidalgo and wrote an edifying message in the visitors' book at Hidalgo's home: "A people who, under God's protection and benediction, founds its independence based on freedom and the law, and expresses one and the same will, is invincible and can therefore hold up its head in pride."[97]

Subsequently, Maximilian would order this book to be "properly bound" at his expense. It had been placed there in June 1863 by the order of President Benito Juárez on his way through Dolores, when he raised this village to the status of a city. He also had Hidalgo's home transformed into a museum.[98] A few pages after Maximilian's comment, an anonymous writer invoked:

> The humblest of your children bids:
>
>> Father Hidalgo from Dolores,
>> be alert, noble and brave,
>> arise from your grave,
>> help your supporters this country to save.[99]

During that same period, in the arid northern territory, President Juárez and a handful of collaborators and militia from the Republic improvised a small celebration on the "night of Father Hidalgo." A few flaming branches served as a lantern, a serape was used by way of a flag, a table served as a rostrum for the orator and "a few scattered shouts . . . omens of (their) victory."[100] A description of the national celebrations in Mexico City during Maximilian's Imperial regime mentions that at night, after the fireworks and all the noise died down, the people went out into the streets, the musical bands in tow, for the public serenades. According to *Pájaro Verde*,[101] although the *grito de Dolores* was not officially held, when the bells rang out at eleven o'clock, everyone let out spontaneous shouts of joy.

When the Bells Spoke

During Porfirio Díaz's regime, since the 15th of September coincided with the birthday of the president, the traditional eleven o'clock ceremony took on a new glitter and the street festivities were resumed. Díaz cheered Independence after a volley of artillery was fired; the military bands and a general pealing of bells evoked the *grito*. Around 11:30, a number of balls and dances were held in different theaters throughout the city: "The most aristocratic families went to El Nacional; the middle class to El Principal; the Arbeu was for the social climbers and parvenus; the Hidalgo for the lower middle classes; and the common people [gathered] in the main square."[102]

Porfirio Díaz and his collaborators undertook the task of reconciling popular spontaneity with the established tradition of using theaters as the most appropriate sites to control the patriotic outbursts from every sector of the population. However, since the celebration of the *grito* once again began to resemble more a routine than a ritual, there were those who, in order to impress General Díaz, proposed a series of new, more spectacular activities to demonstrate that peace and progress now prevailed in Mexico. As of the mid-1880s, Díaz's supporters competed among themselves to uphold the benefits of centralism, presidential power, and his successive reelections as head of the government. One of these proposals came from a group of Mexico City councilmen for whom the Cathedral bells were not enough and who thought it would be a wonderful idea to bring to the capital the original bell from Dolores, which, according to local tradition, had been used to call the parishioners to join the insurrection in September 1810. No sooner said than done: in 1886 a delegate from the City Council arrived in Dolores. A clothing store salesman persuaded the delegate, who had asked him for directions, that Hidalgo's bell did not exist; it had been melted down many years ago. This story became Dolores's official version to defend its precious relic, which hung proudly from one of the parish church's towers.[103] The members of the Mexico City Council were thoroughly satisfied with the results of their delegate's inquiry.

In 1896 yet another City Council committee revived the idea of going to the Dolores church and retrieving the Bell of San José, the official name of the much-coveted relic. The excuse for this fiercely patriotic act was the inauguration of the national exhibit aimed at flaunting Porfirian progress, attended by hundreds of local and foreign dignitaries, and also, the example set by the tour organized the previous year by the U.S. authorities to exhibit their own Liberty Bell. The new City Council committee, now reinforced by another delegation composed of high-ranking military officers personally appointed by President Díaz, went to Dolores to obtain the priceless object. On the occasion of the official presentation of the bell, Dolores's chief political representative, the author of a famous book on the history of the region, justified the release of the Bell of San José with a speech arguing that since the humble parish bell had enjoyed the privilege of "awakening the lethargic Anáhuac from its slumber," it had now earned the honor of belonging to the entire nation. In a burst of lyricism, this same official had the bell itself utter this phrase: "I belong to history."[104]

The bell, now renamed the Independence Bell, was placed on the National Palace's main balcony during an elaborate ceremony. As an act of self-glorification, General Díaz had the pleasure of pulling its clapper for that year's *grito* celebration. In the Republic's capital, no one could stop talking about this innovation, although the *dolorenses* were bitter over losing a cultural legacy in exchange for giving the nation a mouthpiece for the *grito* ceremony. In 1910 the Centennial Independence celebrations were especially spectacular and served to show off President Díaz, who took advantage of the opportunity to compare his image with that of the most prestigious figures in the country. But, in general, once the bell ritual was established in the *grito* ceremony (which incidentally observed its 100th year in 1996), it has undergone few significant redefinitions to this day.

Notes

1. By *history* we mean the discipline which reconstructs events that actually occurred and were experienced, and whose veracity "is guaranteed by controllable, verifiable, and repeatable operations," as Roger Chartier writes in *El mundo como representación. Historia cultural: entre práctica y representación*, trans. Claudia Ferrari (Barcelona: Gedisa, 1992), 77.

2. Myth has been defined as "something invented by someone who attempts to have it accepted as truth, or something which only exists in someone's imagination," in María Moliner, *Diccionario del uso del español* (Madrid: Gredos, 1992), 428. On the other hand, according to Martín Alonso, *Enciclopedia del idioma*, 2 vols. (Mexico: Aguilar, 1991), 2:2854, myth is an allegorical fable, usually of a religious nature. But even though myth is a fable that contains a lesson (Martín Alonso), it is not an absolute invention per se, as María Moliner seems to suggest.

3. Mircea Eliade, *Aspects du mythe* (Paris: Gallimard, 1963), 10.

4. Roger Chartier, op. cit., xi.

5. Regarding the inevitable degree of mythicization that filters into historiography, see Raphael Samuel and Paul Thompson's introduction to the essays published as *The Myths We Live By* (New York: Routledge, 1900), 1–22, particularly when the authors ironically identify rationalistic realism as the unique myth of Western culture. They exemplify this viewpoint by means of "the symbolic categories we use (such as 'nation' or the 'average man') or the great theories we support or, even, our irrational belief in facts."

6. Alfredo López Austin, *El conejo en cara de la luna. Ensayos sobre mitología de la tradición mesoamericana* (Mexico: Instituto Nacional Indigenista–Consejo Nacional para la Cultura y las Artes, 1994), 34. For a more extensive discussion on myths see Alfredo López Austin, *Los mitos del tlacuache* (Mexico: Alianza Editorial Mexicana, 1990), 9–146; and Luis Barjau, *La gente del mito* (Mexico: Instituto Nacional de Antropología e Historia, 1988).

7. To understand the relationship between religious and secular festivities, and the revolutionary celebrations, see Emmanuel Le Roy Ladurie, *El carnaval de Romans* (Mexico: Instituto Mora, 1994); and Roger Chartier, "Disciplinas e invención: la fiesta," in *Sociedad y escritura en la sociedad moderna* (Mexico: Instituto Mora, 1995), 19–36.

8. In regard to the functionalistic and structuralistic trends in sociology and historiography as well as to the economic tendencies endorsing the elitist character, the mechanisms of political domain, and the primacy of economic rationality, Roger Chartier supports the effectiveness of a cultural focus on history that takes into account the dialectical relationship between production, consumption, and reception of physical and imaginary representations, according to the following terms: "The works (or representations) have no stable, universal, fixed meaning. They have plural and movable meanings, generated by the reencounter between proposition and reception, between the forms and the motives that structure them and structure the expectations of the audiences who make them their own." Roger Chartier, op. cit., xi.

9. E. P. Thompson, in *La formación de la clase obrera inglesa*, originated the trend in research focus present in several works and has resulted in theoretical and methodological approaches based on categories such as *cultural hegemony, experience*, and *custom*. These have been quite stimulating in the study of the behavior and attitudes in the protest and seditious actions observed in some rituals, symbols, and theatrical reenactments of traditional and revolutionary festivities; see E. P. Thompson, "The Patricians and the Plebs," in *Customs in Common* (New York: The New Press, 1993). Raphael Samuel has recently analyzed the specificity of *popular memory* in mass society during the cybernetic and electronic communications era. We have taken the list of the main characteristics of the ways people appropriate the past from the introduction ("Unofficial Knowledge") of his *Theatres of Memory: Past and Present in Contemporary Culture* (New York: Verso, 1994).

10. Mona Ozouf, *Festivals and the French Revolution* (Cambridge, MA: Harvard University Press, 1988), 8. Even though Ozouf's contributions to the development and interpretation of the revolutionary festival have been considered in this work, we do not entirely share her notion that the history of the festival is, in itself, the history of a delusion generated by utopian promises of the revolutionary ideology and by the genuine results obtained by the State and by the postrevolutionary French institutions.

11. We agree to a large extent with Mary Ryan's concept of the "nineteenth century parade," but not with her statement that "this type of reenacted celebration seems to be a North American invention." See Mary Ryan, "The American Parade:

Representations of the Nineteenth Century Social Order," in *The New Cultural History*, ed. Lynn Hunt (Berkeley: University of California Press, 1989), 131–53.

12. Mexican presidents have sometimes cheered certain issues considered of national interest or of international scope. In 1935, Lázaro Cárdenas introduced "Long live social revolution!"; in 1975, due to the International Women's Year, Luis Echeverría included Josefa Ortiz de Domínguez with "the heroes who gave us a Nation." We also have to mention the slogans of the political opposition or of the protest movements conducted separately from the official ceremonies: in 1968, Heberto Castillo headed the festivities at the National University in Mexico City, and Cuauhtémoc Cárdenas did the same in 1989.

13. Fernando Serrano Migallón, *El Grito de Independencia* (Mexico: Porrúa, n.d.), 66–67, in Archivo Histórico del Ayuntamiento de la Ciudad de México (AHACM), Libro de festividades de septiembre 1825–1845, vol. *(tomo)* I, file *(legajo)* 2. Nine years later, under Valentín Gómez Farías's administration, the practice of setting off firecrackers and shooting pistols into the air was officially authorized. This authorization lasted several decades. See Arturo Priego Ojeda (research) and Begoña Hernández y Lazo (coord.), *Celebración del grito de Independencia* (Mexico: Instituto Nacional de Estudios de la Revolución Mexicana, 1985), 61.

14. The records of "Hidalgo and other associates' court-martial" (May to July 1811) and those of the Inquisition's indictment of Hidalgo (May to June 1811) were the primary sources for all the important historical works assigning to the *grito* the value of a foundational historic event, and attributing to Hidalgo the paternity of this event. Lucas Alamán and Julio Zárate are, no doubt, two of the authors who used these sources.

15. *Procesos inquisitorial y militar seguidos a don Miguel Hidalgo y Costilla*, foreword by Antonio Pompa y Pompa (Mexico: Instituto Nacional de Antropología e Historia, 1960), 222–25, emphasis added.

16. In a recent article, Guadalupe Jiménez Codinach observes that whereas the large funds and the number of revolutionary leaders provided by San Miguel el Grande—Ignacio Allende's hometown—have been recognized, historiography has neglected Allende's organizational and conspiratorial achievements in San Miguel el Grande in order to glorify Miguel Hidalgo y Costilla. Although we will not yet discuss this point, we do wish to stress the valuable information compiled by the author, which is used here in order to support our interpretation of Hidalgo's deposition in the court-martial. See Guadalupe Jiménez Codinach, "La conspiración de San Miguel el Grande," in *Enfoque,* supplement of *Reforma*, September 10, 1996, 10–11.

17. In the summary of Ignacio Allende's case, there are several statements concerning his disagreement with the lootings, summary trials, and mistreatment inflicted by Hidalgo's followers on Spaniards. Regarding Hidalgo's gradual estrangement from the monarchic principles and his positive stance toward the Independence cause, Allende claimed that he asked Dr. Severo Maldonado and Gómez Villaseñor, governor of the Mitre, "if it would be licit to poison him so as to end these ideas and other such evils he was causing, like the murders that were taking place under his orders . . . and many others resulting from his threatening despotism." See *Procesos inquisitorial y militar seguidos a don Miguel Hidalgo y Costilla*, op. cit., 282–83.

18. After an exhaustive analysis of nineteenth-century historiography concerning the Wars of Independence, Carmen Vázquez Mantecón concludes in a recent article that the *grito*, in its precise sense, was "the voice of alarm marking the beginning of the popular rebellion" and that, confronted with the difficulty of estab-

lishing the watchwords or slogans used by Hidalgo to spread the word about the people's uprising, one must acknowledge that "Hidalgo only summoned the people to rebel against the oppression of the Colonial government" and that, in time, historical accounts and popular tradition have both led to the acknowledgment that "Hidalgo's exhortation [is] one of the main sources of our national identity"; see Carmen Vázquez Mantecón, "Hidalgo y Costilla y 'El Grito' del 16 de septiembre," in *Históricas*, Boletín del Instituto de Investigaciones Históricas, UNAM 36 (September-December 1992): 47–59.

19. Pedro José Sotelo (1790–?) was born and died in the town of Dolores. He was 21 years old when he joined the Independent forces and, according to his own statement, had recently married. His *Memorias del último de los soldados de la Independencia* was published in 1874 and was dedicated to Sebastián Lerdo de Tejada, then president. See Humberto Mussachio, *Diccionario enciclopédico de México* (Mexico: Andrés León Ed., 1990), 3:1939.

20. "Un testigo presencial: Pedro José Sotelo," in *Celebración del grito de Independencia*, op. cit., 29, emphasis added.

21. Ibid., 28–29.

22. Pedro García (1790–1873) was born in Dolores and joined the Independent forces in San Miguel el Grande, where he worked for the Allende family. Arrested in Acatita de Baján, he was sentenced to hard labor but escaped in 1812 and returned to his hometown. He joined the Trigarante Army where he rose to the rank of general. In his old age, he was appointed custodian of Hidalgo's home, which had been turned into a museum in 1863 by President Juárez's decree. García wrote the manuscript, *Memoria de los primeros pasos de la Independencia*, first published in 1929 and republished in 1948 under the title *Con el cura Hidalgo en la Guerra de Independencia*. Before the publication of García's memoirs, the only available source from a popular perspective was Pedro Sotelo. Nevertheless, it is possible that General Pedro García provided considerable information and influenced several historical works prior to the publication of his book, since he was an endless source of details and anecdotes on the early Independence movement. See *Enciclopedia de México*, 2d ed. (Mexico: Editora e Impresora Nacional, 1977), 5:175.

23. Pedro García, *Con el cura Hidalgo en la Guerra de Independencia. El liberalismo mexicano en pensamiento y en acción* (Mexico: Empresas Editoriales, 1967), 1:47.

24. Ibid., 50–51, emphasis added.

25. In an extremely scholarly and creative work, Jacinto Barrera Bassols reconstructs the history of the banner as well as the painted canvas allegedly taken by Father Hidalgo from the Atotonilco parish. See *Pesquisa sobre un estandarte. Historia de una pieza de museo* (Mexico: Ediciones Sinfiltro, 1995), 20–28.

26. "Audiencia de acusación. Escrito del inquisidor fiscal," in *Procesos inquisitorial y militar seguidos a don Miguel Hidalgo y Costilla*, op. cit., 346.

27. Ernesto Lemoine, historical study and documentary selection, *Insurgencia y República Federal* (Mexico: Miguel Angel Porrúa–Banco Internacional, 1986), 22.

28. Lucas Alamán, *Historia de México. Desde los primeros movimientos que prepararon su independencia en el año de 1805 hasta la época presente* (Mexico: Libros del Bachiller Sansón Carrasco, 1985), 1:243–44.

29. Julio Zárate, *México a través de los siglos* (Mexico: Ballesca y C., 1910), 3:191.

30. Ibid., 49.

31. José M. de la Fuente, *Hidalgo íntimo* (Toluca: Gobierno del Estado de México–Dirección del Patrimonio Cultural y Artístico, 1979), 253.

32. Indictment hearings of the Inquisition, February 7, 1811, with Hidalgo being "absent and fugitive," in *Procesos militar e inquisitorial*, op. cit., 36.

33. José Rivera (prologue, selection, and notes) and Rafael Hernández (ills.), "La visita de Chana a Pepa," in *Diálogos de la Independencia* (Mexico: Instituto Nacional de Bellas Artes, 1985), 21.

34. The ecclesiastical authorities in New Spain and the Loyalist writers promptly uttered epithets and used literary metaphors to depict Hidalgo: "monster of strange ferocity," "mercenary priest," "Satan's minister," "frenzied and delirious," "former man and ringleader of bandits and murderers," "theologian of Mr. de la Brié's horseshoe." For a more detailed Loyalist perspective, see Juan Hernández Luna, *Imágenes de Hidalgo. Desde la época de la Independencia hasta nuestros días,* Antonio Castro Leal, int. (Mexico: Universidad Nacional Autónoma de México–Consejo de Humanidades, 1954), 21–69.

35. Ibid., 23, in Diego Miguel Bringas. Sermon preached at the parish church in Guanajuato on December 7, 1810, on orders of don Félix María Calleja, *Antología del Centenario* (Mexico, 1910), part I, 129–47.

36. Ibid., 27, in *Jesús García Gutiérrez,* "Hidalgo y la Virgen de Guadalupe," *Abside* (February 1940), emphasis added.

37. Miguel Hidalgo y Costilla, "Contra el edicto del Tribunal de la Fe" (1811), in Lillian Briseño Senosian et al., *La independencia de México* (Mexico: Instituto Mora–Secretaría de Educación Pública, 1985), 1:143–46.

38. Félix María Calleja's report to Viceroy Francisco Javier Venegas, September 21, 1810, San Luis Potosí, in Archivo General de la Nación (AGN), Secretaría de Cámara, Operaciones de Guerra, Vol. 172, pp. (*fojas*) 14–15.

39. *Procesos militar e inquisitorial*, op. cit., 220.

40. José M. de la Fuente, op. cit., 376–82.

41. *Procesos militar e inquisitorial*, op. cit., 298–308.

42. Ibid., 309–10.

43. While in Saltillo (March 1811), before marching to New Spain's northern frontiers, Supreme Commander Miguel Hidalgo instructed Ignacio López Rayón to assume the political leadership of the Insurgents and appointed José María Liceaga in charge of the military command. While the supreme command was defined, both should take joint action to continue the war; they should also maintain communications with the different factions scattered throughout New Spain. See Ernesto Lemoine, op. cit., 26 et seq.

44. Fray Servando Teresa de Mier, "Segunda carta de un americano al español (1812)," in *Cartas de un americano, 1811–1812,* 2d ed. (facsimile), ed. Manuel Calvillo (Mexico: Partido Revolucionario Institucional, 1976), 136–37, emphasis added.

45. "Elementos constitucionales," in Lillian Briseño Senosian et al., op. cit., 1:216–17.

46. "La Junta Suprema de la Nación a los americanos en el aniversario del 16 de septiembre de 1812," in ibid., 2:354, in E. Hernández y Dávalos, *Colección de documentos para la historia de la guerra de Independencia de México de 1808 a 1821* (Mexico: José María Sandoval Imp., 1889), vol. 4, emphasis added.

47. "Diario de gobierno y operaciones militares de la Secretaría y ejército al mando del Exmo. Presidente de la Suprema Junta y ministro universal de la nación, Lic. don Ignacio López Rayón," by J. Ignacio Oyarzábal, in Carlos Herrejón (introduction, selection, and biographical complement), *La independencia según Ignacio Rayón*, Cien de México (Mexico: Secretaría de Educación Pública, 1985), 69.

48. Ibid., 70.

49. José María Morelos, "Sentimientos de la nación," in Ernesto Lemoine, op. cit., 193–96.

50. "Rapto de entusiasmo patriótico de un americano en el feliz aniversario del 16 de septiembre," *Correo del Sur*, September 16, 1813, in Lillian Briseño Senosian et al., op. cit., 2:65–67.

51. "Exposición de motivos del Congreso Insurgente sobre la declaración de la Independencia mexicana," November 6, 1813, in Ernesto Lemoine, op. cit., 223–25.

52. Exiled in Liorna, Italy, Agustín de Iturbide issued a manifesto (September 27, 1823) where he explained: "I established my plan known as the Iguala Plan; [it was] mine because only I conceived, promoted, published, and enacted it. I was determined to free my country because that was the general and sustained vote of the Americans, a vote based on a natural feeling and on the principles of justice, regarded as the only path to prosperity for both nations." See José Gutiérrez Casillas, S.J., *Papeles de don Agustín Iturbide. Documentos hallados recientemente Episodios nacionales mexicanos* (Mexico: Tradición, 1977), 10:223.

53. Iturbide's proposal was clear and concise. Its goal was to: join the American and Spanish efforts to achieve, as soon as possible, the recognition of "absolute independence" from Spain; establish a moderate ("temperate") constitutional monarchy; summon courts that would draft a constitution allowing for the establishment of an Imperial regime; bring a "ready-made monarch," a member of a reigning dynasty, preferably the Spanish, to occupy the throne of "the Mexican Empire"; and reconfirm the Catholic Church as the official and only religion in the new kingdom. See Plan de Iguala (February 24, 1821) in AGN, *Correspondencia y diario militar de don Agustín de Iturbide, 1815–1821,* Documentos para la historia de la guerra de Independencia (1810–1821), XII (Mexico: Talleres Gráficos de la Nación, 1930), 3:662–65.

54. Ibid., 665.

55. The mayor was the Spaniard Juan José de Acha. See Juan de Dios Peza, "Entrada del ejército Trigarante a México," in *Episodios históricos de la guerra de Independencia* (Mexico: Imprenta de El Tiempo de Victoriano Agüeros, 1910), 2:301.

56. Ibid., 302; Julio Zárate, *Fase final de la guerra por la Independencia, con documentos anexos: Plan de Iguala, Tratados de Córdoba, Acta de Independencia*, Biblioteca Mínima Mexicana (Mexico: B. Costa-Amic Ed., 1955), 8:80–82.

57. Vicente Riva Palacio, "El libertador de México," in *Episodios históricos de la guerra de Independencia* (Mexico: Imprenta de El Tiempo de Victoriano Agüeros, 1867), 1:310.

58. Ibid., 1:311.

59. Juan de Dios Peza, op. cit., 2:302.

60. Zárate, op. cit., 84.

61. Ibid., 84–85.

62. "Acta de Independencia del Imperio Mexicano," September 28, 1821, in Ernesto Lemoine, op. cit., 333. The first signature in the Declaration of Independence belonged to Agustín de Iturbide, president of the Regency and member of the Provisional Council; the second belonged to the bishop of Puebla, Antonio de Pérez; the third was that of don Juan O'Donojú, which was followed by all the members of the Supreme Government Council.

63. Since the thirteenth century, the Oath of Allegiance was a solemn ceremony by which cities and states in a kingdom recognized and promised obedience to the monarch, in the name of the kingdom. As of the seventeenth century, the oath was also used when passing constitutional laws.

64. Luis González Obregón, "La jura de la Independencia," in Lucas Alamán et al., op. cit., 11:310–11.

65. With the inclusion of the Provincial Delegation, popular representation throughout the nation was genuinely and symbolically established.

66. The standard-bearing ceremony was instituted in 1528 to celebrate the fall of México-Tenochtitlan; it also formed part of the colonial Oath of Allegiance ceremonies during the early reign of the Spanish monarchs.

67. Luis González Obregón, op. cit., 11:314.

68. Ibid., 315.

69. Andrés Quintana Roo, "Oda al dieciséis de septiembre," in Ramón Martínez Ocaranza (introduction, anthology, and notes), *Poesía insurgente* (Mexico: Universidad Nacional Autónoma de México, 1987), 30–34.

70. AHACM, Historia, retratos, vol. 2278.

71. AGN, Gobernación, vol. 17, dossier *(expediente)* 10, undated.

72. See Verónica Zárate, "Tradición y modernidad: La Orden Imperial de Guadalupe. Su organización y sus rituales," in *Historia mexicana* (Mexico: El Colegio de México, 1995), 191–217.

73. Jacinto Barrera Bassols, op. cit., 141.

74. *Celebración del grito de Independencia,* op. cit., 141.

75. Years later, in a manifesto to the peoples of the world, Iturbide explained his reasons for opposing the inclusion of the *grito de Dolores* in the secular calendar: "The voice of the insurrection neither meant independence nor fair liberty; its purpose was not to claim the rights of the nation but to eradicate all that was European, to destroy possessions, to prostitute ourselves, to ignore military law and even religion: the parties in conflict fought to the death. . . . If such men deserve statues, what is there in store for those who never depart from the path of virtue?" See "Manifiesto al mundo de Agustín de Iturbide o sean apuntes para la historia" (September 1823), in J. Gutiérrez Casillas, op. cit., 262–63.

76. AHACM, Festividades del 16 y 27 de septiembre, File *(legajo)* 1, dossier *(expediente)* 2, record *(registro)* 1058, year *(año)* 1822.

77. Edmundo O'Gorman, "Hidalgo ante la historia." Speech on the occasion of his appointment to the Academia Mexicana de la Historia, in *Memoria de la AMH* 33, no. 3 (July–September 1964): 227.

78. In Mexico City it was the City Council's responsibility to collaborate with the committee in charge of the festivities. Their meetings were always promptly entered in the City Council Records. A revision of the 1822 Records, at the AHACM, yielded negative results; we can therefore infer that little or nothing was done by way of celebration.

79. Miguel de Beruete, *Elevación y caída del emperador Iturbide*, Andrés Henestrosa (transcription, prologue, and notes), (Mexico: Fondo Paglai, 1974), 63.

80. *La Jornada*, 9/16/96; and *Reforma*, 9/16/96. For the next few days, Felipe Calderón answered the criticism regarding his actions and explained his reasons for revindicating Iturbide.

81. AHACM, Historia, retratos, April 12, 1823.

82. AHACM, Festividades del 16 y 27 de septiembre, File *(legajo)* 1, dossier *(expediente)* 2, record *(registro)* 1067, year *(año)* 1823.

83. Edmundo O'Gorman, op. cit., 228; and Miguel de Beruete, op. cit., 53 and passim.

84. Fernando Serrano Migallón, op. cit., 66–68.

85. Ibid., 68.

86. AHACM, Festividades del 16 y 27 de septiembre, File *(legajo)* 1, dossier *(expediente)* 6, record *(registro)* 1067, year *(año)* 1829.

87. AHACM, Festividades del 16 y 27 de septiembre, File *(legajo)* 1, dossier *(expediente)* 2, record *(registro)* 1067, year (*año)* 1823; File *(legajo)* 1, dossier *(expediente)* 5, record *(registro)* 1067, year *(año)* 1825; File *(legajo)* 1, dossier *(expediente)* 3, record *(registro)* 1067, year *(año)* 1826; File *(legajo)* 1, dossier *(expediente)* 7, record *(registro)* 1067, year *(año)* 1830; File *(legajo)* 1, dossier *(expediente)* 8, record *(registro)* 1067, year *(año)* 1832 et seq.

88. Fernando Serrano Migallón, op. cit., 78–79, in *El Sol,* September 14, 1832.

89. Loc. cit.

90. Timothy E. Anna, *El imperio de Iturbide,* trans. Adriana Sandoval (Mexico: Patria–Consejo Nacional para la Cultura y las Artes, 1991), 25.

91. José Ramón Malo, *Diario de sucesos notables de don José Ramón Malo (1854–1864),* ed. and annot. Mariano Cuevas, S.J. (Mexico: Editorial Patria, 1948), 2:468. In an addendum at this entry of his *Diary,* Malo states: "This bull was rotten and since then, in the caricatures of Comonfort . . . there is always a small bull by his side."

92. Clementina Díaz y de Ovando, "Rostro y corazón de los mexicanos," *México, patria e identidad* (Mexico: Secretaría de Gobernación–Archivo General de la Nación, 1995), 95.

93. Ibid., 35–101.

94. Ibid., 64 et seq.

95. AHACM, Festividades del 16 y 27 de septiembre, dossier (*expediente*) 51, record (*registro*) 1068, year (*año*) 1861.

96. Clementina Díaz y de Ovando, op. cit., 82–84.

97. René Avilés F., *La guerra de intervención en dos libros, El álbum de Hidalgo y la hija de Oaxaca,* Edición Especial para el Primer Congreso Nacional de Historia para Estudios de la Guerra de Intervención (Mexico: Editorial Libros de México, S.A., 1962), 30–31.

98. *Guía Oficial de la Casa de don Miguel Hidalgo* (official guide to Miguel Hidalgo's house) (Mexico: Instituto Nacional de Antropología e Historia, 1960), passim.

99. René Avilés F., op. cit., 32, entry on December 20, 1864.

100. Guillermo Prieto, "El grito," in Carlos Monsiváis, *A ustedes les consta. Antología de la cronica en México* (Mexico: Era, 1980), 80–81.

101. José María Iglesias, *Revistas históricas sobre la intervención francesa en México* (Mexico: Ed. Porrúa, 1972), 476–77.

102. Fernando Serrano Migallón, op. cit., *Apud El Monitor Republicano,* July 31, 1887.

103. For information on the *dolorenses'* attempts to preserve their bell, which included resorting to collective ruses and denying its existence on the grounds that years before it had been resmelted in order to make new bells, see Alfonso Alcocer, *La campana de Dolores* (Mexico: Departamento del Distrito Federal, 1985).

104. Speech by political leader Francisco González Caballero, June 28th. Ibid., 55–56.

CHAPTER TWO

The Junta Patriótica and the Celebration of Independence in Mexico City, 1825–1855*

MICHAEL COSTELOE

E arly in August 1825 a small group of Mexico City residents met informally to consider an idea possibly suggested to them by José María Tornel, private secretary of President Guadalupe Victoria. Tornel's idea was that the anniversary of the Grito de Dolores of 16 September 1810 should be marked with some form of celebration.[1] The residents welcomed the proposal and, having obtained governmental approval to proceed, they decided to form an association that would organize events and festivities to celebrate the date as the beginning of the movement for independence. At first known as the Junta Cívica de Patriotas, the new body soon became known as the Junta Patriótica. Mexicans in other towns and cities throughout the republic, encouraged by their metropolitan compatriots, quickly adopted the idea and formed their own associations.

This essay is concerned with the Junta Patriótica in Mexico City. Despite the ravages of war, revolution, and pestilence, it managed to meet each year without fail for the next thirty years; and with only one exception in 1847, when the U.S. army occupied the city in September, Hidalgo's Grito de Dolores and subsequently, other similar anniversaries, were celebrated with a full program of events organized and financed by the Junta. Although its membership was renewed annually with different volunteers participating each year, the

*From *Mexican Studies/Estudios Mexicanos* 13, no. 1 (Winter 1997): 21–53.

Junta was able to keep an archive together with accumulated furniture, portraits of heroes of the insurgency, and various relics of the war against Spain. Unfortunately, the archive and possessions have not been located and almost certainly have been lost or dispersed. Fortunately, on the other hand, the secretaries of the association were exceptionally diligent in keeping full and detailed minutes of the weekly, and at times twice or more weekly, meetings held from July to September approximately each year. These minutes were published in the press of the time, as were in some years the financial accounts. With only a few exceptions, they have been located for each of the thirty years between 1825 and 1855.[2] They provide us with a comprehensive insight into all aspects of the Junta Patriótica, its principles, objectives, organization, membership, finances, and its sometimes turbulent relationship with the political factions of the day. The history of the Junta Patriótica also provides an unusual, microscopic view of various aspects of the so-called Age of Santa Anna. Its finances, for example, clearly reflect the changing economic circumstances of the country and the growing poverty of the individual Mexico City resident from the early 1830s onwards. Its membership offers an exceptional panorama of the city's social and political elite, and its activities reveal how the celebration of independence developed into the most important secular festival in the Mexican calendar, still celebrated, of course, to the present day.

Foundation and Principles

Prior to 1825, the commemoration of independence seems to have been confined to relatively low-key events on 27 September, the date when Agustín de Iturbide had finally entered Mexico City in 1821 at the head of his victorious army.[3] During Iturbide's period in power, the Grito de Dolores passed almost unnoticed and it was only after his fall that 16 September was formally declared a public holiday. In 1823 the remains of the insurgent hero, José María Morelos, were brought to Mexico City for ceremonial burial on the anniversary and there were some public celebrations. The following year, 1824, however, saw nothing more than brief, formal speeches in Congress.[4] Welcoming the proposal that more should be done to mark the anniversary, one newspaper editor noted that memory of the Grito was already fading in the public mind. Mexico, he said, should learn from the 4 July celebrations in the United States and should use the anniversary to create a sense of national unity and patriotism.[5] The founder members of the Junta Patriótica agreed. Eighteen people attended the inaugural meeting; most represented a specific group—senators, deputies, military personnel, government employees, people in commerce—but two were present as private citizens. They elected General Anastasio Bustamante as their first president or chairman. They soon agreed upon certain basic principles which, though amended or refined over time, remained fundamentally the same throughout the first thirty years of the association.

The first principle was that the association was an entirely voluntary body, open to all Mexican citizens by birth or naturalization who were resident in the capital. No discrimination on any grounds of occupation, profession, or social class would be permitted. In the early years, participation seems to have been restricted to men. By the 1830s, however, women, especially wives of male members, were becoming increasingly important in the Junta's activities. Several of the subcommittees, mainly those concerned with fundraising, consisted entirely of women. In 1849 the association's rules were revised, and Article 2 confirmed the nondiscriminatory nature of the organization:

> This junta is entirely popular. Therefore, all Mexicans by birth or naturalization, without exception on grounds of class, age, sex, or any other distinction, may be members of it. Any responsibilities or tasks they may be given are voluntary, and they shall be accepted or refused, as they wish, without any need to provide reason or excuse.[6]

The second principle was that the Junta was popular and democratic. All of its officers from chairman to secretaries and accountants were elected, and usually there were several candidates for each position. In the early years, the electoral procedure consisted of each voter approaching the presiding committee and "telling the secretary of the committee in a low voice the person for whom they are voting."[7] In later years, secret ballots were used; and by the early 1840s, when political factions began to take an active interest in the Junta, printed lists of candidates became common, as was the case in congressional and other elections.

The third principle concerned finance. It was agreed in 1825 that the association would rely entirely on voluntary donations from individuals or groups. Again, the principle remained unchanged, but in practice, reflecting among other things the economic recession, the

Junta was obliged by the early 1830s to seek financial help from the government. Such requests were not always met, as will be seen in the section below on finance.

Finally, and what was certainly viewed by many of the members as its cardinal principle, the Junta was nonpolitical. This meant that party political affiliation or ideological belief was irrelevant both in its members and in its activities. The 1849 regulations state this succinctly:

> The junta shall never discuss any matters other than those for which it was established, nor shall it involve itself in the politics of the country. Its sole function is to encourage a spirit of independence and the enthusiasm to defend it at all costs.[8]

Once again, this principle was never altered. But perhaps inevitably, given the political turmoil of the time, politics and party rivalries did affect the Junta on more than one occasion. Political intervention is also examined below.

Initially, the objective of the Junta was the commemoration of Hidalgo's Grito de Dolores of 16 September 1810. Within a few years, however, it took on other anniversaries as well. The most important of these, introduced for the first time in 1837, was the celebration of Iturbide's entry into the capital on 27 September 1821. These two dates, 16 and 27 September, always remained the Junta's main concern and soon they were extended to include 15 and 28 September. Others were added from time to time, according to the dominant political group of the day. For example, when Santa Anna was in power, he insisted that 11 September also should be celebrated. That was the day in 1829 when he had defeated, at Tampico, a Spanish invasion force dispatched from Cuba by Fernando VII in a futile attempt to reconquer his former colony. When Santa Anna was not in office, the day passed without any celebration. Similarly, when federal republicans controlled the government, the Junta was occasionally asked to organize events to mark 4 October, the date of publication of the country's first federal republican constitution in 1824.

These anniversaries were celebrated in various ways. Each year the Junta organized a full program of events including parades, concerts, special theatrical performances, military salutes, Te Deums in the churches, poetry competitions, prizes for musical compositions or *himnos nacionales*, decoration of the streets in the capital, and fireworks displays. Most important of all were orations by speakers who were elected in the same way as the association's officers. The orators' duty was to praise the valor of the heroes of the insurgency and, after 1837, of Iturbide and his contemporaries. No control was exercised by the Junta over the content or views expressed, and it was largely the orations that were to generate political controversy and intervention.[9]

Speeches, fireworks, poetry and the like were symbolic illustrations of the anniversaries, but the founder members in 1825 were anxious to have a more tangible demonstration of the significance of independence. They decided, therefore—and again this became the accepted practice of the Junta in all future years—that the group should also perform acts of charity. Noting that a principal benefit of independence had been freedom or liberty from oppression, it was resolved that a very appropriate way to remind Mexicans of that fact would be to arrange for the public emancipation of slaves as part of the 16 September celebrations. The members in 1825 enthusiastically welcomed this suggestion and it was decided to use some of the funds collected to purchase slaves' freedom. Almost immediately, donations began to be offered. One benefactor, who wished to remain anonymous and hence signed his offer only as M.J.A., volunteered to pay for the freedom of one slave. If the latter were a minor, he promised to provide him or her with a home and education within his own family.[10] Several similar offers were received. Responding to the spirit of the time, slave owners also promised to donate their slaves. For example, Senator Manuel Ambrosio de la Vega offered two women, and Minister of Hacienda [Interior] José Ignacio Esteva offered one. Within about a week of the Junta's invitation to slave owners, twelve slaves had been offered, some freely by their owners and others at a price. As one newspaper editor commented, the number demonstrated that there were more slaves in the city than previously had been thought.[11] So many were promised, in fact, that the Junta decided to restrict the money it would allocate for slave emancipation to two thousand pesos. The first slaves were duly given their freedom as part of the ceremonial on 16 September 1825.

The emancipation of slaves became a regular part of the Independence Day celebration until 1829, when the Junta placed the following advertisement in the press:

> The patriotic junta to celebrate the glorious declaration of 16 September is seeking slaves: if any person wishes to sell, he should contact the members of this committee, who are Luis de Urquiaga, Manuel Barrera, Senator José Hernández Chico, Deputy José de Jesús Rada, José Cervantes, and Rafael Mangino.[12]

This produced no response; no slaves were offered for manumission with or without payment. It was also in that year of 1829 that President Vicente Guerrero decreed the abolition of slavery throughout the republic. To emphasize the symbolic significance of that measure and the association of independence with liberty, the law was released on 16 September.

Another charitable act of the Junta that, unlike the manumission of slaves, continued throughout the thirty years under review, was to give cash payments to disabled or destitute veterans of the Wars of Independence and to the widows and children or orphans of insurgents who had died in the conflict. Starting in 1825, each year some of the money collected was spent in this way. The number of those who benefited varied according to the availability of funds, and over the years the number of those eligible, especially veterans, naturally declined. By the 1840s, however, it was decided that dependents of those who died in the 1829 conflict against Spain, the 1838 war against France, and the 1846–1848 war with the United States also were eligible. Potential claimants were invited, usually through a press announcement, to register a claim. For example, the following appeared in the *Aguíla Mexicana* on 14 September 1826:

> The patriotic junta, which promotes the maximum brilliance of the anniversary of the declaration of Dolores, has commissioned me and my companions in arms to undertake the investigation of patriots resident in this capital who have been maimed, crippled or disabled through service to the nation. In consequence, I invite those brave men of the fatherland who find themselves in this situation to come to see me in my room in the mezzanine of the palace until the 14th of the present month. —José María Tornel

Initially a designated member of the Junta, and later a subcommittee, evaluated the claims and recommended each year the list of those to whom a donation should be given. In the first year, presumably because of lack of publicity, only four orphans of insurgents were located. Three members of the Junta—Pedro Terreros, Vicente Filisola, and Francisco Molinos del Campo—volunteered to pay for their education. By 1830, 500 pesos was distributed to widows and orphans; and in 1843, twenty-eight veterans, widows, and orphans were given a total of 500 pesos. Two years later, 250 pesos was allocated at the rate of 25 pesos per veteran or widow; and in 1848 the beneficiaries received amounts varying from 20 to 4 pesos, according to perceived need. Finally, by 1853, the sum earmarked for the donations had risen to 1000 pesos.

Such charitable donations were always a primary objective of the Junta and, when its rules were revised in 1849, they were given priority over all other methods used to celebrate independence. Article 5 reads as follows:

> The exclusive purpose of this patriotic junta is to commemorate the said anniversaries by means of acts of charity in the first place, and second, with fiestas, fireworks, processions, and all kinds of popular entertainment, and with the patriotic speeches which shall be delivered on 16 and 27 September.

This philanthropic aim was achieved in many other ways. For example, in the 1820s, as one of the highlights of the day's events on 16 September, poor children were each given a new set of clothes. Sixty-two children "were completely dressed" in 1827 and thirty-two in 1830. Sometimes, as in 1829, selected poor children were each given a cash sum, presented in that year by President Guerrero. Also in 1827, which seems to have been a particularly affluent year for the Junta, on 16 September every prisoner in the city's jails was given a good meal, a packet of cigarettes, a bar of soap, and one *real*.

In 1830 the Junta accepted a proposal from one of its members that widows and children of Spaniards who had been exiled from the country under the expulsion laws of 1827 and 1829 should be helped to return. Many of the exiled families had gone to New Orleans where it was known that some of the wives and children of deceased Spaniards were living in extreme poverty. No doubt reflecting the change of regime in 1830 when the conservative vice president, Anastasio Bustamante, took control of the government with his main minister, the pro-Spanish Lucas Alamán, the proposal to help the Spanish exiles was warmly received. Those present at the meeting of the Junta at which the proposal was made immediately donated 700 pesos, and it was resolved to launch a nationwide appeal for funds, which eventually yielded 2283 pesos. The idea was to pay the travel costs and general expenses of those widows and orphans in New Orleans who wanted to return. They would be paraded on 16 September and given a cash sum to help towards their reestablishment in Mexico City. José Javier de Olazábal, resident in New Orleans, was appointed the Junta's agent and he quickly reported that he had found ten widows, two with four children and one with five. They were returned to Mexico, 400 pesos being spent on their travel costs and 385 pesos in grants to them.[13] How many others returned in this way is not recorded in the minutes.

Organization

It is clear from these details of charitable activities that the Junta Patriótica quickly developed into a well-organized and well-regulated association. Its basic administrative procedures were devised in the 1820s, and in 1831 a formal set of regulations was drawn up and approved.[14] After each year's celebration was concluded, the Junta elected a nine-member standing committee (*comisión permanente*). It had several important duties. These were to conclude any matters left over from the September events, including making sure that the treasurer presented proper accounts of income and expenditure. If not already done, it had to arrange for the printing of the orations and had to recompense the orators appropriately.

In June of the following year, it had to initiate the procedure for the assembly of a new Junta Patriótica. This involved organizing a place for the meetings, almost always the reception room in the university or the national palace, and placing notices in the press inviting attendance at the first meeting of the year. In most years, this first meeting was held on the second Tuesday of July at 5:00 P.M., though political or other circumstances occasionally caused a delay. At the inaugural session each year, the chairman of the standing committee presented a report of the activities of the previous year. Elections then followed for the officers of the new Junta. A president, vice president, treasurer, and two secretaries were chosen, and the newly elected president took the chair for the rest of the meeting. The retiring secretary and treasurer handed over their respective records to their successors. Members of the standing committee then stood down and took their seats among the membership.

In July of each year, a new Junta Patriótica was installed in this way. Its first task at the inaugural meeting was to appoint a nine-member program committee (*comisión proponente*). Proceedings were suspended for a short time while the program committee prepared two short-lists of three candidates for a public orator for the 16th and 27th of September. The short-lists were put to the meeting, and the orator for each day was elected in the customary low voice or secret ballot. The final business was for the new president to choose a six-man deputation whose job was to inform the president of the republic of the proper installation of the Junta. Another three-man deputation conveyed the same message to the governor of the Federal District.[15]

After this first meeting, the Junta met in most years —again there were exceptions—at least every Tuesday throughout July and August and up to the 16th or 27th of September. During these sessions, the events proposed by the program committee were discussed, amended, and approved. The program committee also was responsible for suggesting the membership of numerous subcommittees, each composed of three to five people, all of whom had to be approved by the full Junta Patriótica. The responsibilities of these subcommittees included decoration of the streets, preparing the platform in the big city park, Parque de la Alameda, where the main events took place, organizing fireworks displays, arranging events such as concerts or special performances in the theaters, or in some years the bullring, from which most of the proceeds were given to the Junta. Other groups commissioned poetry, musical compositions, portraits of insurgents, or plays based on the independence theme. By the mid-1830s, separate women's committees were formed, some to seek donations and others, for example in 1841, to arrange for schoolchildren to line the streets during the parade. By far the largest number of these subcommittees, however, were concerned with fundraising. Again, by the early 1830s, there were forty-three involving more than 180 people. Each had a chairperson who was obliged, according to the regulations, to attend the weekly meetings of the Junta to report progress in their cash collections. Further details of these collecting committees are given below in the section on finance.

This organizational structure developed informally from 1825, and then the procedures so far found to be effective were formalized in the written regulations approved in 1831. They remained in force until 1849 when they were revised. The revision made no major changes but did consolidate some aspects. For example, as already noted, the nondiscriminatory rules for membership were confirmed, as was the participation of women. The number of officers on the main committee was in future to be seven, all elected by secret ballot. The voting rights of members were changed. In all previous years since 1825, all those who had attended a meeting were allowed to speak and to vote. Now it was decided that in June of each year, following the usual press announcements, a register would be opened. Those who wanted to participate in the Junta had to sign the register when they would be given credentials or "letters of invitation." Only those with such credentials would be allowed to speak and vote at meetings. The Junta retained the right to recruit members by invitation. As will be seen later, the question of voting rights quickly became a contentious issue. Finally, the 1849 regulations reaffirmed the principle that the Junta Patriótica would never interfere in party politics.

Membership

There is no doubt that the social and political elite of Mexico City prized membership in the Junta Patriótica highly. From the Junta's foundation in 1825, its officers and committee members formed a perhaps unique gallery of the prominent families as well as the leading political figures of the time. Although determined to retain its nonpolitical character, it is also evident that in several years the membership directly reflected the party or group in power. By the late 1840s, there were definite signs of increased party political intervention. Nevertheless, it must be said that political influence was the exception rather than the rule and that during most of the three decades from 1825 to 1855, regardless of the political affiliation of the members, the celebrations were successfully kept out of the political arena. Table 1 gives the presidents for each year.

This list, together with that of the orators given in Table 3 below, contains most of the top names in Mexican politics in the Age of Santa Anna. The election of Santa Anna himself in 1847, which he accepted with gratitude, was entirely symbolic because he was then leading the army in the war against the United States. He attended none of the meetings in July and August. In contrast, Anastasio Bustamante, founder president in 1825 and again elected in four later years, regularly took the chair, even though during 1837–1839 he was also president of the republic. The insurgent hero, Vicente Guerrero, was twice elected and was also a regular participant. Another prominent name is that of José María Tornel, credited with the original idea for the Junta and three times elected its president. He was an active supporter throughout his long career. Even when not in the chair, he was often on one or more of the subcommittees. The political spectrum is clearly reflected with conservatives like Bustamante, Facio, and Díez de Bonilla, and the liberals Gómez Farías, Alvarez, Riva Palacio, and Rodríguez de Puebla, together with those whose party allegiances and beliefs fluctuated such as Valencia, Almonte, and Tornel, although he was a lifelong supporter of Santa Anna.

With so many of the nation's leading generals and politicians at the head of the association, it is not surprising that many other prominent personalities were anxious to be involved. Literally thousands of people participated over the thirty years and they included virtually every well-known figure of the time, serving on the main committee or on one of the subcommittees. Lorenzo de Zavala, José María

Table 1

1825	Anastasio Bustamante
1826	Vicente Guerrero
1827	Manuel de Mier y Terán
1828	Vicente Guerrero
1829	Anastasio Bustamante
1830	Luis Quintanar
1831	José Antonio Facio
1832	Juan Gómez de Navarrete
1833	Juan Rodríguez de Puebla
1834	?[16]
1835	José María Tornel
1836	Gabriel Valencia
1837	Anastasio Bustamante
1838	Anastasio Bustamante
1839	Anastasio Bustamante
1840	Melchor Múzquiz
1841	José María Tornel
1842	Tranquilino de la Vega (acting)
1843	José María Tornel
1844	Antonio Díez de Bonilla
1845	Mariano Riva Palacio
1846	Valentín Gómez Farías
1847	Antonio López de Santa Anna
1848	Mariano Riva Palacio
1849	Juan Nepomuceno Almonte
1850	Juan Nepomuceno Almonte
1851	Juan Nepomuceno Almonte
1852	Antonio Pérez de Lebrija
1853	Antonio Díez de Bonilla
1854	Leandro Estrada
1855	Juan Alvarez

Luis Mora, José María Bocanegra, Carlos María de Bustamante, Francisco Paula de Arrangoiz, Luis Gonzaga Cuevas, Gregorio Mier y Terán, José María Herrera, Andrés Quintana Roo, Juan de Dios Cañedo, and most of those who achieved ministerial level or political eminence gave their time and their money. There are, however, two exceptions to this comprehensive gallery. The Junta Patriótica was a secular association, and while there is no written evidence in the minutes, it appears that the role or influence of the clergy was kept to a minimum. Hence, no bishop or senior clergyman was voted to the presidency. Instead, the clergy seem to have been restricted to the lower committees, especially those involved in fundraising. Religious services played a part in the ceremonial, and although senior clerics took part in the procession, their presence and influence were limited.

The second exception is personal and individual. Significant by its absence is the name of Lucas Alamán. He made a generous donation of 100 pesos to the first Junta in 1825 but thereafter, apart from agreeing to chair a collecting committee in 1837, he appears to have taken no part. Of course, he did not spend all of his time in the capital but his absence from the Junta when he was there, for example, in the 1830s and late 1840s, is noticeable. His antipathy towards Hidalgo and the early stages of the insurgency was well known; and in his *Historia de Méjico*, published in the early 1850s, he was unequivocal in his opinion of the 16 September celebration: "The purpose of the great national festival is not only to celebrate a lie. It also is an act of ingratitude repeated every year whereby the glory of achieving independence is given to those who do not deserve it, thus depriving the rightful recipient of the justice he is owed. The injustice done to the person of Iturbide is even repeated against his memory."[17]

The number of participants varied over the years and was affected by external circumstances. The early meetings were always the best attended and although the registers have not been located, it is possible to get an idea of the attendance from the number who voted for the various officers and from the minutes. In 1827, for example, over one hundred attended the first meeting; two hundred were present in 1843; and in 1850, when political activists tried to take over the association, there were reported to be between six hundred and one thousand. Later meetings through July and August attracted an average attendance of between twenty and forty. In 1833 a serious cholera epidemic reduced the numbers and forced the postponement of the celebrations until 4 October. On other occasions, notably in 1840 and 1841, rebellions involving military action on the streets of the capital also prevented many from attending, but on both occasions the Junta continued to conduct its business. The procedure for recruiting members has already been indicated. In the first years, notices were placed in the press inviting participation, and by the 1830s invitations also were sent to individuals. By 1843 these had reached sixteen hundred. Not everybody responded positively, and when it came to serving on a collecting committee, the minutes are filled with polite letters of refusal.

Finance

The founder members wanted the association to rely entirely on voluntary donations. With the exception of a few years when government grants were sought and received, it was largely money given by individuals and groups that paid for the Independence Day celebrations. Funds were raised through an elaborate and well-organized system of targeting potential benefactors. A comprehensive range of all the professional, commercial, industrial, and other groups living and working in the capital was identified. A collecting committee (*comisión recaudadora*) of three to five people was allocated to each of the identified groups. The committee's job was to approach the target and solicit donations. In 1825, the first year, the number of targeted groups was small and individual donations from groups such as employees in government offices and from cabinet ministers—each gave 100 pesos—provided most of the money collected. The following year, the collection was more organized. Committees were formed to approach seventeen different groups. These included senators, deputies, ministers and their offices, military units, clergymen, city council members, lawyers and other members of the judiciary, miners, merchants, farmers, doctors, theater owners, and tradesmen. Each year thereafter the number of target groups expanded, reaching forty-three in 1834. Every professional and commercial group now was included, ranging from government employees, ecclesiastical institutions, and military garrisons to butchers, bakers, tobacconists, and pulque sellers.

After the initial enthusiasm of the early years, the amount of money raised by the collecting committees declined, as did the willingness of people to serve on them. From the early 1830s onwards, the association's minutes are filled with letters from designated collectors refusing the job. All manner of excuses were offered including illness, absence from the city on urgent business, lack of time, and other commitments. In 1849, Manuel Luzuriaga, who had been named a collector for paint shops (*tlapalería*), refused because of the abuse or "disagreeable replies" he had received from those he had approached in earlier years.

Another problem was that there were many other competing demands on the pockets of potential contributors. Little research has been done on the topic, but it is clear that with the certain reduction in the charitable activities of the Church after 1821, especially the convents and monasteries, lay philanthropic organizations rapidly expanded, depending for their work on private donations. All manner of such charities were formed from medical care for the destitute to a reform school for delinquent teenagers. In 1839 some of the women asked to arrange a fundraising concert for the Junta declined because they were already engaged in preparing one on behalf of a home for abandoned children. The taxation demands on the middle class from the mid-1830s onwards also rose significantly, and the Junta was reluctantly forced to conclude that there was little point in asking for individual donations. One example of this occurred in July 1847 when, just as the collecting committees were being formed, a tax of sixty thousand pesos was imposed on all the city's main institutions as well as on named individuals. The Junta's members at once decided that it was inappropriate to seek private contributions that year.

Always claiming insufficient funds, the Junta tried a variety of fundraising alternatives. In 1837–1839 it was suggested that because of the widespread poverty then afflicting rich and poor alike, donations should not be sought. Instead, special performances should be staged in the theater, bullring, and cockfight arena with the profits going to the Junta. Such special events became common in the following years, and in 1848, for example, the theater produced four hundred pesos. In 1842 another idea was floated but apparently not accepted. This was for a raffle (rifa) in which all government employees would be obliged to take part with one peso per one thousand deducted from their salaries and with all those earning over five hundred pesos a year included. In some notably difficult years, such as during and immediately after the war with the United States in 1846–1848, the celebrations were scaled down considerably, with the elimination of all "entertainments." In 1846 the Junta decided to donate some of its funds to the war effort with an initial gift of five hundred pesos, gratefully received by Santa Anna.[18]

Individual contributions continued to be received, sometimes in the form of pay credits against the Treasury from military and other public employees whose salaries rarely were paid in cash after the mid-1830s. But it was clear that dependency on voluntary donations was unreliable. Hence, from the early 1830s, the Junta began to ask for government help. The response varied. In 1833, Valentín Gómez Farías, vice president in charge of the government, offered two thousand pesos, although only twelve hundred was received according to the accounts for that year. In 1836, Congress voted to give three thousand pesos but that was not paid; and in 1837, taking advantage of the fact that Anastasio Bustamante, president of the republic, was also their chairman, the Junta put a formal request for help to the government. Bustamante agreed to provide three thousand pesos. As chairman again the following year, Bustamante reported to the association's meeting on 7 August that he and his cabinet had agreed to ask Congress to pass a law authorizing an annual grant of two thousand pesos. Nothing seems to have come from that and by 1840, again in reply to a request from the Junta, the government offered one thousand pesos. This was increased in 1841 to twelve hundred pesos, but Bustamante warned that the Treasury had so little cash in hand that it would have to be paid in weekly installments of two hundred pesos. Santa Anna, in power from 1841 to 1844, was less generous, although in reply to the Junta's now annual request, he did order departmental governors to propose taxes to be used for a regular endowment for the Independence Day celebrations throughout the country. The Junta itself proposed to the governor of the Mexico department a small tax for the same purpose. He passed the idea on to his departmental assembly, from which it never emerged.

None of the fundraising schemes, regular newspaper appeals for support, or pleas to the government provided any constant source of income. Consequently, the Junta had to rely year after year on its members' energy and initiative in extracting voluntary donations from the general public. Then, in 1850, following another appeal to the government, Congress finally enacted a law by which the city council was ordered to give the association an annual grant of four thousand pesos towards the cost of the celebrations.[19] Two thousand pesos had to be spent on acts of charity for the families of those who had died in the Wars of Independence and in subsequent wars against external aggressors. Now, seemingly endowed with "a fixed endowment," the 1850 Junta decided to abandon the practice of targeting groups or "donations by class," and to seek additional funds only from individuals. Ignacio Cumplido, the country's leading publisher and for several years an enthusiastic supporter of the Junta, was elected that year's treasurer. The city's residents were invited to pay their donations to him at his bookshop at No. 1, Calle de Plateros, where they would be given a receipt. The names of all contributors would also be published in his newspaper, *El Siglo XIX*.

The 1850 law did not solve the Junta's financial problems because it was soon discovered that the city council either did not have the money or would not part with it. A couple of years later, in 1853, Santa Anna resumed power and, as in his earlier periods in office, refused to help the Junta with government money; the municipal authority likewise offered no contribution. Hence, the system of collecting committees and appeals for individual donations was reintroduced for the 1853 anniversaries.

According to the rules of the association, accounts of all income and expenditure had to be published each year so that contributors could see how their money had been spent. This requirement does not seem to have been met every year, but enough accounts have been located over the thirty years to 1855 to give a good idea of the sums involved. Minutes of the meetings also provide further details of the money received from the collecting committees and other sources. Table 2 gives some indication of the income and expenditure.

Table 2

	Income	Expenditure
1825	8949	7752
1830	5438	5373
1834	4413	4644
1836	1652	1528
1840	2046	1652
1842	263	170
1850	4200	4200

The sums given above for 1830, 1834, 1836, 1840, and 1842 are taken from the final accounts submitted by each year's treasurer. The figures for the other years are from references in the minutes to money received and spent. These amounts are certainly minimal and are not the final totals. 1842 was obviously a difficult year and the accounts presented for that year by the treasurer, J. R. de Ibarrola, reveal that almost nothing was spent on the celebrations either on 16 or 27 September. This may have had some connection with the fact that Santa Anna, then in power, had ordered lavish celebrations on 11 September to mark his 1829 victory at Tampico. Parades, military bands, and four thousand troops had saluted the "hero of Tampico," who sponsored a sumptuous ball in his own honor on that evening. The infamous burial of his amputated leg in a specially constructed mausoleum also took place in September, with the vice president of the Junta Patriótica among the dignitaries present.

Excluding exceptional years like 1842, or 1846 and 1847 when it was decided that public entertainments were inappropriate in a time of war, the pattern of expenditure of the Junta's funds was consistent.

In each year, the main items of expenditure were on the construction of a platform (*templete*) and decoration of the Parque de la Alameda where the ceremony was held and the orations given; the purchase of fireworks; street decorations from the national palace to the Alameda; gifts to war veterans and their surviving dependents, and other charitable acts. Other costs included printing of the orations and invitations to the ceremony, as well as a cash payment in some years to the orators. Office and secretarial costs were another small but regular item, and prizes often were sponsored with cash and medals for literary works on independence.[20] Musical compositions were sponsored in most years and portraits of heroes of the insurgency sometimes commissioned.

The 1833 accounts show the following costs:

Fireworks	1525 pesos
Street decorations	1420 pesos
Parque de la Alameda platform	1412 pesos
Printing	286 pesos

The fireworks displays were always expensive and clearly regarded as an essential part of the event. Seven hundred pesos—about half the income in 1836—was spent on fireworks and, in most years, the agreed budget proposed by the program committee was around one thousand pesos. After 1837, when the 27 September anniversary was added to the Junta's responsibilities, the costs increased and added to the perceived need and pressure for government assistance. Even so, in 1841, for example, another one thousand pesos was spent, and by 1850 the amount had risen to fourteen hundred pesos.

The money awarded to veterans, widows, and children was also a major expense. Again, the amount varied from year to year but it was rarely less than five hundred pesos. In 1848, thirteen hundred pesos was distributed at the two ceremonies on 16 and 27 September, with three hundred pesos of that total collected by the women's committee. The sums given to the individuals, each selected as a deserving case by a subcommittee which examined all claims, varied from four to twenty-five pesos. Bearing in mind that an artisan's weekly wage was not much more than two pesos, the sums were not negligible.

From the Junta's inception in 1825, its members were always anxious to ensure proper scrutiny of and public accountability for all funds raised and spent. This was achieved in two main ways. First, the amounts collected, including the names of each individual or corporate contributor, were recorded in the minutes as the cash was received by the treasurer from July through September each year. Second, the treasurer was obliged to keep accounts of all income and expenditure. These were checked by the accountant and by the treasury subcommittee. When they were complete, the accounts had to be presented for approval to the succeeding Junta at its first meeting the following year. Then, as a final check, a summary of the accounts usually was published.

This system of checking and public accountability seems to have been very successful and there were remarkably few allegations of peculation or misuse of funds. In fact, only two such allegations have been found between 1825 and 1855 and neither was proved. The first occurred in 1832 when that year's president of the Junta, Juan Gómez de Navarrete, was accused of seeking to make money from his office. He was a publisher and he obtained the contract to print the orations. Charged with abusing his position (by his political enemies, he said), he resigned, but the full Junta refused to accept his resignation. In 1850 the brothers Francisco and Vicente Carbajal, both of whom had been active members of the Junta for several years previously, also alleged financial irregularities. They used the normal medium of an anonymous letter in the press signed "Two insurgents" to state their suspicions and, amidst a brief polemic in the press between rival newspapers, they promised to publish a detailed accusation.[21] They failed to keep their promise—no such document has been found—and it seems that their allegations reflected no more than a quarrel with other members of the Junta. Finally, money very occasionally did go missing or could not be accounted for by the treasurer. In 1841, for example, 394 pesos could not be explained, and two years later, the Junta's accountants were still trying to locate the missing money.

The Celebration

The Junta Patriótica's primary objective was to organize events to commemorate independence. Initially, the celebration was restricted to 16 September. The founder members in 1825 wanted to start the program on the evening of the 15th on the grounds that Hidalgo had launched his Grito at 11:00 P.M. on that night. President Victoria ruled against that idea, however, largely because he was concerned about public order. He warned the Junta that proper policing arrangements would have to be made and the city's garrisons kept on alert throughout the day. He also ruled that all establishments selling alcoholic beverages should close on the evening of the 16th.[22] His fears for public order seem to have been assuaged by the success of the 1825 celebrations, and in all succeeding years, the program of events began at 9:00 P.M. on the 15th. As already explained, the 27th was introduced in 1837 and the following day also was soon added.

The anniversary, therefore, was spread over four days; 15, 16, 27, 28 September. The program of events was formulated largely in the 1820s and the pattern remained much the same for the next thirty years. It began on the evening of the 15th with a series of events from 9:00 P.M. to 11:00 P.M., often held in the university or one of the city's theaters. The officers of the Junta attended and the proceedings were chaired by its president. The first item was usually a speech in praise of the insurgency by a student from one of the city's colleges, often the College of Mining or the Military Academy. A choir from another college then sang a patriotic hymn, especially commissioned by the Junta. This was followed by the distribution of money to selected veterans, widows, and orphans. Finally, in several years the text of the Declaration of Independence and the manifesto of the Congress of Chilpancingo were read. After these formal events, members of the audience were invited to read any patriotic verse or other compositions they had prepared. Finally, at 11:00 P.M., all the churches rang their bells and there was an artillery salute.

In some years other events were added. For example, prizes and medals were awarded for poems, plays, or musical compositions sponsored by the Junta and, in 1849, the banners of Hidalgo, Morelos, Guerrero, and Múzquiz were presented to the Junta in a special ceremony. These had been acquired from the families of the insurgent heroes by the women's committee, chaired by Dolores de Almonte. Her husband, Juan Nepomuceno Almonte, natural son of Morelos, was president of the Junta that year. Often prior to the ceremony starting at 9:00 P.M., there were concerts or performances of new plays about independence in the theaters and a military band played a serenade in the main square.

The program for 16 September began at dawn with a flag-raising ceremony, more bell ringing, and artillery salutes. At 9:00 A.M. all the officers of the Junta met at the city hall and in formal procession walked from there to the national palace to join the already assembled dignitaries representing all the main groups and institutions in the city. Led by the president of the republic and his ministers, the now quite large procession walked over to the cathedral for a service of thanksgiving. Afterwards, there were more artillery salutes, military bands, and other activities until the procession set off for the park, passing through the streets now adorned with flowers, flags, tableaux, and anything else chosen by the patriotic citizenry to decorate their houses. Arriving at the Alameda, in most years lavishly decorated judging from the amount of money spent, the dignitaries mounted the stage and the speeches began. Following what always seemed to have been a brief address by the president, the elected orator of the day gave the main oration. Table 3 lists the orators on the 16th.

Table 3

1825	Wenceslao Barquera
1826	Juan Francisco Azcárate
1827	José María Tornel
1828	Pablo de la Llave
1829	José Manuel Herrera
1830	Francisco Manuel Sánchez de Tagle
1831	Francisco Molinos del Campo
1832	José Domínguez Manso
1833	José de Jesús Huerta (4 October)
1834	José María Castañeta y Escalada
1835	Antonio Pacheco Leal
1836	José María Aguilar y Bustamante
1837	Manuel Barrera Troncoso
1838	Ignacio Sierra y Rosso
1839	Juan de Dios Cañedo
1840	José María Tornel
1841	José Ramón Pacheco (27 October)
1842	Manuel Gómez Pedraza
1843	Mariano Otero
1844	Joaquín Ladrón de Guevara
1845	Andrés Quintana Roo
1846	Luis de la Rosa
1847	Francisco Carbajal
1848	José María Iglesias
1849	Francisco Modesto de Olaguíbel
1850	José María del Castillo Viejo
1851	José María Brito or José María Cortés y Esparza
1852	Juan N. Azcárate
1853	Gabriel Sagaseta
1854	José Ignacio de Anievas
1855	Guillermo Prieto

In some years after the oration more money was distributed to veterans or their dependents and there were other special events such as the manumission of slaves in the 1820s. More artillery salutes and music followed. In the evening, various entertainments were put on in the theaters but the highlight was the fireworks display. Much the same program was followed on 27 September and Table 4 lists the orators.

Table 4

1837	José María Aguilar de Bustamante
1838	Manuel Tossiat Ferrer
1839	Lino José Alcorta
1840	Manuel Micheltorena
1841	Manuel Bermúdez Zozaya (27 October)
1842	Rafael Espinosa or Pedro Tames
1843	José María Lafragua
1844	Guillermo Prieto
1845	Joaquín Navarro y Ibarra
1846	José María Godoy
1847	Guadalupe Perdigón Garay
1848	José María González Mendoza
1849	Santiago Blanco
1850	José María Tornel
1851	Joaquín Rangel
1852	José Mariano Monterde
1853	Bruno Ordoñez (in place of brother Juan)
1854	Agustín Sánchez de Tagle
1855	José María del Castillo y Velasco

The next day, 28 September, there was a service in the cathedral followed by a speech in memory of the victims of the war against Spain and of those who had died in later conflicts. Again, there sometimes were special events. In 1838, for example, the Junta helped collect funds to pay for the ceremonial interment of Iturbide's ashes, which were brought to the capital for burial in the cathedral. A proposal in 1851 to exhume the remains of Hidalgo and Morelos and to carry them in the parade was not adopted.

We have one excellent eyewitness description of the celebrations on 16 September. This is by Fanny Calderón de la Barca, wife of the Spanish ambassador, who lived in Mexico City from 1840 to 1842. She describes the scene in 1840 as follows:

> A speech was made by General Tornel in the Alameda. All the troops were out—plenty of officers, monks, priests, and ladies, in full dress. We did not go to hear the speech, but went to the E's house to see

the procession, which was very magnificent. The line of carriages was so deep, that I thought we should never arrive. After all was over, we walked in the Alameda, where temporary booths were erected, and the trees were hung with garlands and flowers. The Paseo in the evening was extremely gay; but I cannot say that there appeared to be much enthusiasm or public spirit. They say that the great difficulty experienced by the Junta, named on these occasions for the preparation of these festivities, is to collect sufficient funds.[23]

From both Calderón de la Barca's account and contemporary press reports, it appears that the city's population responded in large numbers to the Junta's efforts. The streets were said to be crowded, and although there may have been in some years little "enthusiasm," a large assembly always gathered in the Alameda to watch the ceremony. No instances of public disorder were reported, probably because each year the Junta, in cooperation with the city council, was obliged to see that police and military units were deployed on the streets.

The main problem was usually the weather. Year after year, heavy and at times incessant rain disrupted the proceedings, particularly the parade and the fireworks display, which had to be postponed on more than one occasion. The rain was so persistent and regular on both the 16th and 27th that in 1839 the Junta seriously considered a proposal to move both celebrations to 29 October on the grounds that the weather was likely to have improved by then. In some years, circumstances dictated a change. In 1833, for example, a cholera epidemic had swept the country, and although by September its impact in the capital was declining, the Junta decided it was prudent to postpone the whole program until 4 October.

In 1841 the celebration had to be postponed again, this time because of a rebellion. The Junta had met as usual throughout July and August, but early in September hostilities began in the capital. Government forces and rebels both occupied the rooftops of buildings in the central area of the city, firing at each other and causing many civilian casualties. The fighting continued throughout September but both sides agreed to a cease-fire on the 16th to allow a Mass in the cathedral. Eventually, by the end of the month, the administration led by Anastasio Bustamante was forced out of office and Santa Anna took over the government. The president of the Junta in that year was his loyal supporter, José María Tornel, and he announced on 25 October that the festivities planned for 16 and 27 September were to take place two days later, on 27 October. All the usual events took place on that date.

Finally, in one year, 1847, no celebrations were possible. The Junta and the orators had been elected and had met regularly in July and August, but the U.S. army's occupation of the city on 14 September meant the program had to be canceled.

Politics and the Junta

The Junta Patriótica was intended to be nonpolitical. For the most part, this aim was achieved, but amidst the political turmoil which characterizes the three decades after independence, it was perhaps inevitable that it could not remain entirely isolated from party rivalries. The list of presidents in many cases reflects the dominant political group of the time; and on several occasions, the public orators took the opportunity to promote their own or their party's policy or ideology. In general, conservative orators defended the conquest and the colonial regime, arguing that the Spaniards had brought civilization and the true religion to a barbaric continent. They emphasized the indigenous practices of human sacrifice and idolatry, portraying the colonial past as one of benign despotism which had given Mexicans their social and moral values. Emancipation had been a natural progression, only made possible by the liberal values of their Spanish forebears.

In contrast, liberals and others such as Tornel chose to depict the conquest as a war of aggression against an innocent race, and independence as liberation from three centuries of colonial oppression. Tornel vilified Spaniards in his 1827 speech, reflecting a political campaign then in progress to have all Spanish residents expelled from the country. He described Hernán Cortés, Francisco Pizarro, and Pedro de Valdivia as "names of horror and loathing" who had brought ruin and desolation to millions of innocent victims.[24] Other orators, much to the anger of the pro-Spanish conservative press, praised indigenous society as a terrestrial paradise of "innocent inhabitants, a thousand colorful birds, exquisite flowers, fragrance and scent embalmed the air, crystal clear waters. Happiness was everywhere."[25]

In addition to depicting contrasting images of indigenous society as barbaric or civilized and of the colonial regime as benign or despotic, a few orators also introduced contemporary political ideology or opinion. This brought swift retribution on the individual and on the Junta. The first such instance was in 1843 when the orator for 27 September was the federalist liberal, José María Lafragua. Santa Anna was in power and in June of that year he had sanctioned a new constitution known as the Bases Orgánicas, which had concentrated power in Mexico City, and largely in himself. Following the usual practice, Lafragua's speech was printed in advance.[26] On the day before it was due to be given—26 September—Tornel, minister of war and also president of the Junta, sent a note to the association's vice president, Juan Bautista Morales. He told Morales that the government had reason to believe that Lafragua's speech was subversive, containing "irritating and even seditious expressions." He instructed him to take steps to "avoid the harm" which the speech would generate. Morales summoned the officers of the Junta and they decided that all they could do was to warn Lafragua of the government's view. At 9:00 A.M. on the 27th, the Junta assembled in the city hall for the day's ceremonies only to be told that Lafragua had been arrested and jailed the night before. Moreover, the government, having had its view that the speech was subversive confirmed by a lawyer, had ordered that it should not be given. All copies at the printers and in the city hall where they had been prior to distribution had been confiscated. Faced with this challenge to its autonomy, the Junta promptly held an emergency meeting in the city hall and voted to dissolve itself.[27]

Lafragua had certainly defended the federal system and attacked the Bases Orgánicas in his speech, as well as criticized Santa Anna's policy in Texas and Yucatán. He suffered no long-term consequences, and was released from prison the next day. In contrast, the Junta Patriótica had been dissolved and Santa Anna saw no reason the following year why it should be forgiven. Hence, in the absence of the standing committee, which normally would have initiated the election of a new Junta for 1844, it seemed that there would be no organized celebrations in September. Then in July, Carlos María de Bustamante, in a letter to the press, urged Santa Anna to allow a Junta to be formed.[28] Santa Anna responded by announcing that he would permit an organizing committee appointed by his government from among the city councilors. This committee was quickly formed and met under the chairmanship of the prefect, Antonio Díez de Bonilla. The program of events went ahead on the usual lines though on a much reduced scale. Santa Anna decided to show his magnanimity by ordering that all Texan prisoners of war held anywhere in the republic should be released on 16 September. The following year, 1845, with Santa Anna no longer in office, the popular, elected Junta was restored and the leading liberal, Mariano Riva Palacio, was elected its president.

The 1843 episode was certainly an exception in the history of the Junta Patriótica to that date. Thereafter there were increasing signs that rival political parties were seeking to get control of the association. Elections for the officers were more competitive and the practice of introducing previously prepared printed lists of candidates for each post was used, much to the annoyance of some members.[29] Following the re-adoption of the federal constitution in August 1846, the orator for 16 September, Luis de la Rosa, used this opportunity to launch a bitter attack on the so-called privileged classes and their support for the monarchist form of government.[30] Three years later, in 1849, during a congressional election campaign vigorously contested by conservatives and liberals, the pro-monarchist daily, *El Universal*, edited among others by Lucas Alamán, chose to use the 16 September anniversary to publish a vitriolic condemnation of Hidalgo and the early stages of the insurgency. Hidalgo and his fellow insurgents were described as bandits and murderers, interested only in pillage and destruction. The movement, started at Dolores in 1810, was no more than "a pretence of a national cause," opposed and condemned by all honorable men. It had brought division, conflict, and bloodshed to the country. Published precisely on 16 September, this editorial naturally caused a sensation. It is probable that Alamán and his fellow editors chose to publish it because they knew that the orator for the day, Francisco Modesto Olaguíbel, a radical liberal, had used his speech to denounce the conservatives and their monarchist supporters.[31]

It is clear that by the late 1840s, the main political groups looked on the Independence Day festival as a political opportunity. Throughout 1850, the polemic between *El Universal* and the liberal press over the nature of the 1810 uprising continued unabated. It was also in that year, as part of its campaign, that *El Universal* attacked the financial probity of the Junta and criticized the quality of the orations with their persistent attacks on "the supposed tyranny of the Catholic Kings."[32]

In 1851 this intervention by the political factions reached its peak. The president of the republic was General Mariano Arista, elected in January as the candidate of one section of the *moderados*, or moderate liberals. His main rival in the election campaign had been Juan Nepomuceno Almonte. Together with his wife Dolores, who was chair of the women's committee, Almonte had dominated the Junta as its president in both 1849 and 1850. The first meeting in 1851 was held at the university on 1 July and, according to some press reports, between six hundred and one thousand people attended. This very large turnout was due to the fact that for weeks beforehand Almonte's political rivals, recruited and encouraged by Eligio Romero, had plotted to take over the Junta. Romero was a prominent *puro* or radical liberal but he was also a close friend and ally of Arista.

In the absence of Almonte, the chair was taken by the vice president of the standing committee, the publisher, Ignacio Cumplido. He struggled to maintain order as it became clear that the rival factions had come well prepared for the elections of the new Junta. Four printed lists of candidates were being circulated, each printed on different colored paper. The blue list proposed Valentín Gómez Farías for the presidency; the yellow, Miguel María de Azcárate; the pink, Antonio Haro y Tamariz; and the purple, Almonte. When the first round of voting was counted, it was discovered that there were more votes than names in the register. Cumplido invoked the 1849 regulations which stipulated that only those who had registered in advance and received a credential were eligible to vote. He ordered another vote taken and the group headed by Almonte was declared elected. The program committee and the orators then were chosen.[33]

During the next few days, the defeated factions, aided by *El Universal*, campaigned to have the elections annulled on the grounds that the 1849 regulations were invalid because they had not received the government's formal approval. A petition was circulated, attracting a reported 1246 signatures, and the government was asked to abolish "that club which is usurping the title of patriotic junta."[34] On 11 July, Arista responded by ordering the dissolution of the elected Junta and its replacement by a committee of thirty members appointed by the governor of the Federal District.

During the remaining weeks of July, Almonte and his Junta tried to defy Arista and to maintain what they argued was the popular, democratic tradition of the association. They continued to meet at the university until they were refused admission. After this, they met at Almonte's home. They composed an impassioned plea to the nation and brought court charges against Arista, his ministers, and several members of the judiciary. Almonte, Cumplido, and the other defiant officers of the Junta were warned that their meetings were illegal but they persisted. In reply, Arista brought charges against them in the courts and both Almonte and Cumplido were fined one hundred pesos. Almonte refused to pay, and bailiffs forcibly entered his house and removed goods to that value, namely, one silk-covered sofa and two armchairs. Cumplido's house likewise was visited and he paid the fine under protest. Both were senators at the time and enjoyed a certain immunity but others were less fortunate. Francisco Zarco, for example, was sacked from his job as a translator in the Ministry of Relations and jailed for a month. Others also were dismissed from their jobs in government offices. Several were imprisoned. Some army officers were demoted or retired. Both Almonte and Cumplido appealed to Congress to defend them against the arbitrary actions of the executive, but while the issue was raised, the legislators did nothing to stop Arista. After weeks of bitter recrimination, mostly published in the press, Almonte and his colleagues accepted defeat and their Junta was disbanded. Their court cases were pursued as far as the Supreme Court, which eventually found that some of the magistrates used by Arista had acted illegally and they were suspended from office.[35]

The saga of allegation and counter-allegation, letters to the press, court cases, and congressional appeals dominated the headlines throughout August and September, inevitably obscuring the efforts of the new, official Junta Patriótica. Of its thirty appointed members, which included Almonte and Cumplido, who never attended, about half turned up for the regular meetings. Much of the program of the elected Junta was adopted and the celebrations in September passed off in the usual way. Perhaps concerned about possible popular demonstrations, the Federal District governor banned all street parties without prior authorization and also the use of live ammunition by those who joined in the festivities, either civilian or military. Apparently, in earlier years, enthusiastic participants on the rooftops and in the streets had fired live rounds, causing injuries and even deaths.

The government-appointed Junta Patriótica, renewed annually, continued to organize the Independence Day events for the following three years. In 1852, Arista appointed a new thirty-member Junta; and Santa Anna, during his 1853–1854 dictatorship, continued the practice. He refused to give any grants, and donations were solicited by letter as well as through the now traditional collecting committees. The orators adopted their pro- or anti-Spanish attitudes regarding the conquest and indigenous societies and *El Universal* maintained its criticism of the quality and bias of some of the speeches.

Finally, the overthrow of Santa Anna and his flight from Mexico City in August 1855 enabled the victorious liberals to demonstrate their democratic credentials almost immediately. They abolished the recently instituted official Junta and restored its popularly elected counterpart. On 20 August a new Junta Patriótica was elected with General Juan Alvarez chosen as president. Other members included long-standing liberals such as Juan Bautista Morales, Ignacio Cumplido, Mariano Riva Palacio, and Valentín Gómez Farías. The celebrations were much as before with speeches, religious services, decorated streets, fireworks, and cash gifts to deserving widows and dependents of Mexico's now many wars. The history of the Junta Patriótica had come full circle.

Conclusion

The Junta Patriótica was an unusual, and possibly unique, association in the years between independence and the Reform. It was democratic, voluntary, nondiscriminatory in its membership (it included women), self-financing, and, at least for the most part, nonpolitical. It owed its longevity to the flexibility that annual renewal of members gave it and to the existence of the written and published regulations of 1831 and 1849 that provided a framework of procedures and objectives. It was, in general, very successful in achieving its aims, namely, the commemoration of independence and its heroes by means of festivities and philanthropic activities ranging from the manumission of slaves to gifts of money to widows and orphans.

For the largely Creole elite which took control of Mexico in 1821 and whose leading personalities dominated the Junta, it also served a broader purpose. They were acutely aware of the fact that outside the confines of their own social group and in the distant regions of the country, the concept of Mexico as a single nation-state was at best tenuous. They were always anxious, therefore, to support anything that could create or help a sense of national identity to supersede regional and local loyalties. They knew the value of the celebration of military victories, of monuments, portraits, and regular, visible reminders on the streets with bands and parades. The annual public ceremonial centered on independence and its heroes was an obvious way to achieve a historical tradition of their own making and to develop their concepts of patriotism and national unity.

On several occasions, supporters of the Junta expressed this broader aim. In 1825 the editor of the *Aguila Mexicana* urged that there should be a Junta Patriótica in every town in the republic with a triumphal arch erected in every public square to remind the people of the benefits of independence and the need for national unity.[36] In an 1839 letter to the government asking for money, the Junta emphasized the importance of maintaining public morale amidst the endemic party factionalism. Independence, it said, was "the only point of contact and harmony among Mexicans" and it was essential to preserve "this uniform feeling."[37] Again, in 1843, Juan Bautista Morales, president of the standing committee, told the members of the association that he and his fellow committee members were convinced of the value of the Junta's work because "republics cannot exist without patriotism and patriotism cannot be sustained without public spirit."[38] Finally, in 1850, again appealing to the government for money, the Junta reminded Congress that its role since 1825 had been to give the people "a feeling of nationality in order to defend independence."[39]

It is also appropriate to view the Junta Patriótica, as A. Lempérière has recently suggested, in the context of the growing secularization of Mexican society, a process which certainly accelerated in the post-independence years. All kinds of secular associations were quickly established. There were, for example, Academies of History and Language, a Society of Geography and Statistics, a national archive, numerous lay institutes of education and science as well as myriad charitable societies. These organizations all were established in the same context of secular nationalism as the Junta Patriótica, with its aim of creating a sense of patriotism, unity, and national identity. It is no surprise, therefore, that many of their members were also regular participants in the Junta. Most liberals, of course, such as Zavala, Mora, and Gómez Farías, were also anxious to achieve similar aims by reducing the influence of the Church and, above all, the dominance of external religious observance seen daily on the streets of every town and village. Secular associations and secular festivals with a pantheon of national heroes of independent Mexico provided an alternative to the constant parade of ecclesiastical images and patron saints. Hence, the Independence Day events were almost entirely nonreligious and the role and intervention of the clergy always kept to a minimum. As the Junta itself put it, while due regard has to be paid to divine help, "all nations, both ancient and modern, have tried to perpetuate the memory of those events to which they owe their existence or which have had a benign and important influence on their destiny, by means of public festivals, entertainments, and various ceremonies."[40]

Notes

1. Tornel was credited with the idea of the Junta Patriótica in the meeting held on 11 July 1843; see *El Siglo XIX*, 28 July 1843.

2. Except where otherwise indicated, the information in this article is taken from the published minutes. The location of the minutes as published each year in the press is given as an Appendix. There is also a very informative collection of documents relating to the 1825 celebrations in folders 10–11 of the García Collection in the Benson Library, University of Texas at Austin. These are the papers of Juan Wenceslao Barquera, who was the inaugural orator for the 16 September celebrations in 1825.

3. W. Beezley, "Recreating the Creation of Mexico: Pondering Nineteenth Century Celebrations of Independence," unpublished paper. R. Warren, "The Construction of Independence Day, 1821–1864," unpublished paper. For further details of the early celebrations, see F. Serrano Migallón, *El Grito de Independencia. Historia de una pasión nacional* (Mexico, 1995), 39–46.

4. For example, see the congressional record of 16 September 1824 in *Aguila Mexicana*, 18 September 1824.

5. *Aguila Mexicana*, 28 August 1825.

6. *Reglamento de la Junta Patriótica* (Mexico, 1849).

7. *Proyecto de reglamento para gobierno de la Junta Patriótica del Grito Glorioso de Dolores, presentado a la Junta del año de 1831 por la Comisión Permanente* (Mexico, 1831).

8. *Reglamento* (1849), art. 6.

9. The texts of the orations usually were published in the press and also as separate pamphlets. The Lafragua Collection (Biblioteca Nacional, Mexico City) has many of the latter both for Mexico City and for elsewhere in the republic; see *Catálogo de la Colección Lafragua, 1821–1853*, ed L. Moreno Valle (Mexico, 1975).

10. *Aguila Mexicana*, 5 September 1825.

11. Ibid., 10, 12, 13, 15 September 1825.

12. *El Sol*, 2 September 1829.

13. These details are from various reports published by the Junta in *Registro Oficial*, 7 July 1831.

14. *Proyecto de reglamento* (1831).

15. According to Lempérière, the Junta's relations with the city's municipal authorities were not always harmonious: A. Lempérière, "¿Nación moderna o república barroca? México, 1823–1857," in *Imaginar la Nación*, ed. F. X. Guerra and M. Quijada (Hamburg, 1994), 164, n. 53.

16. Reports of the meetings held in 1834 are in *El Telégrafo*, August-September 1834. Unfortunately, these refer to the officer, i.e., the president, and do not give the holder's name.

17. L. Alamán, *Historia de México*, 5 vols. (Mexico, 1969), 4:483–84.

18. Santa Anna's letter accepting the donation is in the minutes of 4 November 1846, published in *Diario del Gobierno*, 9 July 1847.

19. *Exposición que la Comisión Permanente de la Junta Patriótica de México dirige al soberano congreso* (Mexico, 1850). The text of the congressional law is in M. Dublán and J. M. Lozano, *Legislación mexicana*, vol. 5 (Mexico, 1876), 699–700.

20. For an example, "Himno cívico para toda orquestra o forte-plano" by F. Sánchez de Tagle and Mariano Elizaga. See *Correo de la Federación*, 16 September 1827.

21. *El Universal*, 6 September 1850.

22. J. M. Tornel to A. Bustamante, 11 September 1825, in *Aguila Mexicana*, 13 September 1825.

23. F. Calderón de la Barca, *Life in Mexico* (London, 1970), 258–59. There is also a good description of the events on 26–27 September on p. 443. Enterprising retailers advertised the latest fashions for Independence Day. See, for example, the advertisement by Duval & Cía offering "un surtido completo de adornos y plumas" for women to wear on the day; *Diario del Gobierno*, 9 September 1835.

24. The text of Tornel's oration is in *Correo de la Federación*, 20 September 1827, and in Lafragua, no. 2269.

25. J. M. Brito, *Discurso pronunciado por el ciudadano José María Brito el 16 de septiembre de 1851, comisionado por la Junta Patriótica para orador del pueblo* (Mexico, 1851), There is a copy in Lafragua, no. 5945. *El Universal* (30 September 1851) criticized the speech, calling Brito a charlatan.

26. There is a copy in Lafragua, no. 4404.

27. Details of the Lafragua incident are in *El Siglo XIX*, 28, 30 September, 6–7 October 1843.

28. The letter is signed CMB in *El Siglo XIX*, 9 July 1844.

29. In the meeting on 11 July 1843, José María Iturralde complained about the use of printed lists: *El Siglo XIX*, 28 July 1843.

30. Rosa's speech is in *Diario del Gobierno*, 20 September 1846, and in Lafragua, no. 5050.

31. The Junta commissioned a reply to *El Universal*'s editorial: *Refutación en la parte histórica del artículo de fondo publicado en el número 305 del periódico titulado El Universal el 16 del pasado septiembre, por una comisión de la Junta Cívica de México* (Mexico, 1849). This was apparently written by Anastasio Zerecero. See Lafragua, no. 5492.

32. *El Universal*, 3 October 1850. As part of the polemic with *El Universal*, the Junta was involved in the publication of a collection of works arising from the Independence Day celebration: *Colección de composiciones en prosa y verso pronunciadas en los gloriosos aniversarios de nuestra independencia en mes de septiembre de 1850* (Mexico, 1850).

33. All the main newspapers carried detailed accounts of what happened in the meeting. The fullest account is in *El Siglo XIX*, 2 July 1851.

34. See the letter in *El Monitor Republicano*, 10 July 1851.

35. For the various documents, letters, appeals to Congress, etc., see *El Monitor Republicano, El Siglo XIX*, and *El Universal*, July through October 1851. Many of the documents were published as broadsheets or pamphlets, for example, *La Junta Patriótica a la Nación* (Mexico, 1851).

36. *Aguila Mexicana*, 28 August 1825.

37. Text of letter in minutes of 23 July meeting, in *Diario del Gobierno*, 2 August 1839.

38. Minutes of meeting of 11 July in *El Siglo XIX*, 28 July 1843.

39. *Exposición* (1850), 4.

40. Ibid., 3.

Appendix

The minutes of the meetings of the Junta Patriótica, reports on them, and various miscellaneous documents referring to its activities are in the newspapers given below. All newspapers customarily carried a description of the events on 16 and 27 September in their following issues. The dates given are those of the newspaper, not the meetings.

1825   *Aguila Mexicana*, 25, 28 August; 3, 7, 8, 10, 12, 13, 15 September.

1826   *Aguila Mexicana*, 2 September.

1827   *Correo de la Federación*, 10, 18 July; 8 August.

1828   *Correo de la Federación*, 28 July.

1829   *El Sol*, 25 July; 18, 22 August.

1830   *Registro Oficial*, 14, 21, 24 July; 4 August.

1831   *Registro Oficial*, 7, 13, 22, 23 July; 4–6 August; 15, 24 September.

1832   *El Sol*, 15, 19 September.
         Registro Oficial, 1, 21 August.

1833   *El Fénix de la Libertad*, 27 July; 7, 19 September; 2, 5 October.

1834   *El Telégrafo*, 29 July; 3, 23 August; 7, 10, 21 September.

1835   *El Sol*, 15, 28 July.
         Diario del Gobierno, 5, 16 September.

1836   *Diario del Gobierno*, 28 July; 8 August.

1837   *Diario del Gobierno*, 9, 11, 22, 28 July; 7, 11, 22, 29 August; 2, 24, 27 September.

1838   *Diario del Gobierno*, 13, 27, 31 July; 7, 13, 20, 29 August; 10, 14, 25 September.

1839   *Diario del Gobierno*, 13, 18, 28 July; 2, 13, 16, 24 August; 1, 13, 27 September.

1840   *Diario del Gobierno*, 24, 31 August; 8, 9 October.

1841   *Diario del Gobierno*, 25 July; 2, 11, 14, 29 August; 1, 26 October; 17 November.

1842   *Diario del Gobierno*, 5, 7, 15, 28, 30 August; 1, 9, 24 September; 6, 11, 15 October.

1843   *El Siglo XIX*, 13, 28 July; 2, 7, 14, 24, 30 August; 7, 12, 18, 22, 27–28, 30 September; 6–7, 15 October.

1844   *El Siglo XIX*, 9 July; 4, 6 August; 8 September.

1845   *El Siglo XIX*, 9, 24, 31 July; 12, 22 August; 26, 29 September; 7, 10 October.

1846   *Diario del Gobierno*, 11, 13 August; 13, 18 September; 9 July 1847 (minutes of 4 November 1846).

1847   *Diario del Gobierno*, 10, 14, 19, 22, 28 July; 4, 9, 13 August; 4 September.

1848   *El Siglo XIX*, 12, 22, 31 July; 5, 12, 19, 21, 27 August; 1, 15, 24 September; 2–3, 7, 10 October.

1849   *El Siglo XIX*, 12, 23, 31 July; 8, 11, 22 August; 1–2, 4–5, 10–11, 14–15, 22, 30 September.

1850   *El Siglo XIX*, 8, 10, 19, 30 July; 3, 9, 14, 18, 20, 24–25 August; 2, 9, 12, 14–15, 19, 28, 30 September; 2, 7 October.

1851   *El Monitor Republicano*, 3–4, 10, 13–17, 19, 30 July; 1, 3, 15, 28 August; 10, 14, 30 September; 1, 10 October; 13 November.

          El Siglo XIX, 2, 3, 7, 9, 10, 14, 16, 18–31 July; 3–6, 10–11, 13, 19–20, 26, 29 August; 5–6, 15, 21, 25, 28 September; 9, 13 October; 29 November; 2 December.

          El Universal, 6, 13, 15–17, 19, 22–24, 27, 29, 31 July; 2, 9–10, 13, 16, 21, 23, 27 August; 8–9 September.

1852   *El Siglo XIX*, 13 August.

1853   *El Siglo XIX*, 3 August.

          El Universal, 17 August, 16, 28 September.

1854   *El Universal*, 9–10 August.

          La Verdad, 13, 27 September.

1855   *El Siglo XIX*, 15 July; 15, 19, 21 August.

          La Verdad, 24 August; 10, 15 September.

CHAPTER THREE

The First Independence Celebrations in San Luis Potosí, 1824–1847*

SERGIO ALEJANDRO CAÑEDO GAMBOA

In San Luis Potosí, the heroes and martyrs of the Independence movement first received recognition in the public celebration of 1823: "It was the first time that September 16 was solemnized with *dianas* [bugle calls], pealing of bells, music, fireworks, and the Te Deum. . . . The parish, to honor Hidalgo, Allende, Morelos, and others who sacrificed their lives, held honorary funerals on the following day."[1] This first celebration of Independence on September 16 and on September 17 followed the custom of holding commemorative funeral services to glorify the heroes of Independence begun during the struggle. The celebration on September 17 in 1823 reflected events in Mexico City, where the remains of Miguel Hidalgo, Ignacio Allende, and José María Morelos were transported from Chihuahua to the Cathedral on September 16; these heroes were honored with a special Mass on the 17th. For several years after 1823, the tradition continued of celebrating Independence and exalting its martyrs on two separate days.

National political reorganization began the following year, 1824, with the creation of the Republic. Implementing the federal decree of January 18, 1824, the Mexican Congress had proceeded to establish a legislature in the newly created state of San Luis Potosí. This action replaced the civic institutions founded under the colonial

---

*Selections from "El discurso político en la fiesta de la independencia en San Luis Potosí, 1824–1847" (Master's thesis, Universidad Iberoamericana, 1997), 19–24, 156–67. Rachel Kram, University of Arizona, translated this selection.

administration and the short-lived empire, although it made no change in cultural affairs. The state now began to function through the three branches of administration: the legislature, the executive, and the judiciary.

The national legislature initiated the national celebration of September 16, as well as a similar ceremony on October 4, to commemorate Mexico's first republican constitution. Other legislative actions, including those by earlier regimes, affected the celebration of national holidays, including September 16. For example, the Provisional Government Council had earlier declared national holidays on February 24 (Iturbide's proclamation of the Plan de Iguala), March 2 (signing of the Plan de Iguala), and September 27 (entrance of the Trigarante Army into Mexico City). This list did not include September 16 because the members of the Council had sympathized chiefly with Agustín de Iturbide and not with earlier insurgents. This calendar of holidays needed the approval of the Congress; and its members, among whom were many former insurgents, revised the holiday list to include September 16. The decree was then forwarded to the states.

The holiday law arrived in San Luis Potosí near the end of 1824. The state governor, Ildefonso Díaz de León, and the mayor of the capital city determined the proper celebration of the holidays established by the Congress. Thus, to carry out the order sent by the Congress of the Federation, September 16 and 27 of every year would be a national holiday. The Cabildo agreed that on the first day a Mass would be solemnly prayed, and on the second day, another would be sung.[2] Cost remained an issue, but the schedule included various events. Among them, the theater performance in the Plaza de los Gallos stood out. During one of the acts, a fire broke out backstage; it could not be contained and burned down much of the surrounding area of town.[3]

Little evidence remains of the celebration of Independence in 1825, although one account reports the allocation of city funds for the holiday. The councilmen gave 118 pesos to Ignacio Eguia and don Andrés Barroeta for the expenses at the church to celebrate the glorious *grito de Dolores* and the anniversary of the nation's martyrs.[4] From 1824 to 1826 the cost of the city's celebration fluctuated each year from between 100 and 500 pesos. By way of comparison, at this time, the governor's salary was 2,000 pesos annually, or about 166 pesos per month.

The celebrations during these early years had four constants. First, the celebration was institutionalized as part of the political life of both the nation and the state of San Luis Potosí. The new national government removed it from the control of the state government, city council, or patriotic associations.

Second, the significance of celebrating these first holidays can be seen as a declaration of merriment about the new national political situation. The existing documents reflect the interests and objectives of the elites, but hints of the way that the lower classes observed the festivities survive. The people anticipated the coming of the holiday with the hope of grabbing one of the coins tossed to the crowds, of igniting fireworks, and of watching the procession.

Third, patriotic leaders during the struggle and early years of Independence had taken steps—the Independence oaths, the installation acts of the Congress, and other political activities of the new federal regime—that became part of the commemorations. Thus, Independence was celebrated not only on September 16 and 17 but also with the constitutional oath, the installation of the state congress, and, in general, in each political action of the new government. Moreover, the concepts of Independence and federation could not exist separately in Mexico after 1824. As one of the Oaths of Independence declared, "the sacred federation was the product of our Independence." The issue of a Republic was settled; and, in the following years, debate in the Independence Day celebrations turned to the proper form—federal or central government—best suited to Mexico.

And fourth, the Catholic Church also commemorated Independence in the years after 1826, thus giving a distinct character to the celebration of September 16. The new political faction, sometimes supported by Church leaders, used the holiday to promote their views.

The celebration of September 16 has had an influence on ritual, which did not arise spontaneously but rather had to be invented. The meanings of objects and actions changed with time and circumstances, although the celebration has remained an invariable entity. On some occasions the authorities have made changes, but these modifications were usually inspired by tradition and acquired a social commitment. Those who previously had honored the king subsequently yielded to Emperor Agustín, and later to Independence. In the majority of these cases, the celebration served as an agent of cohesion, of union, and of transcendence of the single goal: the formation of the new nation.

Protocol

The protocol for Independence Day originally was based on vicere-gal rituals—the commemoration of the Oath of the King, with its procession of the royal banner, and the celebration of Corpus Christi. These festivals shared precise and common rituals: a procession and Mass were celebrated, edicts were published, coins were tossed to the crowds, streets and buildings were illuminated, and sermons were preached. Other commemorations, such as the birthday of the king and the honoring of the Virgin of Guadalupe, were similarly based. These ceremonies drew on Iberian traditions as part of the life of the Viceroyalty. The leaders who wanted to observe Independence appro-priated some of these activities but instilled in them new meaning.

For Independence, each part of the ritual had significance. For example, attendance at Mass reflected a symbiosis: the civil authori-ties attended church to gave thanks and to receive the priest's bene-diction (a sign of divine recognition and support from Church leaders); in turn, the Church was recognized as a pillar of the new society and as a mediator with the divine. The September 16 celebration repro-duced the mutual recognition of civil and Church authorities through the commemoration of Independence. Members of the state and city governments attended the Mass of Thanksgiving, or Te Deum, to make public the relationship between these governing bodies and their shar-ing of authority.

As part of the colonial celebrations such as the procession of the royal banner, it was traditional to place a portrait of the king in a pavilion. Thus, the first Independence celebrations included the swear-ing of the Oath of Independence before a portrait of Emperor Agustín. Later, the tradition continued on September 15, 16, and 17, but the crowds swore allegiance to Independence before the portrait of a pa-triot, usually of Hidalgo but on occasion of some other insurgent hero. The display of the portrait helped to put a human face on the patriots of Independence.

The procession through the streets can be considered as the dem-onstration of official control over public space. It was also the occa-sion for the people to show their enthusiasm: they shouted, sang, and cheered. The procession was one of the rare moments when the civil authorities and the public came into direct contact by sharing a com-mon space. The procession of the royal banner had allowed the crowds to show their loyalty and to recognize the king through acts of merriment. After Independence, the civic processions gave spectators (many of whom had earlier sworn allegiance to the king) the opportunity to express their support for the new state. Again, the procession was the point of contact between town authorities and the public.

The Spanish monarchy survived as long as the people believed in the institution; thus, the Crown sought to strengthen loyalty through the celebration of the coronation and other rituals. Spain needed to demonstrate royal control due to the internal problems in New Spain, and one way of showing its control was to promote certain holidays. The commemoration of the king was not necessarily dedicated to the person but rather to the power of the state and the symbol of royal majesty. The first Mexican republicans, after Independence, utilized festivals to promote a cluster of ideas that fortified the new nation.

The September 16 holiday came to have importance as it began to seize this precise moment to show the different political views, thoughts, aspirations, and desires of the new nation. The motive of celebrating began to take on meanings of its own. Some people celebrated to remember the heroes of the country, to offer them homage, and to follow their example. Others found it a time of reflection, a time to put away arms, and a time to pursue national unity. Thus, the celebration came to express various meanings.

During the early years, the public speeches at the commemorations expressed anti-Spanish sentiments as one of the functions of the September 16 holiday. Speakers recalled first, that the Spaniards had controlled mining, commerce, and lands, and second, that they had planned to reconquer Mexico several times. For example, there was the conspiracy of Father Arenas, who intended to return the country to the rule of Fernando VII. Another instance was the Plan Montaño to bring the Spaniards back to Mexico, and then there was the invasion of 1829, when Isidro Barradas led Spanish troops into Tampico in an effort to reincorporate Mexico into the Spanish empire. In the celebrations, speakers uttered harsh words to judge the Spaniards. Even "pilferers," for example, showed that they blamed the Spaniards for much of the suffering of the new nation.

Within the festival organizations, arguments developed over the nature of the celebration. Plans for a dance performance, for example, resulted in a major dispute. The controversy revealed that the passions associated with different phases of the Independence struggle still remained. The compromise solution moved the dance to September 17, on the anniversary of the death of the victims of the struggle. September 16 was reserved for the expression of federalism, education, freedom of the press, and national sovereignty.

Two public speakers, Luis Gonzaga Gordoa and Luis Guzmán, represented the division of views of Independence. Gonzaga Gordoa in 1831 expressed his commitment to federalist ideas at a time when a group of moderates governed the state. His speech called for tolerance of differing political views. Gonzaga Gordoa took examples from the pre-Hispanic and the colonial pasts to demonstrate the roots of the Mexican nation and to propose that this heritage be recognized. Guzmán, for his part, attacked the Spaniards. His speeches of 1828 and 1833 reflected political circumstances. In 1828, both in the lines he read and between those lines, he spoke for the second expulsion of the Spaniards and expressed apprehension of Spanish efforts at reconquest. His speech of 1833 took up the theme of "public opinion" as the expression of the thoughts of the Mexican people.

The people and government of San Luis Potosí celebrated Independence Day with trepidation during the war with Texas. The public feared a total dismembering of the country together with an economic crisis. Indeed, wartime required forced loans to meet the army's expenses. Thus, the celebration in 1836 reflected the wartime circumstances. Poetic compositions expressed the sentiments of the people in a city at war. Other texts, such as sermons and proclamations, also revealed the concerns of the embattled citizens. Now, the image of the enemy changed: the Spaniards were no longer the principal adversary. During this conflict, the people of the Texas colony became the enemy until 1838, when the focus shifted to the French, who were blockading the port of Veracruz. The Hispanophobia found in the earlier patriotic discourses diminished after the Spanish government recognized Mexican sovereignty in 1836, and as new enemies appeared.

Mexico's adversary was always present during the speeches offered on Independence Day. This adversary—whoever it might be—took the blame for the political and economic chaos in Mexico. The Plan Montaño, the Arenas conspiracy, the Barredas invasion, the Texas revolt, and the French blockade were the scapegoats for any national misfortune.

Antonio López de Santa Anna used similar techniques to make himself a living hero of Independence. He introduced the idea that the hero did not have to be dead to be celebrated and, in the process, restored the public status of Emperor Agustín. The city of San Luis Potosí followed with celebrations of Iturbide's successful conclusion to the Wars of Independence.

Changes

The Independence Day celebrations reflected the society that organized them. Changes in the festival tradition were caused by both political and social developments. The political changes revealed the group in power and the social class that identified with it. The social developments reflected trends copied from Europe, such as the opera or the singing of patriotic hymns, that became part of the September celebrations. The new nation searched for a universal song, one recognizable to the rest of the world. Composers of the era provided a myriad of new hymns, some characteristic of the group in power and others that expressed the sentiments of different sectors of society.

Organizers of Independence Day celebrations also integrated new dates into the festivities. For example, Iturbide was redeemed and placed on the heroes' altar for the official celebration by General Santa Anna. Later, Santa Anna fostered the interpretation that Independence had been secured with his victory at Tampico on September 11, 1829, over the Spaniards, so this date joined the list of patriotic holidays. All of these modifications or, better, these enrichments of the September festivities reflected the desire to give the nation a face, a distinctive personality, or, as historian Ernesto de la Torre Villar said, a "national conscience." Further, during the U.S.-Mexican war, in the Independence celebrations the theme of defending the nation took both physical and ideological forms. Each contributed to the depiction of the enemy as a barbarian, the destroyer of the Catholic religion, the usurper of the nation, and the violator of women.

Vicente Chico Sein in his speech on Independence Day in 1846 praised the union and called for the defense of the nation. He also revised Mexico's history as an independent nation, dating it from the first republic in 1824. Then, during August and September 1847, the people of San Luis Potosí followed reports of the efforts to defend the national capital against the U.S. troops. The invaders defeated the Mexican defenders and occupied the city. As a result, both the governor of San Luis Potosí and the editor of the city's newspaper, *La Epoca*, in their patriotic addresses, compared the U.S. commander Winfield Scott with Hernán Cortés.

Conclusion

Three characteristics slowly emerged in the patriotic celebrations in San Luis Potosí. First, the protocol of Independence celebrations had its origin in viceregal traditions, although the components of the commemoration, such as the procession, Mass, and the tossing of coins, experienced some changes as, of course, did the portraits of the principal personages. The image of Agustín replaced that of the king, then Hidalgo's likeness took center stage, and, in the middle of the decade, Santa Anna brought back the emperor's portrait. Another change was the disappearance of the royal lieutenant who had played a principal role in the procession of the royal banner. Iturbide's Flag of the Three Guarantees replaced the royal banner, which was replaced in turn by the new national flag. Some viceregal traditions remained, such as the tossing of coins, the procession, and the flight of hot-air balloons, but the images on the coins, as the portraits, were altered. The coins no longer carried the king's profile but that of Iturbide, Hidalgo, or some other hero of Independence. At the same time, the procession on September 16 had a character distinct from that of the procession of the royal banner and now reflected the new nation. The Independence commemoration also underwent changes in its protocol. For instance, in 1839 the people celebrated September 27, which marked the entrance of the Trigarante Army into Mexico City, a date that therefore referred to the conservative hero, Agustín de Iturbide.

Second, the public addresses given during the celebrations of Independence revealed the political ideals of the principal groups who were disputing control of public life. Thus, following the first expulsion of the Spaniards, Luis Gonzaga Gordoa proposed education, art, industry, commerce, and mineral exploitation as the means necessary to develop the new nation. National politics also resulted in themes for the Independence Day speeches. Thus, in 1833, Luis Guzmán assailed the Spaniards and looked to public opinion as the "solid support of just and beneficent governments." Beginning in 1835, the Texas rebellion became a constant in the speeches as the fear of Spanish reconquest was replaced by the fear of national disintegration. The implementation of a highly centralized national government with Anastasio Bustamante as president in 1835 also resulted in a resurgence of the name of Iturbide, the hero of conservative Mexicans, in holiday celebrations. For example, in 1838, Mariano Romero dedicated a part of his speech to refer to Iturbide as the consummate figure of Independence. Reading between the lines of the text written by Ponciano Arriaga, one finds the liberal political views in the same year, with special emphasis on the problem of Texas. In 1846, Vicente Chico Sein used his Independence Day speech as an occasion to harangue against the U.S. invasion. Generally in this year, the central themes in the Independence addresses were the defense of the nation and the search for unity.

Third, one final characteristic of the Independence Day celebrations was the identification of a national enemy. In the second half of the 1820s and the early 1830s, the enemy was the Spaniard, an identification made real by fears of the Spanish plans of invasion and reconquest. Once the Spaniards recognized Mexican sovereignty in 1836, the national enemy became the colonists in Texas who were demanding independence. The colonists, a combination of Mexican and U.S. settlers, were identified as traitors to Mexico. In 1838 the conflict with France created another adversary, one that was perhaps the most ephemeral of all. Then in 1846 the U.S. invasion of Mexico resulted in a new foreign enemy, defined as the barbarian Anglos, Protestants, and violators of women.

The three characteristics found in the political discourse of the Independence celebrations are only examples; many others exist. These examples suggest further lines of investigation of holiday celebrations. However, the constant element in all kinds of festive activities through the early years of independent Mexico was political debate. Politics was manifested in the processions, in the proclamations, and in the public addresses. The political statements expressed a combination of the changing ideas that gave personality to the celebrations, which were, above all, political.

Notes

1. Manuel Muro, *Historia de San Luis Potosí* (San Luis Potosí: Sociedad Potosina de Estudios Históricos, 1st ed. 1910, facsimile 1973), 1:373.

2. Archivo Histórico del Estado de San Luis Potosí (AHESLP), Sección General de Gobierno, 1824.4, unnumbered.

3. Muro, *San Luis Potosí*, 1:384.

4. AHESLP, Ayuntamiento, 1825, 1.

CHAPTER FOUR

San Angel as the Site of
National Festivals in the 1860s*

VERÓNICA ZÁRATE TOSCANO

Civic commemorations have acquired a far-reaching role in the history of different peoples, identifying individuals and events that occupy significant places in the national memory. Each country has its own way of celebrating events, selecting a civic calendar, and constituting a pantheon of heroes. This process forms part of the effort to establish a uniform national historic memory. Once authorities have reached an agreement on the calendar, they endow each festival with specific characteristics that are repeated until they become habits associated with the celebration. Nevertheless, even though officials strive to eliminate improvisation, spontaneous features always find their way into festivals, aided by the particularities of the events and individuals being commemorated.

This essay examines the ceremonies dedicated to the birth of independent Mexico. The festivals under consideration took place in the village of San Angel, a suburb of Mexico City, during the 1860s. The celebrations reflected the interests of the political authorities, whose attitudes found expression in behavior ranging from unquestioned submission to stubborn resistance to the governments in the capital. By investigating the organization and the implementation of the Independence festivals, it is possible to uncover political commentary on national leaders and events (such as opposition to the French occupation regime, 1863–1867).

*This essay comes from an investigation into the process of the nature and impact of civic festivals during the nineteenth century in the villages surrounding Mexico City. This research project has received assistance from the Consejo Nacional de Ciencia y Tecnología (CONACyT). The essay was translated by William H. Beezley.

When and Where

San Angel, situated south of Mexico City, today still preserves its colonial and nineteenth-century atmosphere. Only in recent years has the capital of the republic grown excessively, absorbing the surrounding towns that had their own characteristics and life-styles. One such community was San Angel, which was recognized at midnineteenth century for its agreeable climate and community. The town occupies an area of uneven terrain cut by rivers and gullies. These physical features shaped the distribution of buildings, resulting in the integration of man-made structures with the charming topography.[1] Fanny Calderón de la Barca, who visited the town in 1841, in one of her letters described it as follows:

> San Angel is pretty in its own way, with its fields of maguey, its scattered houses that look like the *beaux restes* of better days, its market-place, its parish church of Carmen with the monastery and high-walled gardens adjoining, its narrow lanes, Indian huts, profusion of pink roses, little bridge and avenue, and scattered clusters of trees; its houses for *temperamento constitución* (as they call those where Mexican families come to reside in the summer), with their grated windows, and gardens and orchards.[2]

Since the colonial era, wealthy and noble families had bought haciendas and houses in the San Angel area as holiday get-aways. In addition, liberals who had used the desamortization laws of the 1857 Constitution to acquire extensive properties competed with each other in building country homes there. Many present-day mansions stand as testimony to the splendor of these previous residents, thanks to later owners who have carefully maintained them.[3] Further, the churches and the Carmelite monastery, attached to the parish church of San Jacinto, gave a particular rhythm to local life. The religious devotion of the people, who took part in church-related celebrations and activities, added to the religious character of this community.

One midnineteenth-century assessment of San Angel appeared in *El Estandarte Nacional*. The editor noted in the March 13, 1957, issue that the town, located three leagues from the capital, had grown both in population and buildings. He attributed the growth not only to the town's fertile soil and beautiful location but also to the action of a local judge who had eased regulations for renting land and who had encouraged public works. Nevertheless, the author reported that next to the new homes of powerful families, there still existed hovels where people of meager means lived, thus making the town one of contrasts.

After Independence, San Angel formed part of the jurisdiction of Coyoacán. In 1854, President Antonio López de Santa Anna divided the Federal District into three zones. San Angel was placed in the southern prefecture, with its administrative center at Tlalpan. In the next year, the Santa Anna government redefined the Tlalpan district to encompass twelve municipalities including San Angel. Then in March 1862 the district capital was moved from Tlalpan to San Angel, but after two months it was moved back.[4] With San Angel as the seat of the district, the twelve subordinate villages were Tizapán, Contreras, San Jerónimo Aculco, La Magdalena, San Nicolás Totolapan, San Bernabe, Tepectipac, San Bartolome Ameyalco (also known as San Bartolo), Santa Rosa Xochiac, Tetelpa, Tlacopac, and San Sebastián Chimalistac. In addition, there were several haciendas (including Anzaldo, Huicochéa, Guadalupe, La Cañada, and La Eslava) and several ranches (Olivar, Sánchez, Rancho Viejo, and Padierna). Furthermore, according to an 1865 report, the district contained 79 urban and 467 rural houses.[5]

San Angel, shortly after midcentury, underwent a transition with the opening of some industries in the region. The presence of various arroyos, rivers, and waterfalls favored the construction of manufacturing enterprises using water power. Among these new industries were the factories of Loreto, La Hormiga, La Magdalena, and La Abeja producing cloth and the El Aguila and Puente de Sierra mills weaving goods. Other new enterprises included the Santa Teresa paper factory, the San José del Batancito wheat mill, and a hardware shop. These industries benefited from San Angel's location astride major transportation routes. In the colonial era, the town lay along the road from the colonial capital to Acapulco, New Spain's principal port on the Pacific. The town's proximity to Coyoacán favored the construction of additional roads. Then, in 1869, the railroad arrived in San Angel (it passed through Tacubaya, Mixcoac, Coyoacán, and Tlalpan).[6]

Turning from the geographic description, let us consider the population of San Angel and the social and ethnic mixture that characterized the town from the colonial era. According to an 1865 report, the municipality contained 7,329 people,[7] distributed in San Angel proper with 1,027 residents, in the dependent villages of La Magdalena with 955, San Nicolás Totolapan with 786, and San Bartolo with 553, and several smaller settlements.[8]

Each region imprinted its own peculiar character on these festivals. Participating in a national celebration reaffirmed the community's place in a larger whole while including local characteristics that ranged from financial resources to membership in local patriotic committees to the unique nature of festival locations. Thus, María Ana Portal explained for the national capital: "Each zone in Mexico City constructs its identity in a particular manner, therefore we cannot talk of a single homogenous standard. The factors reflect the condition of class, work, places of origin, and the ownership of land, among others."[9]

Now that we have set the scene, the question remains: Why examine the decade of the 1860s? First, archival sources are readily available in the Historical Archive of Mexico City, which contains records for San Angel and Tlalpan. Here the oldest surviving documents come from the 1860s—thus the impossibility, at the moment, of analyzing events in the municipalities for the earlier years of the Republic. Moreover, the decade of the 1860s not only witnessed the great civil war known as the War of the Reform (1858–1861) but also the invasion and occupation of Mexico by French troops (1862–1867). The latter events culminated in the coronation of Maximilian I as emperor of Mexico, constant war against the troops of the occupation, and, finally, the restoration of the Republic. Therefore the 1860s offer a propitious moment for examining the change and continuity of customs and attitudes by using this suburban society as a test case during an era when it was convulsed by civil war and occupied by foreign troops.

Independence Day celebrations, especially the annual speeches, reflected national concerns. In 1862, for example, Manuel Payno delivered the Independence Day address. He quickly reviewed five hundred years of history in the Central Valley, from the first arrival of a small band of Aztec settlers in search of land where they could live "free, independent and happy," to the arrival of the French in 1862. Payno justified his historical review because it was an occasion "when the people should be told the history of their homeland and their nationality." He reprimanded Napoleon III, the French emperor, for sending troops into Mexico, especially because France's influence would be better achieved through its citizens' talent and knowledge. He recalled that Mexicans had learned a great deal from the French by imitating their literature and adopting their customs. Faced with French aggression, however, he declared that Mexicans would have "to repel force with force," adding that "only the united effort among the sons of Mexico" could save national independence.[10] The invasion complicated the holding of Independence celebrations throughout the French era.

Patriotic Juntas and Finances

Before a festival took place, a group of residents needed to take charge of organizing an appropriate celebration. From the earliest years of the Republic, the capital city had relied on patriotic juntas or committees to oversee the necessary arrangements, ranging from organizing recreational activities to assuming the role of hosts for various events to raising funds.[11] Within a short time, these patriotic committees became common in nearly all the towns and villages based on the model of the ones in the capital.

Maximilian, as emperor of Mexico, wanted to use the Independence holiday to promote his regime, so he issued a decree requiring that all "cities, towns, and villages of the empire" appoint a patriotic commission to direct the celebration of Independence.[12] Maximilian's decree resulted in the creation of a patriotic junta in San Angel that was charged with organizing the Independence Day celebration in 1863. The local ayuntamiento, or town council, appointed the committee two weeks before the scheduled fiesta. Tomás Orozco, a 47-year-old merchant, headed the committee; Fortín Aguilar functioned as secretary and Genaro de la Garza as treasurer. In addition, several other persons were named to head subcommittees to handle the details of the commemoration.

Perhaps the most important of these subcommittees took charge of the fireworks display intended to entertain the public. The chairman of the committee, German de Olmos, eagerly developed a brilliant pyrotechnical design accompanied by his proposal of costs, which included 60 pesos for castles (one of the most common and spectacular of Mexican fireworks constructions) and 35 pesos for thirty gross of firecrackers. The cost for this pyrotechnical display represented over one-half of the total budget proposed for the celebration. It should be remembered that since colonial times, governments had spent enormous amounts on fireworks as part of festivals. According to Angel López Cantos, fireworks served as "the condiments that seasoned all of the brilliant manifestations of the collective character." Fireworks were always set off at the transcendent moment of the festival, either at the beginning or at the end. No major festival occurred without at least one burning, exploding castle.[13]

Carl Christian Becher, a German traveler, attended a fiesta in San Angel, where he was duly impressed with the quality and quantity of the fireworks. He commented that in Mexico more fireworks were consumed for festivities than in all the nation's military drills and battles taken together.[14] (It should be noted that even today, huge quantities of fireworks, especially firecrackers and skyrockets, explode during the September Independence celebrations.)

Apart from the spectacular displays of fireworks, two other facets of the celebration required considerable attention. The patriotic committee illuminated the town's streets and its municipal building. A certain Señor Fernández took charge of this task, and he estimated the cost of oil for the lamps at 8 pesos. The other considerable expense related to the holiday music, and German de Olmos spent 30 pesos to hire musicians. Crispin Nava, a day laborer from San Jerónimo, was assigned the task of decorating the town, except for illuminations. He was in charge of the architectural ornaments, street decorations, and lights in the plaza. He had nothing to do with private homes whose owners assumed the responsibility of adorning the exteriors.

Juan del Castillo, a 58-year-old clerk, organized the program according to the elaborate instructions from the junta. He also sent out invitations to all the events and posted announcements of the celebration in the surrounding towns and in the capital. The budget for his committee, of course, was critical. The decree of August 1863 ordered that money be obtained from the office of revenue and from donations, which the committee should promote by arousing "the patriotism of the local residents."[15] The junta named Sr. Aguilar, Bernardo Olmos (a 35-year-old merchant), José María Giron (a 31-year-old employee), and Genaro de la Garza as a committee to solicit donations from their fellow townsmen, the local literary salons, and the factories of Tizapan, Loreto, and Santa Teresa. On September 10, a few days after beginning their collection, the men had gathered 87.75 pesos. Since estimated costs totaled 161 pesos, it was necessary to solicit another 73 pesos from the office of revenue to cover the difference. From all indications, the commissioners accomplished their task because the celebration occurred as planned.

In 1864 the city fathers followed similar procedures with some modifications. The patriotic commission comprised Rafael Ulibarri, German de Olmos, José María Ordóñez, Pedro Gaitan, Manuel Eslava, Rafael Eslava, and Rafael Rizo, with Marciano Giron as treasurer. The junta also solicited the assistance of several other residents to help on subcommittee assignments. The full group was divided as follows:

Decorations and Program—Jacobo Carrera and Tomás Gardida
Fireworks—José María Ordóñez
Illuminations—Manuel and Rafael Eslava
Architectural Decoration—Eugenio Rizo and Rafael Ulibarri
Music—Gerardo de Olmos
Circus Entertainers—German de Olmos and Pedro Gaitan
San Angel—Manuel Moreno and José María Giron
Tizapán—Ausencio Lira and Fortin Aguilar
Contreras—?
San Jerónimo—Quirino Mayagoitia and José María Giron
La Magdalena—Julio Ruiz and Jesús Hayad
San Nicolás—Margarito Bassoco and Guadalupe Alvarez
San Bernabe—Juan Nava and Atanasio Reyes
San Bartolo—Antonio Olmos and Pablo López
Santa Rosa—José María Gutiérrez and Guadalupe Gutiérrez
Tetelpa—Paulino Rivas and José María Velasco
Tlacopac—Cruz Lara and Guadalupe García
Chimalistac—Roque Arredondo and Cristobal Rivas
Hacienda Anzaldo—Quirino Mayagoitia and José María García
F. la Magdalena—Cristobal Ortiz and Valente Guerrero
F. Santa Teresa—Guilibaldo Arena

If we compare this committee to the previous one, we find that the number of persons increased to thirty-five, with only three names repeated. The committee took the opportunity to include more members of the community and to incorporate individuals representing neighboring villages and factories. While enlisting more people did not guarantee the success of the celebration, it did ensure wider participation in the holiday.

The records provide the following information on the commissioners for 1864:

Name	Residence	Age	Status	Occupation
Bassoco, Margarito	San Nicolás	36	Married	Blacksmith
García, José	María Magdalena	26	Married	Brick mason
Gardida, Tomás	San Angel	42	Married	Merchant
Giron, José María	San Angel	42	Married	Scribe
Gutiérrez, José M.	San Bernabe	32	Married	
López, Pablo	San Bartolo	28	Married	Farmer
Mayagoitia, Quirino	Magdalena	41	Married	Carpenter
Moreno, Manuel	San Angel	40	Married	Merchant
Nava, Juan	San Bernabe	57	Married	Blacksmith

Olmos, Antonio	San Angel	30	Widower	
Ordóñez, José María	San Angel	30	Single	Merchant
Reyes, Atanasio	San Bernabe	48	Married	Day laborer
Rizo, Eugenio	San Angel	24	Single	Clerk
Ruiz, Julio	Magdalena	20	Single	Weaver
Velasco, José María	Magdalena	24	Married	Farmer

This list shows clearly that the residents of San Angel as well as persons from the surrounding villages took an active part in the planning of the holiday. On examining the occupations of committee members, two patterns appear: the diversity of occupations; and the fact that each member could contribute directly through his profession by working on the festival's site, transporting materials, contributing goods, and even assisting with the paperwork required in the planning.

During both the colonial and the early republican eras, government officials, local clergy, and community elites participated in the planning of celebrations. As the Liberals began to reduce ecclesiastical power and privileges, clerical participation in festivals declined. This development had far-reaching effects on Mexican communities because parish priests had always been influential in civic matters, ensuring the cooperation of community members. As Church participation declined, persons from the local social, political, and labor sectors had to take more active roles in celebrations, even though the mechanisms for "voluntary cooperation" remained the same.

Upon returning to the commission for 1864, we find that the members approved the following budget (in pesos):

$60	Musicians
120	Fireworks displays, September 16 and 27
60	Firecrackers and skyrockets, September 15, 16, and 27
40	Decorative facade for the main salon
25	Lighting
50	Laborers, wood for construction, miscellaneous costs
40	Horsemanship company
$395	

The commission, according to the 1863 decree, should have received an allowance of 200 pesos from the administrative office in charge of taxes. The members also were counting on a considerable amount of money donated from local residents and neighboring factors. Unfortunately, eight days before the celebration, the commission had collected only 6 pesos and one-half *real* from the towns of Chimalistac,

San Nicolás, and Santa Rosa. Moreover, the office of revenue denied the commission's request for monies.

The committee members at this point returned the paltry donations and notified San Angel's president that because of "the insurmountable obstacle" created by the lack of funds, it was impossible for them to complete their duties. As a consequence, the commissioners resigned. The official 1864 commemoration of Independence was apparently canceled, although private, spontaneous celebrations may have taken place. In this incident, we can detect the reluctance on the part of local residents to collaborate with the invading regime. Donations dramatically fell from 87 pesos in 1863 to 6 in 1864. No economic crisis accounted for the drop, so that the only explanation can be the change of conscience on the part of the people. How could anyone support an Independence celebration at a time when the nation had lost its independence as a result of foreign invasion?

Municipal officials did not want the same embarrassing experience to happen in 1865, so that we learn from the local registers that the administrators established a budget for festivals. They still called for donations but had a minimum amount to defray costs. In 1867, three months after Emperor Maximilian's execution on the Hill of the Bells and the ensuing restoration of the Republic, the residents of San Angel generously donated funds totaling 268.67 pesos. The celebration, which also reflected the nation's recovered independence, cost 210.60 pesos. For the first time since well before the French intervention the municipality had a balance after the celebration.[16]

The creation of a budget did not guarantee a successful celebration of Independence. Indeed, committee members were forced to seek other sources of revenue. In some cases, they donated their own funds for the festival, hoping for reimbursement. For example, the town's financial records reveal the amount of 5 pesos registered in the month of December 1868 for "a salary allowance for the patriotic junta for September 15 and 16."[17] The need for funds probably dictated the appointment of several merchants who could afford to donate money for the celebration with the hope of receiving some future municipal benefit.

The Program

The program for the "festival of those glorious days when emancipation was announced" specified that the celebration should last three days. Although the August 10, 1863, decree stipulated only September 16 and 27 as the official holidays, the program proposed by the commission added that the celebration should begin on the evening of September 15. Since the founding of the Republic, leaders had debated what dates to celebrate. Depending on the regime in power, whether Conservative or Liberal, the holiday changed days. The different dates also determined the audience who participated. During the era of Santa Anna, the celebration on September 15 was reserved and private, held in enclosed spaces, in contrast to the popular festival on the next day. It was during the private celebration in the National Theater in Mexico City that the national anthem made its debut on September 15, 1854.[18]

According to the 1863 San Angel program, on the night of September 15 the municipal buildings and the main plaza were illuminated. At nine o'clock the bells from the churches and chapels in San Angel and the surrounding towns commenced to ring, accompanied by bursts of fireworks and strains of music. Next, the members of the commission met in the municipal hall and, together with local officials, walked to the plaza for the official speeches on the Act of Independence. Finally, they, along with the assembled members of the community, listened to a "discourse appropriate to the celebration" pronounced by a designated orator, although the participation of other speakers was permitted. In 1863 a teacher, Susano Alvarez, delivered San Angel's civic oration. Once the speeches had ended, the commission retired and the festival ended for the evening.

At dawn on September 16 the residents of San Angel awakened to an artillery salvo, followed by the pealing of church bells. Given the fact that most of the residents had spent much of the previous evening strolling through the streets and listening to music, the morning noise was probably necessary to wake them up. Independence Day was again remembered with another civic oration on the stage in the central plaza at 11 A.M., attended by local authorities, with Luis G. Del Villa as the speaker. The program noted that "cheers and music" would continue until 4 P.M. and that musicians would serenade the crowd until 9 P.M., when the fireworks display began.

A week after these two events came a third festival with the celebration of the culmination of Independence. The 1863 decree ordered the commemoration of September 27, marking the entrance of the Army of Three Guarantees into Mexico City. San Angel residents repeated the same pattern of celebration, only with a different orator. This celebration of September 27 occurred when the regime in power supported the image of Mexico that included Emperor Agustín I. Generally, more conservative regimes promoted this holiday. Anastasio Bustamante as president in 1837 initiated the commemoration of this date. According to Enrique Plasencia, in 1864, Emperor Maximilian officially decreed the suppression of the September 27 holiday.[19] Despite Plasencia's statements, the day was still honored in San Angel. Moreover, the date was celebrated with various holiday events, including the ascension of a hot-air balloon.

During the early Independence Day festivals, the events centered on the main plaza. The exception came in 1864 and continued for the next ten years, as September 15 was celebrated in private locations. For example, in 1864, the holiday events took place in the home of Señor Orozco, who had served in 1863 as the president of the patriotic junta. Although the records reported that the event took place in Orozco's residence, the location actually was the San Nicolás Hotel, owned by Orozco. The hotel, facing the San Jacinto Plaza, contained various salons, a restaurant, a theater, baths, and bowling allies, with an orchard and stables. While in theory any town resident could have gone to the hotel to attend the celebration, in fact the festival took place indoors under the watchful eye of authorities who controlled admission.[20]

The celebration occurred within an architectural and geographic space of distinct scale,[21] uncovered but enclosed. Perhaps the reason for choosing these locations came from the methods of social control: defined and enclosed space was easier to regulate, or the major issue may have been to provide a location with good acoustics. Furthermore, the use of an enclosed space meant a smaller area for the general population to fill, thus making possible greater control over access and prohibiting undesirables from participating.

In 1864 one aspect of the celebration stands out. The program called for the members of the patriotic junta to attend Mass together and hear the singing of a solemn Te Deum. The political prefect made attendance at this service a requirement for the neighboring population.[22] This measure reflected an old tradition that had been suppressed by recent regimes in which government officials participated at the church in a homily that constituted a fundamental part of the festivities. During Maximilian's reign, the Roman Catholic Church and the empire had a close relationship reflected in the incorporation of religious services as a fundamental part of Imperial ceremonies. The 9 A.M. Mass on September 28, 1864, was intended to complement the Independence Day festivities. The religious services equated the sacrifice of the heroes of Independence, who had shed their blood for the nation, with the Catholic belief in the sacrifice of Jesus Christ, who had died for mankind. This conflation gave a religious character to the pantheon of heroes who, each year, were remembered with thanks for their sacrifice.

Conclusion

In examining public ceremonies, Marcos González Pérez identified preparatory, central, and complementary sequential stages and plans of the celebrations.[23] Organizers acted during the first stage to create the appropriate atmosphere through selection of the right location. For the festivals in San Angel, the members of the patriotic junta began the preparations at initial meetings usually early in August. In these meetings, the members formed various subcommittees and discussed the planning of the celebrations, the approval of programs, the raising of funds through donations, and the naming of orators. Municipal authorities assisted by recommending that residents adorn their houses and assist in decorating the streets. Many residents placed decorations and illuminations on the facades, windows, doors, and balconies of their homes. In public places, painters and carpenters built stages to transform the principal plazas into central festival sites. In addition, days before the festival the junta directed the construction and placement of symbols that helped to establish local and national identity.

The festival's events included honoring the national flag by public display, listening to an oration on the meaning of Independence, and participating in a parade. Activities for the September celebrations varied from place to place and from year to year. For example, according to the 1864 program, the residents of San Angel witnessed an equestrian display on September 16 and a hot-air balloon ascension on September 27. In other towns, the celebrations provided the occasion for the inauguration of public buildings.

In San Angel, the festivals combined both private and public, civil and religious, and personal and corporate spaces. For example, in San Angel in 1863 and in 1864 the committee members used the main plaza, the parish church, the city council's meeting rooms, the town buildings, a private home, and a hotel salon—each one for distinct activities of the Independence holiday. The principal actors in the festival would meet in one place, form a delegation, and walk to another location, passing through the streets to provide a spectacle for the people gathered as an audience, who sanctioned the festivals by participating in them.

A group of determined citizens thus called together townspeople and encouraged them to celebrate. The patriotic juntas acted even though they could not always count on the assistance of the government or of private institutions. In some cases, the junta members themselves had to provide the funds for the celebrations. And, of course, in 1864 it became evident that in spite of the substantial actions by notable citizens, the majority of the people opposed the Imperial regime and would not support a celebration. In other words, their actions demonstrated that they had no intention of cooperating in a festival promoted by a government created by foreign occupation. It was not a simple case of there being no public interest in the holiday, but rather an act of defiance against an emperor who ordered the people to celebrate.

Notes

1. Carlos Mijares Bracho, *San Angel* (Mexico: Clio, 1997).

2. Marquesa Calderón de la Barca, *La vida en México* (Mexico: Editora Nacional, 1958), 2:136–37.

3. Francisco Fernández del Castillo, *Apuntes para la historia de San Angel (San Jacinto Tenanitla) y sus alrededores. Tradiciones, historia, leyendas, etc.* (Mexico: Imp. del Museo Nacional de Arqueología, Historia y Etnologia, 1913), 98.

4. Archivo Historico de la Ciudad de México (hereinafter cited as AHCM), Tlalpan, Estadística, inv. 89, caja 3, expediente 14, "Datos estadísticos del Distrito de Tlalpan reunidos por el C. Antonio Carrion, asociado corresponsal de la Sociedad Mexicana de Geografia y Estadística conforme a la circular del Ministerio de Fomento de 9 de julio de 1873." I thank Ignacio Hernández García and Jovita Elena Ramos Cruz for their help in locating much of the documentation found in the AHCM.

5. Ana Lau J., "Tlalpan: una nueva organización administrativa, 1824–1903," in *Población y estructura urbana en México, siglos XVIII y XIX* (Jalapa: Universidad Veracruzana/Instituto Mora/UAM-Ixtapalapa, 1996), 311; AHCM, Tlalpan, Estadística, inv. 90, caja 4, exp. 27. I am grateful to Ana Lau J. for her generosity in sharing documents that she has collected concerning San Angel.

6. María Ana Portal Ariosa, "Identidad urbana y religiosidad popular" (Ph.D. diss. in Antropología, UNAM, 1995), 85; Mijares Bracho, *San Angel*, 29–31.

7. Lau, "Tlalpan," 311.

8. AHCM, San Angel, Padrones, inv. 191, exp. 3.

9. Portal Ariosa, "Identidad urbana y religiosidad popular," 24.

10. Manuel Payno, "Discurso pronunciado en la plaza del pueblo de San Angel por el ciudadano . . . el 16 de septiembre . . . en celebración del aniversario de la independencia nacional," *Monitor Republicano*, September 28, 1862.

11. See Chapter One of this volume, Michael Costeloe's "The Junta Patriótica and the Celebration of Independence in Mexico City, 1825–1855."

12. *Boletin de las Leyes* 97 (August 10, 1863): 1:221–22.

13. Angel López Cantos, *Juegos, fiestas y diversiones en la América española* (Madrid: Editorial Mapfre, 1992), 50–61.

14. Carl C. Becher, *Cartas sobre México. La república mexicana durante los anos decisivos de 1832 y 1833* (Mexico: Facultad de Filosofía y Letras, NMAM, 1959), 122.

15. *Boletin de las Leyes*, 1:221–22.

16. AHCM, San Angel, Diversiones y festividades, inv. 96, exp. 16, 1867.

17. AHCM, Fondo Tlalpan, Ramo Hacienda, Presupuestos, inv. 148, exp. 7, 1868.

18. Enrique Plasencia de la Parra, *Independencia y nacionalismo a la luz del discurso conmemorativo 1825–1867* (Mexico: Consejo Nacional para la Cultura y las Artes, 1991), 172; Serie Regiones, 68.

19. Plasencia de la Parra, *Independencia y nacionalismo*, 12, 70, 119.

20. *El Pajaro Verde*, May 2, and June 28, 1866; AHCM, San Angel, Padrones, inv. 191, exp. 3, "Estado general de la población de San Angel, ano de 1866."

21. See Mijares Bracho, *San Angel*, 80–81.

22. *El Pajaro Verde*, September 26, 1864.

23. Marcos González Pérez, *Bajo el Palio y el Laurel. Bogotá a traves de las manifestaciones festivas decimononicas* (Bogotá: Fondo Editorial Universidad Distrital Francisco José de Caldas, 1995).

CHAPTER FIVE

Conservatives Contest the Meaning of Independence, 1846–1855

JAVIER RODRÍGUEZ PIÑA

> Who were those men to whom Mexico owes its Independence? Our history says it and everybody knows it, *El Siglo XIX* confessed it not too many days ago: they were the men from the Conservative Party. To them we owe the fortune of being independent, if one can call fortunate this miserable existence that we have had ever since we became independent.[1]

During much of the nineteenth century, the Mexican political scene was characterized by rancorous debate between Liberals and Conservatives. While it is true that the development of these two ideological trends into political groups was a slow process lasting several decades (from before Independence until, at least, the Liberal triumph in 1867), we find expressions of these two tendencies from Independence onward. In some instances they were well defined, in others barely distinguishable. In general, this central debate divided the great majority of the political actors of the time and stirred arguments that kept the country constantly on the verge of chaos.

Although the ideological differences between the Liberal and Conservative positions often may not seem great, they were, in fact, two alternative conceptions of the road that the country should follow in order to develop. Thus, from the first moments of independent existence, discussions about the best possible political organization for the country resulted in major struggles between supporters of centralism and federalism and between proponents of monarchy and republic. Later on, these struggles began coalescing into liberalism and conservatism, with each group developing a distinct and coherent perspective not only about the political organization of Mexico but also about its social and economic structure. Certain issues, such as the role of the Church in society, the importance of the army, the tasks of the social classes, the issue of private property, to name a few, were intensely debated—at times with the support of firearms—between members of the two factions.

In the emergence of this great division in the Mexican polity, the debate over the achievement of Independence stands out. This controversy, born in the first years of independent life, was to end only with the Liberal triumph of 1867. From its inception, the debate over the meaning of Independence featured two groups: one that vindicated the genesis of the movement of Independence and the "first insurgents" (Miguel Hidalgo and José María Morelos), and another that championed the end of that popular movement and the image and spirit of Agustín de Iturbide. Evidently, this dispute was not about the Liberals and Conservatives' personal likes or dislikes but instead was a true ideological battle that only became more distinct with time.

As the consolidation of the Liberal and Conservative groups was achieved around the middle of the nineteenth century, their ideological definitions become more precise and rigid. At the same time, the discussion about Independence-period heroes took shape as a fundamental conflict over the kind of country proposed by each group. For Liberals, the Independence movement had been in its origins the beginning of a democratic and republican project for building the country. This tendency had been thwarted at the end of the process by Iturbide's monarchical claims. For Conservatives, the movement led by Hidalgo and Morelos was a clear demonstration of the violence and anarchy that had sent the struggle for Independence down a blind alley in its first decade. To Conservatives, Iturbide was a hero who not only had brought the process of Independence to a conclusion but also had done so without violence while not destroying any fundamental structure.

In the long run, this ideological dispute was won by the Liberals. The triumph that overcame the Conservatives by way of arms in 1867 meant the political defeat of the Conservative group. It also defined the history of a country in which the Liberal vision prevailed, and where ideological enemies of the Liberal project became enemies of the whole nation and were denied their right to express their opinion or take part in a more open way in the destiny of the country.[2] In the long run, the proscription of the Conservatives from Mexican history prevented their interpretations of the past and their proposed alternatives to be thoroughly known. This end was brought about by ignorance, by the manipulation of history, and by the creation of dominant national myths.[3]

The aim of this essay is to access a small segment of the almost forgotten Conservative view of the world. It is an effort to rescue their opinions of the meaning of the Independence movement and the position advanced by this group between 1846 and 1855, when it enjoyed more political and intellectual presence.[4] Research was conducted through the Conservative newspapers *El Tiempo* (1846) and *El Universal* (1848–1855), propaganda media that revealed a great deal about Conservative thinking. The present work not only gathers the fundamental ideas expressed in these publications but also reviews the background of the discussion and Lucas Alamán's contribution to the subject.[5] My intention is to show that, behind the controversy on the heroes, what was really at stake was a model for the country that was every bit as valid as that of the Liberals.

The Background of the Debate

The beginnings of the debate on the paternity and the meaning of Independence appeared in the last moments of the war itself. Iturbide insisted on establishing a marked distinction between the First Insurgents, whom he considered "a pack of thieves and murderers who were after their own profit and personal grandeur only," and his own movement. According to Iturbide, the revolutions of 1810 and 1821 were two different and opposing events and, thus, the merit of Independence belonged only to him. Whereas the early Independence fighters had instilled violence and alienation among the inhabitants of New Spain, his movement—without the recourse to violence—had vindicated the union of all inhabitants without distinction of origin or race.[6]

Such a self-serving view from the author of the Plan de Iguala came from an evident reality: the Independence war in its first stages had implied a frontal attack against colonial power and had, at the same time, given way to a tense period of social unrest that threatened the organization and stability of the future independent country. The outcome of the movement led by Iturbide, especially after the signing of the Plan de Iguala, in contrast, was a peaceful, shared, and organized transition toward Independence that offered the country a political establishment very similar to the one enjoyed during the colonial period. In the end, to put it simply, it was a collision between a project of social revolution and one of ratifying Independence. The two processes involved radically different projects for the building of a country and engendered a dispute about Independence that would stay alive for many decades.

It should not come as a surprise that, as soon as he could, Iturbide tried to deny the First Insurgents the right to be honored through a celebration. On March 1, 1822, during the Provisional Government Junta—assembled and presided over by the victorious Iturbide in order to found the independent country—the days to be declared national holidays were discussed. The chairman, José María Fagoaga, proposed February 24, the day of the proclamation of the Plan de Iguala; March 2, the signing of the Plan de Iguala; and September 27, the date of the entrance of the Trigarante (Three Guarantees) Army, with Iturbide at its head, into Mexico City.[7]

Fagoaga's recommendation set off a debate over the heroes of Independence in which representatives of different factions, whose presence in the Provisional Government Junta had apparently been accepted by Iturbide, participated. According to Lucas Alamán, this debate was the origin of a growing opposition to Iturbide:

> The deputies who had belonged to the insurgents as part of their government and the Congress or had been active under their banners were joined by those who had been advocates, albeit in secret, of that revolution as well as by those who showed little affinity for Iturbide or his ideas and were trying, even then, to tarnish his glory while enhancing that of the promoters of the 1810 revolution, who started to be known as "old patriots." This contributed to the growing influence of that party as was evidenced by the establishment of the national holidays that the Provisional Junta requested from the Congress upon its dissolution.[8]

Partisans of this view asked that September 16 be observed in order to honor those "old patriots" whose objectives, they argued, had been similar to the ones brought by the culmination of Independence:

> Dr. Argandar tried to claim that "the revolution started that day in the town of Dolores, just as the Iguala Plan, had had as its objectives independence, religion, unity, and monarchy. Because this was not the general opinion, all of this would later become confusing and horribly disorganized." He ended up requesting the designation of "a committee in charge of deciding upon the way to honor

the memory of those first defenders of the country and the principal leaders who, proclaiming the memorable Iguala Plan, consummated its glories." . . . Once the committee had been appointed, it embraced all the questions concerning the subject, but because of the urgency of deciding upon the national holidays—March 2, one of them, was coming up soon—this was the only topic discussed. To the three suggested dates, September 16 was added. The rest of the discussion was postponed. This delay encouraged Colonel Ochoa, representative for Durango, to make a suggestion that touched on the core of the matter, namely, that "the committee in charge of the ways in which the heroes were to be honored should examine closely, and file by file, who the real heroes were."[9]

Finally, after a long debate, September 16 was included and thus, says Alamán, the insurgents "succeeded in placing themselves in the same standing as the leaders of the Iguala revolution, with no little exasperation on Iturbide and the company's part."[10]

With this first official decision on the Independence holiday, we can say that there was a momentary tie between the protagonists. This does not mean, nevertheless, that the debate had come to an end. As Alamán points out, the debate was a daily occurrence in the press:

> This affair was not only discussed in the Congress; the press was also involved. Dávila and Fernández de Lizardi, also known as the "Mexican Thinker," in a series of questions on daily affairs, had promoted the assessment of the merits of the old patriots and their part in the achievement of Independence. Joaquín Parres answered each and every one and, speaking of Hidalgo, [Ignacio] Allende, and other leaders of the insurrection, maintained that "the only thing that our freedom owes them is their small contribution, made with serious harm to the country, to the idea of Independence." He went on to question: "What was to be found in the Iguala Plan that pertained to the system or the project of the old leaders of the independent party? Is death to the gachupines the same as unity? Is looting the same as preserving and defending property? Is establishing a liberal government and sparing blood remembering a practice of desolation and rivalry?"[11]

Any linking of the two dates, propitiated by what Edmundo O'Gorman has called Iturbide's tacit mistake of allowing the creation of a collegiate power, could last only a fleeting moment.[12] As soon as Iturbide fell in 1823, the republican opposition hastened to cancel not only the validity of the Plan de Iguala and the Treaties of Córdoba but also any acknowledgment of Iturbide as an essential part of Independence. What is more, Iturbide was decreed to be a traitor and an outlaw as well as a public enemy of the State, and he was banned from the country and never allowed to set foot again on Mexican soil.[13]

As soon as the Constitutional Congress was formed, however, the republicans decided to avenge the offense that, according to them, Iturbide had perpetrated against the First Insurgents. They promulgated the Decree of July 19, 1823, that declared Hidalgo, Morelos, Allende, Juan Aldama, Mariano Abasolo, Mariano Matamoros, Leonardo and Miguel Bravo, Hermenegildo Galeana, José Mariano Jiménez, Francisco Javier Mina, Pedro Moreno, and Víctor Rosales "meritorious in the heroic degree," and that awarded pensions to their widows and closest relatives. Their names were to be written in gold letters in the Hall of Sessions in the Congress. Later, their mortal remains would be exhumed and taken to Mexico City where they would be laid to rest in the Cathedral during a fine ceremony on September 17.[14]

To crown this vindicating process of the republicans, when a Decree on civic holidays was issued on November 27, 1824, the 27th of September, as well as all other dates associated with Iturbide, was erased from the holiday calendar.[15] Thus annulled, for a period of almost twelve years, was the possibility of celebrating the culmination of Independence and the heroes of that period. This act officially terminated, for the time being, the debate over Independence. When the 27th of September was rejected as a commemorative date, it not only canceled the celebration but put off momentarily the possibility of discussing the subject in the newspapers as well as in civic speeches associated with this date.[16]

In fact, after 1825, the first year that the 16th of September was celebrated, civic speeches became opportunities to honor the First Insurgents. During the next five years, as Spain tried several times to recover its old colony, the speeches became a common means to spread a Hispanophobic attitude that went very well with the context of the first stages of Independence. This attitude of rejection toward everything Spanish became a motive for questioning the Conquest, the three hundred years of life as a colony, and the vindication of a kind of Mexican nationalism where the First Insurgents in their struggle against Spain fitted neatly but where Iturbide could not be clearly positioned.

Nevertheless, beyond failing to mention Iturbide and thus simply attempting to forget him, there was no explicit intention to revile his image. Actually, the greater part of the civic speeches of the 1820s, far from provoking antagonism, were invitations to the Mexicans to unite. At the beginning of the 1830s, once Spain's goal of recovering its old colony had faltered, the anti-Spanish attitude diminished and the negative disposition toward Iturbide also became more subdued.

The political events of the 1830s prepared the ground for bringing the leader of the Trigarante Army back into the debate. This change appeared first as a reference during a civic speech given by José María Tornel on September 16, 1827. While mentioning those who carried through Hidalgo's movement, he said: "Morelos, Matamoros, [Francisco] Victoria, [Ramón López] Rayón, the Bravos, Terán, [José Sixto] Verduzco, [Vicente] Guerrero the indomitable, and so many other caudillos as well as the caudillo of Iguala, fired up with wrath, maintained for ten more years and until victory Hidalgo's promise and his sacred faith." Later on, while referring to the closure of Independence, Tornel said: "September 27 of 1821 is the complement to the great day, a source of intense joy for the Mexicans. Blood and tears ceased to water this privileged land. Night picks up its somber veil: confusion and disorder disappear with the first rays of the sun."[17]

Tornel does not mention Iturbide by name but succeeds in turning him into a follower of the movement initiated by Hidalgo. The 27th of September would have the same fate, becoming a complement of September 16, 1810. From this speech onward, Iturbide's name would reappear on different occasions during the celebration of Independence. Speakers would try to find a common thread between Hidalgo and Iturbide to reconcile the contradictions between their respective movements. Iturbide would be vindicated as a *libertador*, but no mention would be made of his subsequent performance while in power.

The 1830s were an even more propitious time for the rehabilitation of Iturbide's image. The federalist failure to organize the country had allowed the growth of a centralist-conservative opposition. In this decade, Conservatives made their first concerted attempt to organize the country from a position of power and based on conservative principles. During the regime of Anastasio Bustamante (January 1, 1830–August 14, 1832) and during the phase started in 1835 in response to Valentín Gómez Farías's reformist attempt, Conservative initiatives gave rise to the Centralist Constitution of 1836 and the creation of the Supreme Conservative Power. In both instances, centralism was only a small fragment of an extensive program (that included the vindication of Catholicism and the defense of the Church's privileges as well as those of the Army and the "upper classes") with which Conservatives hoped to establish the basis of a far-reaching project within an atmosphere of political stability.

During the Conservative ascent of the 1830s, Iturbide's image had a chance of being finally restored. In fact, it was Antonio López de Santa Anna, during his first administration, who would make the initial attempt to place Iturbide in a privileged niche in history. This he did by issuing the Decree of November 3, in which it was ordered that "D. Agustín de Iturbide's ashes be brought to Mexico and placed in the urn destined to the heroes of Independence." The reason for this act was that "the Mexican nation, being as fair when chastizing those who take over her rights as when rewarding the great endeavors of her children, recognized him as one of the authors of its Independence, [his] having proclaimed it in Iguala and secured it with his wisdom and courage."[18] Nevertheless, for reasons undoubtedly related to the recently declared independence of Texas and the uprisings in various parts of the country, the transfer of the remains could not be completed.

Beyond this failed attempt, the legal process toward Iturbide's complete rehabilitation was begun on February 27, 1835. In the context of Santa Anna's return to centralism and the integration of a Congress with a majority of the *partido del orden*, a Decree was issued whereby the exile of Iturbide's widow and children was revoked.[19] Two months later, the same Congress issued a law whereby the Iturbide family would be paid one million pesos and granted land in Nuevo México and the Californias.[20] Finally, on May 20 of the same year, the Congress determined that Iturbide's name should be written in gold letters in the Chamber of Representatives, matching his image to that of the First Insurgents.[21]

This reparation process entered its decisive phase around 1837, when Bustamante's Conservative government decided to reinstate September 27 as the second Independence holiday. Although the celebration was reinstated in a nonofficial manner, as no corresponding Decree was issued, it soon caught on in the main capital cities of the country as a supplement to the celebration of September 16. At the beginning, civic speeches underlined the continuity between the onset and the conclusion of the process of Independence, but very soon they started differentiating between the two. As had been the case at the beginning of the period, Conservative commentators would emphasize the inherent violence of the first stages of Independence, contrasting it unfavorably with the peaceful approach of the final process.

Bustamante's government continued to ingratiate itself even more with the people by honoring Iturbide's memory. In the year following the restoration of September 27 as a holiday, and before the new anniversary of that date, Bustamante issued the Decree to transfer Iturbide's remains to the Mexico City Cathedral, "the site destined to heroes."[22] This transfer became an event full of opulence and significance.[23] Iturbide had been reevaluated and placed—this was the belief at the time—face to face at last with the other insurgents. Alamán describes the occasion:

> the remains were received with great pomp, at the entrance of the city on the afternoon of September 25, and then placed in the Convent of San Francisco in the Chapel of the Stairs until October 24 when, with great solemnity, they were taken to the Cathedral. The next day, after a vigil and a Mass sung with magnificent circumstance, they were interred in the grave in the San Felipe de Jesús Chapel and not where Hidalgo and company's ashes are contained. Bustamante and Iturbide's followers would have thought, by coming in touch with them, that they would have been desecrated. Thus they were as distant in death as they had been in life.

Alamán concludes his account of the reburial a little resentfully: "This has been the only tribute of recognition paid to the memory of Iturbide. While, by the effects of the passing of time, a man's errors are forgotten and only the benefits received through him are present, the founder of Mexican Independence seemed to have deserved other proofs of gratitude from the nation that he raised to that position; but the will to dispossess him of this honor has caused him to be seen with much indifference."[24] Thus, finally rehabilitated under the influence of Bustamante's Centralist-Conservative government, Iturbide made a comeback in public discussions. The fact that September 27 could be celebrated undoubtedly contributed to the renewed distinction between the beginning and the closure of the Independence movement. Moreover, the vindication of Iturbide became stronger as years went by. The majority of civic speeches on the occasion of this holiday reiterated Iturbide's right to be presented as a fundamental hero of Independence.

Nevertheless, in most civic speeches of the 1830s the feeling of frustration toward what had been left unaccomplished after the breakup with Spain began to emerge. The optimism of the 1820s had disappeared and given way to the disappointment with the results of the clashes among the opposing "parties" in their aim to impose different forms of government. This new move is apparent, for example, in the speeches given on September 27, 1839, and on September 16, 1840. A pessimistic tone regarding the situation of the country two decades away from Independence can de detected here. In the first one, General Lino José Alcorta says:

Eighteen years have gone by since the time that the problem of independence was solved. If we then had had the experience acquired through the evil resulting from that fatal civil war, we would have enjoyed an equivalent period of peace and fortune. . . .

The origin of those evils we deplore has been the lack of unity, of that precious support to society; and if unity was sworn in Iguala vis-à-vis the foreigners (establishing thus one of the Three Guarantees of our troops), we should find even more motivation in preserving it among us, children of the same country and brothers by nature, by blood, friendship, and association!

May the parties disappear then: let us hold each other in brotherhood: may all grudges and opinions be buried and may our country be our only insignia so that as free men her noble emulation may be reduced to providing the highest benefits. May the rivalry among the social classes be banished from politics as they exist as long as they serve a common goal and the idea of one being superior to the others does not arise. This verdict only brings discord and with it the separation or, more precisely, the division of the community of all Mexicans who would thus become armed combatants and destroy each other, bringing about the extermination of our society when we should be supporting it.[25]

Slightly more elaborate and more clearly identified with the Conservative persuasion is the speech of September 27, 1840, by José María Tornel. Here we also find disillusionment with the progress of the country after Independence, although Tornel attributed the country's ills to the origins of the Independence movement: "The Mexican nation, mutilated and sickly, is still alive; but its life is a torment because even the hope of happiness eludes her. Here I recall thirty years of continuous sufferings, thirty years of sailing on a sea of tears and blood without ever coming to port. The helmsmen have perished, steering the broken ship through wind, obstacles, and storms." At the same time, Itubide is vindicated over Hidalgo and Morelos.[26] Tornel questions Iturbide's fate:

The angel of the Lord urged Iturbide and took him, as if by the hand, in order for him to become the instrument of Providence on that day of health and redemption. But, oh, eternally regrettable misfortune! The glorious conqueror of his country's Independence is overpowered and murdered by the same men he had freed, by those who owed him the vilified title of citizens! The basest ingratitude did not allow that life—the ultimate and least considered of human rights—be granted to the creator and leader of this country. As hero and as genius, Iturbide marched as do the heavenly bodies, eclipsing their satellites. The Mexicans, deaf to the cry of recognition, saw without blushing how the valiant soldier, who had separated one world from the other and given it life, freedom, and honor, died.

For Tornel, the responsibility of all evils that came after Independence lay in the search for models unsuited to the national reality:

> Vacillating and unsteady have been the footsteps of the nation from the dawning of its political existence. We have tried all forms of government, from absolute monarchy with its dazzling pomp, to the federated republic and its dangerous excesses. In the adoption of laws, those habits and customs, whose roots are strong and ancient, have been tenaciously disturbed. Without first preparing the soil, we have planted exotic flowers that died at birth. While keeping the old legislation of our elders, we have disfigured it with extravagant addenda that have altered the scheme without improving it.

Finally, in light of the balance resulting from what happened after Independence, Tornel rejects—as would the Conservatives later— the possibility of questioning the pertinence of the breakup with Spain:

> Will I ever curse the day of the birth of the Republic? Will I dare execrate the night when the new political conception was proclaimed to the universe? Oh, no! Forgive, my friends, the ravings of an imagination pained and agitated by the dismal images of sterile and calamitous dissension. The truth is that Independence has been bought with all the goods that a society can long for, but it is in itself such an important and necessary asset that it was worth the resolution and sacrifice of an entire generation.[27]

These are examples of the changing style of civic speeches going into the 1840s. The pessimism in regard to the critical situation of the country and the questioning of the country's lack of unity—provoked by constant political dissension—would dog the policies of both Liberals and Conservatives. Nevertheless, as will be seen below, the latter would soon radicalize their interpretation of Independence and the process that followed on its appeals.

The Debate over Independence in *El Tiempo* and *El Universal*

During the 1830s, under the shadow of centralist regimes, Mexican conservatism had ample possibilities for political growth. Nevertheless, while the construction of Conservative thought grew considerably during the 1840s and 1850s, its possibility of offering the country a way out of its critical situation was substantially reduced. This was not the result of a lack of a coherent political project on the part of the Conservatives. Rather, it was due to the impossibility of carrying it out in a country burdened by all sorts of conflict.

Conservatives worked to define their ideology at the same time that they pursued the power necessary to execute their projects. In this connection, two specific moments are of interest: the first one fell under Mariano Paredes y Arrillaga's regime in 1846; the second one, in the period between 1848 and 1855, during the last presidency of Santa Anna. In both cases, solutions for the country were proposed and principles clearly defined through the two principal Conservative journals, *El Tiempo* and *El Universal*. Both periodicals emanated from the mind and actions of the Conservative genius, Lucas Alamán. Their importance lies in the possibility of finding in their pages ideological definitions fundamental to the understanding of the Mexican Conservative thought of that period.

El Tiempo published several articles on Independence and its heroes as well as on the national frustration over the events that followed the separation from Spain.[28] For *El Tiempo*, belonging to Spain for three hundred years was a source of pride because the inhabitants of New Spain had lived in peace and tranquility and had been able to create the wealth of the colony. Nevertheless, the germ of Independence had appeared naturally due to the maturity of the society:

> to our country came one of the highest ends that a country can achieve, independence. Early or late, prematurely or in a timely fashion, Mexican independence carried within it the seed and elements of prosperity. To be part of a Monarchy whose government resided two thousand leagues away could not be, in time, the formula for our happiness nor the aim of our ambition. We had been born and could not fit in our old dwelling. The child had become a man and did not need tutelage. At the same time we demanded a seat in the congress of the nations.[29]

With the country facing the inevitable dilemma of Independence, *El Tiempo* makes a clear distinction between its first stage, highlighting its violence and anarchy, and its conclusion, which would leave the country prepared for a future full of promise:

> A disastrous revolution that for ten years had transformed our continent into the battlefield of a bloody fratricidal war put an end to Spanish domination after three hundred years of a peaceful occupation of Moctezuma's empire. A happy combination of circum-

stances allowed us to achieve, in only seven months, an independence that had taken its toll in all the blood that flowed from 1810 to 1821 to no avail. Mexico sang its anthem to liberty and prepared to enter the numbers of the sovereign nations, to come together in a way befitting her dignity, and to rise to the standing that Providence had destined her to by providing her with the elements present in all countries of the globe. Great talents, an utmost respect for religion, an innate docility of the people, valor, morality in all State divisions, patriotism, education, submission, obedience, and respect toward the authorities; a strong love of order, a cordial union among families, an innate hospitality for the foreigner: this is the moral frame of those who inhabit this blissful soil. And the sweetest climate, varied and suitable for all kinds of crops, a favorable sky, mountains brimming with gold and silver, large rivers, virgin soil, people who had already shown their good disposition toward all sorts of commercial, agricultural, and manufacturing enterprises made up the physical component of the beautiful and promising perspective of our country.[30]

Naturally, during the course of the movement for Independence, Iturbide plays an outstanding role in defining the route to be taken by events. For the writers at *El Tiempo*, he is the only one to be credited with giving the country its freedom:

The immortal Iturbide declares liberty in Iguala, proclaims independence,[31] suggests the most pertinent plan to bring together in a common center the most divergent rays. In a moment his straight steps, his fortunate plans, his well-combined actions, his most difficult but promptly executed endeavors bring all disturbance to an abrupt end; and, after the fraternal embrace, everybody enrolls in the *libertador*'s army. Success is swift, complete, and glorious. All the complexity of events happening in less than a year is an embodiment of leniency, valor, foresight, and patriotism, a sign that shows the superb disposition of the inhabitants of Anáhuac coming together in a solid and befitting way, a bright augury of the prosperity that awaited our blessed country! . . . Once occupied by the Trigarante Army, received with an enthusiasm and joy never to be seen again, as the defendant of our adored religion, the guardian of our rights, and the support of our freedom, he established the first national government in Mexico. Everybody set his gaze upon him; the society as a whole stared at his lips; Mexicans believed that they had seen in that reunion of choice citizens, the Fathers of the Country who would lay the foundations of their future, magnificent social edifice.[32]

At any rate, despite the reception that the Mexicans gave to Iturbide, he was unsuccessful, due to Spain's refusal to send a representative

to govern its former colony, which brought about the fall of the leader
of the Plan de Iguala:

> when Independence was achieved, the caudillo from Iguala under-
> stood well the needs of the country he was to organize with his
> powerful hand. The refusal from Spain to send a prince from its
> dynasty, the seduction of flattery, and the fear of seeing his country
> sink in commotion and disturbance compelled him to wear the crown
> of the empire he was founding. . . . That was the cause of Iturbide's
> fall, and not the ambitious mistake of his projects.[33]

For *El Tiempo*, the disintegration of the Iturbidist project gave way to
an era of disaster caused by the introduction of ideas alien to the
national idiosyncrasy and the incorporation of foreign models, such
as the ones coming from the United States:

> the new ideas had had more impact than expected on . . . a multi-
> tude of Mexicans, as was observed immediately in more than a few
> of the members of the first *junta soberana*, and later on in the Con-
> gress. The press was completely occupied by the supporters of the
> new theories. An inexperienced people was seduced and the old
> Constitution of the country substituted by a new one that failed to
> conform to its old habits or customs or the unity that until then had
> been its religious and political banner. The North American form
> of government, the sole example of a particular kind of organiza-
> tion, was transplanted to our soil. If that institution had not been
> demolished by universal clamor, the evils caused by it would by
> now be irreparable, and the stars that now wave over the buildings
> in Texas would probably flutter on its flag over the high towers of
> our Cathedral.[34]

For the editorial writers at *El Tiempo*, the disaster that followed
Independence, brought on by the Liberals, betrayed the noble principles that had guided the Fathers of the Country in their decision to
break up with Spain while seeking the betterment of the Mexican
people. In an editorial addressed to these Fathers of the Country, the
newspaper called:

> Come and see what the destructive spirit of the so-called Liberals
> has done to your country. You who undertook the glorious endeavor
> of making of this a new nation with the noble ideal of improving
> what good it possessed and correcting the evils it suffered from,
> see what they have done with it—those who, unable to imitate your
> valor and virtues, have taken advantage of your heroic labors to
> enslave the nation you wanted free; to drown in misery, ignorance,
> and anarchy the citizens for whom you sacrificed your life wishing
> they would peacefully enjoy the benefits of education and wealth.

The probable answer from the Fathers of the Country would be, according to them, to abandon any Liberal attempts and direct the nation along the path of tradition:

> We, they would say, wanted to give Mexico a country and not to see it devoured by dissension. By declaring its independence, we did not wish to destroy, nor thought of destroying, what good was in it: it was not in our plan to establish an anarchic, revolutionary government. Our aims were always directed to establishing a regime based upon the country's customs. And because we achieved its independence with our blood, it is up to you to make good its benefits. You, who in twenty-five years have not known how to enjoy it and are about to lose it, shall be able to save yourselves by abandoning once and for all the harmful and absurd ideas that you have followed up to now and by establishing instead the only institutions suitable to you that have brought happiness to the most civilized and cultivated peoples of the Earth.[35]

For the Conservatives gathered around *El Tiempo*, the only possibility of resolving the huge problems created by the Liberal deviations following Independence was the monarchical alternative. On February 12, 1846, the newspaper published an editorial titled "Our Profession of Faith," where a monarchy was championed as the most suitable form of government for Mexico. Monarchy would come paired with an aristocracy, a strong army, and the vindication of Catholicism as the sole religion so that the country would leave behind its sufferings and walk a steady path:

> we believe that our republic has been a costly experiment, a hard lesson, but also that it can still be mended. Now, if you asked us what it is that we want or desire, we will say it frankly. We want a Representative Monarchy; we want the unity of the nation and order paired with political and civic freedom; we want the integrity of the Mexican territory; we want, finally, all the promises and guarantees of the Iguala Plan in order to secure our glorious independence on stable foundations.[36]

Toward this goal, *El Tiempo* argued that if indeed the First Insurgents had not come up with any model for organizing the country,[37] Iturbide had done so by propounding the constitutional monarchy: "Let us leave behind our petty disputes. . . . By doing so we will be putting our freedom and Independence to their best possible use. This is what Hidalgo, Morelos, and Iturbide wanted. This is the gift that they gave us by making us autonomous and the owners of our country and our destiny. They certainly did not want us to tear each other to shreds in frivolous disputes that result in nothing but wretchedness, weakness, and devastation."[38]

Summing up in 1846, the Conservatives, by way of their newspaper, developed an outline of Independence, its heroes, and the events that followed that can be reduced to six points:

1) during three hundred years, Spanish colonialism was, in every sense, highly positive for the society of New Spain;

2) the idea of Independence had been the outcome of a natural process resulting from the maturity of Mexican society and its reaction against the liberal policies developed in Spain;

3) differentiation between the movement of the First Insurgents and the one led by Iturbide at its conclusion was established;

4) once Independence was achieved, the failure of Iturbide's project to organize the country was a result of the lack of support and not of the inadequacy of his project;

5) the lack of stability as well as the chaos and anarchy rampant in the country after Independence had resulted from the adoption of styles of government that, promoted by the Liberals, had nothing to do with Mexican reality;

6) the only possible alternative for the country at the moment was a representative monarchy, which amounted to going back to Iturbide's original formula.

To the Conservatives' misfortune, Paredes y Arrillaga's government did not survive the onset of the war against the United States. The attempt to impose a monarchy through a Constitutional Congress caused a division in the country that was impossible to resolve in the midst of the hostilities. Conservatives would have to wait for another opportunity. By 1848, after the traumatic experience of war and with a country dispossessed of almost one-half of its territory, the Conservatives found themselves in the same situation as the Liberals. Neither faction had a convincing grip on power. Nevertheless, the Conservatives could boast of having long foreseen the danger that the United States posed for the country. This advantage gave them, at least, the moral right to play a more openly active role in national politics.[39]

Under these circumstances, Lucas Alamán founded *El Universal*, a newspaper that would reflect Conservative thinking during its eight years of existence.[40] In this publication, many topics that had appeared in *El Tiempo* were revisited, albeit in a more elaborate and open manner. The topics that concern us here—Independence, its heroes, and the fate of the country after the breakup with Spain—

were the subject of articles published on the occasion of the holidays celebrated on the 16th and the 27th of September. The resulting debate on these topics, joined by the Liberal newspapers *El Siglo XIX* and *El Monitor*, supplies information on Conservative constructions.

To begin with, in *El Universal*, in contrast to *El Tiempo*, there was an unequivocal rejection of the First Insurgents and their movement on account of the violence and chaos to which it had given rise. In an article published on September 16, 1849, "Anniversary of the Summons of Dolores," the editors of *El Universal* defined what would be their final interpretation of Independence.[41] After pointing out that if indeed the 16th of September were to be a day of joy and happiness for Mexicans, it only stirred up doubts and fatal memories for the country.

The Conservative analysis can be summarized as follows:

1) It denies to the 16th of September—and thus to the First Insurgents—the merit of being the birth of Independence and the first day of political autonomy on the grounds that the interpretation of the words and acts of the protagonists shows that their movement did not aim at liberty:

> the 16th of September of 1810 was not the first day of our political life, nor was the *grito* the origin of our independence; and because of the disgraceful and calamitous use given to the resulting Independence. No matter how superficially the nature and the circumstances of that insurrection are looked into, it will become apparent that the *grito de Dolores* did not aim at the independence of the country nor was it the expression of the thoughts of the Mexicans. The leader of the insurrection's words and actions did not display this inclination.[42]

2) The day and the men who should be celebrated and who deserve all the credit for Mexican political freedom are those who came after, with Iturbide and the consummation of Independence: "The truth, the day, the men came later on, when Iturbide—enemy of the insurgents and friend of Independence—accomplished the great task braced on the true principles and advised by the men who were able to understand the essential requirements of the new political entity."

3) Those men deserving all the credit for Independence are the Conservatives: "They provided the new edifice with a solid and stable foundation based on the customs, the habits, the needs already three centuries old. Is it its fault that the genie of our misfortunes had come to introduce anarchy and destroy these foundations on which the social edifice should have been erected and maintained?"

4) The evils that came after Independence as a result of dissension, disproportionate greed, and the imposition of models extraneous to Mexican reality do not diminish its value, for "the evil lies not in Independence but in the pitiful use it has been put to":

> When contemplating the sad events of the stormy and ill-fated period we have gone through from the 21st on, some critics say that Independence has been an evil for Mexico. We have answered them, already more than once, by corroborating that our evils do not come from Independence, but that the good results it should have rendered if the favorable circumstances that the country enjoyed had been put to good use have become an illusion. These circumstances have been squandered in a pitiful way, and it would seem that our intention had been to thoroughly suffocate it [our nation], without taking into account that our aim has been to suffocate it completely. Ignoring its background, character, and customs, our nation was hurled recklessly into a new and unknown path, filled with obstacles and difficulties, where it has tripped at every step, losing in each attempt the little vigor that it had left. Abandoning public affairs to the hands of petty ambitions, with tainted power having been the patrimony of shameful rebellions, the ties to obedience and respect for authority slackened, . . . wherein, the law ignored and those in charge of enforcing it weakened, we have walked from revolution to revolution without ever finding solace, unable to allude to even one period of our independent existence that could be considered as better than any that went before.[43]

As could be expected, such an open statement against the First Insurgents and, as was customary in the Iturbidist period, against the 16th of September, could not go unnoticed in the middle of the century. Three days after the appearance of these opinions, a group of Congressmen—"two or three men very well known for their ultra liberal ideas" (Guillermo Prieto, Ponciano Arriaga, José Joaquín Herrera, and Lorenzo de Zavala)—asked Secretary of Foreign and Interior Affairs José María Lacunza if there had been any charges brought against the newspaper on account of the editorial. Even though the representatives' proposal was not confirmed by two-thirds of the voters, the initiative remained pending for resolution. During the September 21 session, the same representatives brought up the article in question once more. After virulent attacks against *El Universal*, the debate was resolved through a vote with which, with 39 cast in favor and 32 against, the proposal of condemning the newspaper was discarded.

The writers at *El Universal* defended their convictions in the following fashion:

In the final analysis, what is it that Srs. Prieto, Arriaga, Herrera, and Zavala found so questionable in our editorial of the 16th? Could it be that we revealed ourselves little inclined toward Independence? . . . Independence has no detractors, being such a deep-rooted feeling in the hearts of men and as instinctive to all nations as the revulsion, hatred, and contempt it produces in those who turn its precious fruits into the poisonous seeds of all kind of misfortunes. Are we accused of having established that we owe nothing of the immense benefit of our emancipation to the First Insurgents on account of their plan, their policies, and the means they used? Where is it written that we are not allowed to think this way and express it through the press? Is there defamation when the public behavior of the men whom a nation takes as its leaders is looked into? Is the sanctity of religion being attacked on that account? Are the bases of our present system damaged in the very least? Which is, then, the crime against freedom of speech we are deemed responsible for? We may collide against the opinions and beliefs of the whole Republic; we may be bizarre men who look at objects upside down; we may preach in the desert, and universal revulsion may crown our efforts. But, no matter how hard we have tried, we have not been able to find where the law was broken or freedom of speech defiled. Fundamentally, this is all about a fact, a historical fact, a fact that was witnessed by great numbers of people and, this should be kept in mind, a fact that, regardless of what is being said, has been prejudged already by national justice. . . . If we are mistaken, we are mistaken about history, and it seems to us that we should be refuted through history and not through accusations. Why is it that the representatives who aspire to make a statement through our humble editorial do not seize the tools of education and of their talents that we sincerely deem superior to ours? Proscribing and condemning only implies power that does not always go hand in hand with reason and enlightenment. Discussion and persuasion is a job worthy of civilization, the task of someone who acknowledges truth and fairness in his cause.[44]

Two days later, on September 23, after the favorable results of the ballot in the Congress, *El Universal* insisted again on the need to discuss Independence and its meaning:

Let us examine those facts in light of reason and of unbiased criticism, and it will be evident that what we have said is accurate— that the great undertaking of Independence was not begun until 1821, when the nation unanimously accepted this notion becoming

therefore essential to carry it on. Could it be said that the first uprising prepared the ground and that the desire to be independent
was awakened in the Mexicans at that moment? Fair enough: but
this cannot keep the events of that period from being judged by
those who desire true and firm glories for Mexico: this cannot stop
us from saying that the Summons of Dolores was not the call to
independence of 1821, or else it would have had the same ardent
and resolute reply from those who responded at a later date. . . .

Mexico has unwithering glories, but it is essential that these
accomplishments be vindicated from the offense caused by placing
next to them other unfortunate events. Mexicans who love their
country, who remember with satisfaction the magnificent undertaking that made us independent and who think of a future have to
take this task in their hands.[45]

The debate that ensued regarding the editorial of September 16
spread to the newspapers of the opposition. *El Siglo XIX* had published a letter by José María Tornel questioning the opinions published in *El Universal*. On September 24 this daily discussed the letter
in which, according to the writers, there was a shortage of ideas and
an excess of intolerant and chauvinistic discourse:

We find it strange that, with all his knowledge of history, S.E. Tornel
could not see the folly of adding his voice to the unpleasant yelling
of a throng of jingoes who, less educated than S.E., believed to be
proving their love for their country by vindicating the memory of a
man to whom the glory of our Independence has been wrongfully
attributed by some. S.E. believes to have seen us anointing a criminal in our article because we reject Hidalgo's role in our Independence, which is exclusively the achievement of the immortal Iturbide
and his companions of 1821. If there is a crime in this, and while
this is finally established, the persons who take away from Iturbide
and his companions the glory of having fathered Independence to
attribute it to Hidalgo are as criminal as those of us who deny
Hidalgo and attribute it to Iturbide.[46]

On September 27, *El Universal* published a long article in which,
besides analyzing the Iturbidist process, the Conservative vision of
Independence continued to be refined. *El Universal* championed the
27th of September as the "great national holiday" because it was on
that date that Independence was achieved: "If all modern nations have
a grand, glorious holiday, of fair and noble pride and immortal memories, that should be in our case the *Twenty-Seventh of September*. On
this day, Mexicans proved to the world what they are capable of when
acting united, inspired by an authentic national feeling, and led by

such a man as the *Great Iturbide*. On this day our country, radiant in its glory, appeared before the nations of the world to occupy among them a distinguished place."[47]

For the writers at *El Universal*, the Mexicans' sentiment for Independence had been numbed as a reaction to the violence and chaos that the first stage of the movement produced. This gave rise, in the great majority, to a closer identification with Spanish interests and not with the promises of the breakup:

> The sentiment of independence, innate in all peoples of the globe, lay dormant in the breasts of the Mexicans, happy and content with the wealth they enjoyed thanks to a wise and strong government. The opposition, the cruel war they were engaged in against the movement of 1810, was not the result of the death of that noble sentiment but of the means employed to achieve Independence— an unacceptable means that alarmed all sensible men in the country and made them decide in favor of the metropolitan government. It was not Independence that these men were against. It was the means, the excesses, the horrors that the men of the year 10 [1810] engaged in to achieve their triumph—excesses and horrors of such proportions that even the advocates of Independence were forced to resign themselves to it and even fight it, feeling that its success might be followed by the institution of the most terrible and antisocial principles. Proclaiming himself as the champion of the Indians and the avenger of their humiliated race, and crying "Death" against those called their oppressors, Hidalgo encouraged from that moment onward the terrible and bloody battle of the castes. By attacking property wherever his troops found themselves, the leader of 1810 drove away from the cause precisely those men who could have made it succeed but who, on the contrary, declared themselves against it. The men belonging to our race as well as the landlords, alarmed at the atrocious principles involved in that movement and the vandalism practiced by the insurgents, united against them, preferring the rule of the metropolis to their government. They joined the metropolitan government by contributing their resources and enrolling in its ranks to take part in a deadly war that, after seven years, resulted in the complete annihilation of the revolutionaries.

Actually, Hidalgo's movement was a failure. Because of the means through which he attempted to achieve Independence, he only succeeded in jeopardizing it and postponing it for a decade:

> The movement was fecund in sacrifice, calamities, and horrors of all sorts, but failed in its results. If what he wanted was, as they say, Independence, not only did he fail to achieve it but, with the revolution drowned in rivers of blood, the Spanish government came

out victorious and strengthened, ready and outfitted with the enormous resources that it had created and displayed during the struggle at the end of which all men were under its rule, further hindering any attempt toward Independence. Hidalgo's movement, we insist, was absolutely null; and, far from attaining its aim or annihilating the Spanish government, it succumbed, leaving that government stronger than ever and the cause of independence utterly lost.

Under such conditions, and given the impotence of the insurgent movement, Independence could only be achieved through the creation of a revolutionary movement founded on totally different principles. This movement was to be led by Iturbide who, having Independence as his only aim, gathered around him all Mexicans to guide them peacefully and in an orderly fashion toward a new reality:

> In order to achieve this, a new revolution was called for—a revolution based on entirely different principles, given that experience had clearly shown that those proclaimed in the first one were absolutely ineffective. But who will dare to fight against the colossal power of the triumphant government? Who? Iturbide, the great leader, the same one who had fought against the leaders of 1810, not out of hatred of Independence but because he could see the deep abyss toward which these men were dragging the country by proclaiming its Independence coupled to the most atrocious and destructive of principles. Iturbide, then, raised the standard of the new revolution, a great and glorious banner that would give shade to all Mexicans, a pure and bright ensign where neither words of proscription and blood to soil or darken its splendor nor lies to deceive the masses and make them fight and die for an unachievable goal had been written. Iturbide wrote on his banner just one word, a magical word that found echo in the hearts of all Mexicans. The word was "Independence."

The promotion of the 16th of September as the national holiday of Independence had been, in the eyes of the Conservatives, a futile attempt on the part of the Liberals to expropriate Iturbide's credit and mar his image:

> And this movement so great, so fair, so glorious—it is a shame to say it!—has been looked upon with spite and even outright aversion by some ungrateful sons of that party that owes its existence to this same movement. Ungrateful to the great man who initiated and sustained it to the extreme of instituting, as if only to aggravate him, the holiday of the 16th of September in an attempt to deprive him of the undying glory due to the promoter and achiever of our

Independence. They opposed the institution of what we celebrate today, and thanks only to the firm standing of President D. Anastasio Bustamante, was it possible to celebrate it in 1830 and establish it as a national holiday. . . . But it is not the Mexican people who have been ungrateful. Their dear hero, their great leader, the immortal Iturbide has a shrine in the heart of each of his countrymen. They bear in mind his worth, know how much they owe him, and idolize his memory. And maybe before long, the modest and almost forced display that during many years we have observed on this day, our great national holiday, will be the one that commemorates the glorious September 27 of 1821.

On the 30th, as a closure to the September celebrations, *El Universal* embarked on a debate with *El Siglo XIX*—a debate that would be continued on October 3—regarding the intentions of Hidalgo and his movement of 1810. After thanking the daily for accepting the invitation that appeared in their editorial of September 16, *El Universal* arrived at its conclusion, returning to its article of the 27th: Hidalgo could not succeed through lies, and that is why he failed. His aim was not the revolution of Independence but the upheaval of society. The three symbols displayed by Hidalgo at the beginning of Independence were only the means to achieve his spurious ends: the expression "Long live Fernando VII," the image of the Virgin of Guadalupe, and the battle cry of "Death to the gachupines" were only an excuse to undermine social stability without a clear idea of what to substitute it with, at the cost of much violence and death. Thus, Hidalgo and his movement did not actually represent a revolution; their trend of destruction only strengthened Spain and postponed Independence another ten years.[48]

The year of 1849 was undoubtedly the richest regarding the discussion of Independence. In the years following the touchstone article in *El Universal*, writers did not publish anything related to the 16th of September, except for the year 1854. At that time, when Santa Anna was dictator and censorship made impossible any political discussion in the newspapers, *El Universal* printed a new article in a neutral style, leaving behind its usual fiery rhetoric: "The anniversary marking the day when Mexico proclaimed its independence is celebrated today by the nation. September 16 of 1810, the beginning of the struggle that aimed at achieving a government with institutions parallel to our needs and the realization of the promises of hope to improve our society, can only awaken pleasant memories, although these may go sour at the evidence of the scant fruits reaped."[49]

This moderate criticism, however, was not only manifest in articles concerning the 16th of September; from that moment on, those on September 27 were also more discreet. In 1850, other than some glorifying phrases about the 27th of September of 1821, the annual notice did nothing but reiterate Iturbide's merits:

> To emancipate a country, any country, is always a huge undertaking; to emancipate it without shedding streams of blood on the battlefield is a glorious undertaking. Emancipating Mexico, subject of a nation famous for its eternal glories, when Mexico was content with the colonial system and when Mexico must have shriveled at the idea of a breakup as it remembered the horrors undergone during eleven years, was not only an colossal undertaking, not just a glorious endeavor, but also a heroic venture, worthy only of a privileged spirit.[50]

On September 27, 1851, *El Universal* reproduced only Iturbide's declaration of the Plan de Iguala of February 24, 1821.[51] In 1852 there was no mention of the 27th of September, due to a law that prohibited the publication of unsigned articles as well as those that promoted political controversy. In the next year, 1853, in the shadow of the repressive Press Law issued by Santa Anna's government, there was only a small comment: a poor homage was paid to the significance of the 27th of September. On the next day, the civic speech by Luis G. Gago in Veracruz was reproduced. By September 1855 the newspaper had ceased to appear; *El Universal* was a victim of continuing political strife. By tying their fate to that of Santa Anna and supporting his return to power, the Conservatives lost the influence that they had been attempting to develop with Mexican society. Finally, the death of Lucas Alamán on June 2, 1853, deprived the Conservatives of their main ideologue and a key element in their political strategy. Under those circumstances, the debate around Independence and its heroes came to an end. The fall of Santa Anna's dictatorship marked the conclusion of the debate and initiated the armed struggle between Liberals and Conservatives whose outcome, favorable to the Liberals, decided not only the fate of their enemies but also the existence of a single, dominant interpretation of the events of 1810–1821.

Conclusion

The Conservative assessment of Independence has been ignored throughout official Mexican history. Nevertheless, its recovery is urgent because it represents a source of interpretation that will help us to understand the worldview developed by the Conservatives in the nineteenth century. It is evident that the Conservative assessment of this and other issues was hardly irrelevant to contemporary and even current affairs in Mexico.

Conservative ideas about Independence may be reduced to several points. First, New Spain lived happily for three hundred years under Spanish colonialism. Thus, the idea of Independence was the result, not of discontent, but of a natural process whereby a society reached maturity. The events themselves were precipitated by the Liberal policies implemented in Spain in 1820.

Next, there are two well-defined processes concerning the Independence of Mexico: the one initiated by the First Insurgents in 1810 that, through violence and chaos, led the country to stagnation; and the one where Iturbide, through the Plan de Iguala in 1821, made final the breakup with Spain by means of a peaceful and orderly movement. Since Hidalgo's movement, plagued with violence and anarchy that sought to destroy society, only made Spain stronger and postponed the desirable conclusion of the process, it is to Iturbide that all the credit for the Independence of Mexico is owed. Therefore, the date that should be celebrated as the "great national holiday" is the 27th of September of 1821. Indeed, the attempt to impose September 16 as the day of Independence was a maneuver of the Liberals who, from the onset of independent existence, devoted themselves to mar the image of Iturbide and his plan for the nation.

It is more than evident that behind this interpretation there existed more refined ideas that built up Mexican Conservative thinking throughout the middle decades of the century. What stands out is the championing of an orderly and peaceful transition toward an independent existence and the need on the part of the Conservatives to have a favorable influence on the preservation of the pre-existing social structure. The interpretation of Independence is a thread that runs through many other interesting subjects considered by the Conservatives in the nineteenth century.

Notes

1. *El Universal*, Sunday, September 16, 1849.
2. In his speech of admission to the Academia Mexicana de la Historia in 1964, Edmundo O'Gorman synthesized this Manichaeism of Mexican history regarding the heroes of Independence. See Edmundo O'Gorman, "Hidalgo en la historia.

Discurso de ingreso pronunciado por el Sr. Dr. don Edmundo O'Gorman," in *Secuencia: Revista Americana de Ciencias Sociales*, México (September/December 1986): 171–85.

3. An example of this Manichaen vision is offered by Reyes Heroles, undoubtedly the most important ideologist of the system in the last decades, when, while explaining the basis of the Mexican political tradition, he alludes to Liberals only in order to describe an ascending line for liberalism in the Mexican political system. See Jesús Reyes Heroles, *El liberalismo mexicano* (Mexico: Fondo de Cultura Económica, 1974), 3 vols.

4. For a review of the formative process of Mexican conservatism in the period between 1821–1855, see Javier Rodríguez Piña, "De los orígenes del pensamiento conservador europeo y mexicano," in *Sociológica* 9, no. 26 (September/December 1994): 11–38.

5. As a matter of fact, it could be said that it all comes together in one entity, since behind all Conservative interpretations of Independence lies the genius of Lucas Alamán, who finished his monumental work on the history of Mexico in 1852, one year before his death, in the midst of the strengthening of the Conservative Party. In the fifth volume he developed many subjects that would later become part of the debate in the newspapers. See Lucas Alamán, *Historia de México desde los primeros movimientos que prepararón su Independencia en el año de 1808 hasta la época presente* (México: Instituto Cultural Helénico-Fondo de Cultura Económica, 1985) (facsimile edition published in 1852 by J. Mariano Lara).

6. Edmundo O'Gorman, "Hidalgo en la historia," 174. In Iturbide's proclamation on the day after his triumphant entrance into Mexico City, he confirmed the fact that his movement had been a peaceful one: "now you see me in the capital of the most opulent empire, not having left behind me rivers of blood, or devastated fields and inconsolable widows or forlorn children who would forever curse the assassins of their fathers."

7. Lucas Alamán, *Historia de México*, 5:491.

8. Ibid., 506.

9. Ibid., 507.

10. Ibid., 508. The final text of the Decree is as follows: "Number 283. Decree of the 1st of March, 1822—National holidays. In order to perpetuate the great events of the establishment of the sovereign Constitutional Congress; proposal to the old government of the Iguala Plan; the oath of allegiance of the Trigarante Army in that town; the first summons to liberty in Dolores; the occupation of the capital city by the national Mexican army; and to honor the memory of the first defenders of the country and the principal leaders who, proclaiming the Iguala Plan, achieved its glories. These will be February 24, March 2, September 16 and 27. The celebrations will include artillery salvos and a Mass of Thanksgiving attended by the Regency and the rest of the authorities and where the Court will dress sumptuously and the ceremony of congratulation will be displayed. This Decree will be applied throughout the empire." Manuel Dublán and José María Lozano, *Legislación mexicana o colección completa de las disposiciones legislativas expedidas desde la Independencia de la República* (Mexico: Imprenta de Comercio, under the charge of Dublán and Lozano, 1888), 1:599.

11. Lucas Alamán, *Historia de México*, 508.

12. Edmundo O'Gorman, "Hidalgo en la historia," 175.

13. All of which would cost Iturbide his life when, unaware of the contents of the Decree, he came back to Mexico, where he was detained and then shot on July 19, 1824.

14. "Number 344. Decree of July 19, 1823." Dublán and Lozano, *Legislación*, 1:660.

15. "Number 442. Decree of November 27, 1824. . . . The sovereign Constitutional General Congress of the Mexican United States has seen fit to declare that: 1) The national religious holidays from now on will include only Holy Week Thursday and Good Friday, Corpus Christi, and the celebration of [the Virgin of] Guadalupe on December 12. The civic holidays will be September 16 and October 4, anniversary of the first summons to Independence and the sanction of the constitution." Ibid., 745.

16. For an analysis of civic speeches, see Enrique Plasencia de la Parra, *La visión de la Independencia a través de los discursos conmemorativos (1825–1867)*. (Licenciatura thesis, Facultad de Filosofía y Letras, UNAM, 1989), 161.

17. José María Tornel, *Oración pronunciada por el coronel José María Tornel en la plaza mayor de la capital de la federación, el día 16 de septiembre de 1827, por acuerdo de la junta de ciudadanos que promovió la mayor solemnidad del aniversario de nuestra gloriosa independencia* (Mexico: Imprenta del Aguila, 1827), 22.

18. Lucas Alamán, *Historia de México*, 802.

19. "Number 1523. February 27, 1835." Dublán and Lozano, *Legislación*, 3:25.

20. "Number 1547. April 18, 1835." Ibid., 41.

21. "Number 1566. May 20, 1835." Ibid., 48.

22. "Number 1971. August 6, 1838 Law." Ibid., 539.

23. "Number 1991. October 20, 1838. Circular—Regulations to be observed during D. Agustín de Iturbide's funeral. The Honorable President of the Republic, in compliance with Item 2 of the General Congress Decree of August 6 of this year, has seen fit to approve the following Ordinance presented to the Commission named to take part in the ceremonies of transportation and relocation in the Cathedral of Mexico of the remains of the hero of Iguala, D. Agustín de Iturbide; consequently it has ordered that it be executed in all its parts." Ibid., 554–56.

24. Lucas Alamán. *Historia de México*, 803–4.

25. Lino José Alcorta, "Oración cívica que pronunció, en ocasión de la consumación de la Independencia el c. general . . . el 27 de septiembre de 1839," in Ernesto de la Torre Villar, comp., *La conciencia nacional y su formación. Discursos cívicos septembrinos (1825–1871)* (Mexico: Universidad Nacional Autónoma de México, 1988), 152. General Alcorta was very close to Anastasio Bustamante and Antonio López de Santa Anna, for whose government he was secretary of War and the Navy in 1847 and later from 1853 to 1854.

26. Contrasting with this vindication of the memory of Iturbide, Guillermo Prieto's speech of September 27, 1844, stands out. After stating that he would not be the one to cast a shadow over the memory of the 27th of September of 1821 by recounting the tragedies that the nation had gone through ever since, he refused to question the later performance of the caudillo of Iguala: "Shall I depict Iturbide asking for shelter as a mendicant would in the plazas of this country that owed him its existence? Should I depict the commander of that army of heroes expiring? . . . Would you be able to hear the last intimate moan of Padilla's victim? Ah, no! His blood was shed over that ludicrous throne already shattered, and the tragic outcome of the parody became a terrible lesson for the tyrants." Guillermo Prieto, "Discurso pronunciado en la Alameda de México el día 27 de septiembre de 1844," in Ernesto de la Torre Villar, *La conciencia nacional*, 223.

27. José María Tornel y Mendivil, *Discurso que pronunció el exmo. señor general d . . . , individuo del Supremo Poder Conservador, en la Alameda de la ciudad*

de México, en el día del solemne aniversario de la Independencia (Mexico: Imprenta de Ignacio Cumplido, 1840), 16. Tornel y Mendivil was repeatedly, but always for Conservative governments, secretary of War and the Navy between 1834 and 1846. At the time he delivered this speech he was, as the title indicates, a member of the Supreme Conservative Power.

28. *El Tiempo* was first printed in the context of the monarchical attempt of General Mariano Paredes y Arrillaga in 1846. He had rebelled against José Joaquín Herrera's presidency, vindicating with this action the war against the United States over Texas and thus the rejection of the negotiated peace desired by President Herrera. Once in power, Paredes y Arrillaga, together with Spanish ambassador Salvador Bermúdez de Castro and Lucas Alamán, decided to found a newspaper that, while serving as an instrument for spreading the monarchical proposal, would also become the print medium for the Conservatives. The newspaper started appearing on January 24, 1846, and continued through 134 issues until June 7 of the same year. Besides Alamán and Bermúdez de Castro, the contribution of other Conservative personalities such as Ignacio Aguilar y Marocho, Manuel Diez de Bonilla, José Hilario Elguero y Guisasola, fray Manuel de San Juan Crisóstomo Nájera, Mariano Tagle, and the Spaniard José Dolores Ulibarri is certain. For reviewing the subjects on the government of Paredes y Arrillaga as well as on *El Tiempo*, see Jaime Delgado, *La monarquía en México (1845–1847)* (Mexico: Editorial Porrúa, 1990); Donald Fletcher, *The Diplomacy of Annexation: Texas, Oregon, and the Mexican War* (Columbia: University of Missouri Press, 1975); Frank Samponaro, "Mariano Paredes y el movimiento monarquista mexicano en 1846," *Historia Mexicana* 37, no. 125 (1983): 39–56; Miguel Soto, *La conspiración monárquica en México, 1845–1846* (Mexico: Ed. Offset, 1988); and Javier Rodríguez Piña, "De los orígenes del pensamiento conservador."

29. "Al público," *El Tiempo*, April 27, 1846.

30. "Parte política," *El Tiempo*, March 30, 1846.

31. The explanation offered by *El Tiempo* itself on the causes of the independence of New Spain is the rejection of the liberal changes promoted in Spain: "The sensible and reasoning part of the nation saw with horror the innovations undertaken in Spain on the principles of its government; pious people, in view of the attacks directed by the Spanish Cortes against religion, had pronounced themselves against that kind of institution; and with their influence and power had efficiently contributed to the success of Independence so that, among other aims, that system of government and those political principles that had for three centuries made Mexico one of the happiest countries in the universe, would not be altered." Ibid.

32. Ibid.

33. "La República y la Monarquía. A La Reforma. Artículo Primero," *El Tiempo*, February 6, 1846.

34. "Parte política," *El Tiempo*, March 3, 1846. In a different editorial regarding the events following Independence, the writers of *El Tiempo* would say: " . . . when it (Mexico) started to exercise the faculty of self-government, it made a terrible mistake of disastrous and lamentable consequences. Heedless of what it was and had been, neglectful of its habits and deepest rooted customs, it eagerly embraced unfamiliar doctrines and welcomed as worthy that which, in all countries that have suffered its contagion, has caused countless evils." "Parte política," *El Tiempo*, January 25, 1846.

35. "Los padres de la patria," *El Tiempo*, February 18, 1846.

36. "Nuestra profesión de fe. Al Memorial Histórico," *El Tiempo*, February 12, 1846.

37. "Post-scriptum. Cuatro palabras a La Reforma," *El Tiempo*, January 26, 1846. This editorial was published before the monarchical definition of February 12. Some time later, once its position had been ascertained, it would say: "Once our emancipation from the metropolis was proclaimed in Iguala, the constitutional monarchical system was appointed more explicitly in that famous decree as the only government that would rule over us." "Parte política," *El Tiempo*, February 26, 1846.

38. "Parte política," *El Tiempo*, February 23, 1848.

39. For example, in 1849 the Conservative Party was formally founded and in that same year it won the elections to govern Mexico City.

40. *El Universal* came out for the first time on November 16, 1848, and kept on appearing without interruption until June 1855.

41. "Aniversario del grito de Dolores," *El Universal*, September 16, 1849.

42. Curiously enough, for *El Universal*, the analysis of events that only resulted in disaster, such as the hatred between brothers, was not worth the effort since they have already been judged by the nation's thinking men.

43. This last interpretation of the pertinence of Independence is quite close to that by Lucas Alamán, *Historia de México*, 903–05.

44. "Proyectada denuncia de *El Universal*," *El Universal*, September 21, 1849.

45. "Triunfo de la razón," *El Universal*, September 23, 1849.

46. "Discurso del Sr. Olaguibel," *El Universal*, September 24, 1849.

47. "El gran día nacional," *El Universal*, September 27, 1847.

48. "La revolución de 1810. Al siglo XIX," *El Universal*, September 30, 1841.

49. "El 16 de septiembre," *El Universal*, September 16, 1854.

50. "Aniversario del día 27 de septiembre de 1821," *El Universal*, September 27, 1850.

51. "Día 27 de septiembre," *El Universal*, September 27, 1851.

CHAPTER SIX

New Celebrations of Independence
Puebla (1869) and Mexico City (1883)

WILLIAM H. BEEZLEY

> When you look back at your life, you discover, or you invent,
> points in time that seem to be tightly knotted nodes of possi-
> bility. Out of the seemingly endless options that present them-
> selves in a given situation, you choose one in particular, and
> your life and the lives of those around you start moving re-
> lentlessly toward a particular outcome.[1]

Independence celebrations during the nineteenth century reveal much about Mexican society, politics, and values—about what Mexicans thought Mexico was and what they wanted their country to become. This brief examination of Independence Day celebrations speculates on the meaning of this holiday for those who organized it—both the meaning for the organizers themselves and the meaning that they wanted to convey to the general public through dramatic didactic visual expressions. The analysis does not discuss in any systematic way the fascinating but difficult question of what meanings or experiences the participants or the audience chose to draw from these Independence festivals. Certainly their responses varied greatly during the nineteenth century, when no radio or television announcer, using a prepared script, explained to the people what they should see and what each allegory represented. Above all, it was the performance of the festival that made Independence a living memory.[2]

Independence had to be invented by the new administrators, and in its invention they projected the interpretation that they wanted the public to accept. This projection evolved over the nineteenth century, so that in witnessing the celebration we can see the changing nature of what Mexico meant to these administrators. Independence celebrations during the nineteenth century had elements in common in the effort to build a national community of Mexicans.[3] This essay discusses two episodes in 1869 and 1883, chiefly from the administrators' perspective, and, in doing so, recognizes the equivocal character of the patriotic holidays.

The appropriate date for the Independence holiday remained contested into the 1860s. Conservative politicians, many of whom can be clearly identified with the monarchist party,[4] struggled during the three decades preceding the 1860s to replace September 16 (commemorating Miguel Hidalgo) with September 27 (memorializing Agustín de Iturbide), as they opposed the beginning of a popular struggle and the military imposition of a Mexican criollo authority. Despite their efforts, no regime ever replaced September 16. Rather, a few leaders tinkered with the Independence holidays by adding celebrations, especially for September 27, until 1863.

Until the Wars of the Reform, the Patriotic Junta established a regular pattern for the celebration of Independence. In Mexico City the Junta's subcommittees arranged for the decoration of the streets, erected a speakers' platform in the Alameda, hired the fireworks technicians, commissioned musical and theatrical performances, and invited the principal orator. Other committees organized competitions for plays, poems, essays, or portraits based on the theme of the Independence struggle or on individual patriots. From the mid-1830s onward, women's committees sought donations and occasionally arranged for schoolchildren to line the parade route. By far, most members served the Junta as fundraisers.[5]

Patriotic holidays took on a different character during the period of civil war and foreign intervention that followed the final overthrow of Antonio López de Santa Anna. Benito Juárez had opposed the September 27 holiday, but ironically it was the French puppet emperor, Maximilian, who permanently eliminated this celebration from the civic calendar. His action added one more disappointing decision to the growing list being kept by disenchanted Conservatives. Maximilian even went to the village of Dolores to celebrate Padre Hidalgo's 1810 call for independence on September 16. He and the empress, Carlota, also funded the construction of an Independence monument in Mexico City that incorporated statues of the major patriots. Among the Fathers of the Country, José María Morelos received special attention from the emperor. Besides this Independence Day holiday on September 16, the imperial couple also brought new enthusiasm to the celebrations of both Corpus Christi and the Virgin of Guadalupe.[6] Maximilian, Mexico's second and last emperor, undoubtedly wanted to put as much distance as possible between himself and Iturbide's failed empire, whose image was summoned by the September 27 date. Consequently, Maximilian and his regime ignored this holiday. Thus the earliest celebrations of Independence marked out the boundaries and established customary performances that continued throughout the century, even though the date itself was not completely resolved until the 1860s.

The Independence celebration in 1869 incorporated striking new features into the old traditions. Ignacio Manuel Altamirano, who wrote a chronicle of these events, began his account by repeating what he said was the widespread complaint against the patriotic celebrations of Independence. He stated the general hostility to the same rather weary festival forms that had been used for the previous two decades. This hackneyed celebration resulted, he explained, because the membership of the planning committee had remained the same, and these "immortals" would not die or alter the details. The Independence celebrations from 1849 to 1869 had declined in people's esteem as well as in their participation because each year's commemoration had faithfully replicated the previous one. Thus, if the dead returned, according to Altamirano, the only differences they would notice would be the formal tailcoat worn by men and the dancing of waltzes. Moreover, genuine popular participation was lacking.[7]

A dramatic revival of the Independence holiday came in 1869, with the focus on the completion of the railroad line from Mexico City to Puebla and the centennial of Alexander von Humboldt's visit to New Spain. The latter resulted in a gathering of savants and professors hosted by the Sociedad de Geografía y Estadística in the salon of the School of Mines; the former, in an innovative celebration of Independence. The inauguration of the completed rail link took place on September 16 as the major part of the day's events. In Mexico City, following a twenty-one-cannon salute at dawn, the Congress officially opened and Guillermo Prieto gave the traditional speech in the Alameda. National leaders and their guests then rushed to the Buenavista station for the 10:30 departure of the train to Puebla.

The locomotive and its open coaches gave bystanders the opportunity to observe a "steam-powered procession" that reflected the hierarchical views of the regime.[8] Immediately behind the locomotive came the coach carrying the official police guard, followed by the coach for guests and family members of government officials, the coach for deputies of the Congress, the coach for judges of the Supreme Court, and, in the last car, the cabinet members and the chief executive, Benito Juárez. As this train chugged through the states of México, Tlaxcala, and Puebla, the only official delegations to meet the travelers before their arrival in the city of Puebla were the local militia units from several towns in Tlaxcala and Puebla who stood at attention along the tracks to salute the president.

Despite heavy rains, when the train arrived in Puebla there was a tremendous reception that followed the Mexico City pattern of patriotic speeches and, in the evening, a grand dinner and dance, here in the Teatro Guerrero. The evening's celebrations included guests representing all the political factions—not because of a sense of national unity but because the host of the entertainment was the railroad company. Railroad officials had ignored politics and invited every civilian of influence, including religious leaders, in the community. Patriotic speeches concluded with toasts to the restoration of Mexico's national greatness. But the highlight of the evening was the music, which reached a climax with the performance of a new composition by Puebla's Melesio Morales.[9] He had written "La Locomotiva" especially for the occasion and had invented new instruments to recreate the sound of the steam engine, its blaring whistle, and the click-clack of the wheels on the track. (The piece proved so popular that it was repeated in the early hours of the morning.) On the following day, September 17, President Juárez placed the first stone in a monument on one of the main plazas dedicated to General Ignacio Zaragoza, the commander in 1862 on the fateful day of Cinco de Mayo, when patriotic troops loyal to Juárez defeated the French invaders. The travelers returned to Mexico City the next day.

Now, what should we make of this 1869 celebration? Obviously, Mexican progress was given a real dimension with the steam excursion from the capital city to Puebla. The journey back and forth took only a few hours, with the only inconvenience caused by the rainstorm. This official excursion linked progress based on steam and steel to the restored, authentic Mexican regime that had deposed the European imperial imposter. Moreover, the railroad (at least the railroad company) united political factions, bringing them together for the Independence dinner and dance. Modern technology and enterprise thus could achieve what individuals had not been able to do before, even during the darkest days of foreign intervention.

There is something more here, however. This celebration vividly states Benito Juárez's iron-willed commitment to civilian rule of Mexico. His belief in Cincinnatus—the Roman patriot-farmer who became a warrior in times of crisis and then returned to civilian life, with no demands beyond the chance to serve his nation when he was needed—received clear expression. A police unit, not a regiment of regular soldiers of the line, traveled as guards for the presidential party. Moreover, the official party did not include officers in a military capacity, nor did they receive invitations to the evening dinner and dance. Some attended as notables, not as soldiers, of Puebla. Where the official delegation was received along the tracks, it was met, as noted, by local militia units—the Cincinnati in the flesh. And these men received reinforcement in their commitment to militia service and their attitudes about what has been called "folk liberalism" from the reception that they provided for the president.[10]

The career of Zaragoza, to whom the monument in Puebla was dedicated, also provided the stuff of Liberal myth. Zaragoza had entered military service through the militia, which fact Juárez could trumpet; and later, during the crisis created by the French intervention, he had resigned his cabinet post to return to the command of troops. The tribute to Zaragoza also brilliantly displayed what Benedict Anderson calls "collective amnesia," the purposeful forgetting of contrary, negative, or unfortunate facts. Here, for example, the portrait of Zaragoza as a civilian soldier-hero ignored two facts: that he had been secretary of war; and that he had been born in Texas, the lost territory of Mexico.[11]

Moreover, it should be noted that Juárez linked Mexico's struggle for its independence from Spain (celebrated on September 15–16) with his own generation's struggle to maintain Mexico's independence from France, as symbolized in the Cinco de Mayo. The president, by laying the first stone in the monument to Zaragoza, dramatically made this connection. (Porfirio Díaz returned to Puebla in 1894 to dedicate the statue of Zaragoza when it was completed. Of course, the unveiling took place on Independence Day.)

Finally, the music should be mentioned. In Mexico the widely played holiday tunes were waltzes, and in Puebla, during the dinner, guests heard dance music with the exception of Morales's special composition to celebrate the locomotive. These festive dances, as opposed to martial airs and the rousing sounds of the national anthem that created a watchful audience and uniformed men in step together, gave the public a chance to participate. The marching troops represented unified hierarchy, and the dancers the individual liberty of Liberalism. Thus, the nature of Independence celebrations at this time focused on the expressions of material progress, the unity of social and economic elites, and the decision to downplay the military, especially taking no account of veterans, who combined patriotic zeal with wartime camaraderie.

A new direction in the celebration of Independence came on September 16, 1883, in Mexico City. This civil holiday became the first to be treated as a tourist event. Because some 1,200 miles of track had been completed for the new railroads, provincial Mexicans now had the opportunity to become spectators at the Independence fete, just as many of them, no doubt, had at one time been pilgrims to the shrines at Tepeyac and Chalma.[12] In 1883 these first-time civic pilgrims were veterans of the Wars of the Reform, survivors of the fight against the French occupation, and the products of the new secular schools. They were, in fact, the heirs of Benito Juárez—although he ignored many of them—and Liberalism as it was popularly understood.

For the September 16 holiday more than 30,000 Mexicans came to the capital to witness a grand cavalcade of their nation's history. The parade featured fourteen floats designed to represent the national, Liberal heritage. These mnemonic devices were meant to "educate" the onlookers and to remind them of patriotic milestones in their proper sequence.

The floats constructed for the 1883 Independence Day parade were a new feature, although floats, or *carros alegoricos*, had long been found in religious processions dating from the sixteenth-century Corpus Christi processions, which had included *tarascas* representing the seven deadly sins.[13] These allegories moved from formal academic art to popular lithographs to broad references known by the people in general.

Let us describe several floats. The first, "The Discovery of America," featured Columbus and his caravel arriving in the New World. Columbus stood on deck, dressed in the short black jacket, hat, and tights of a Castilian nobleman. He was flanked by two Spanish sailors and several soldiers who wore helmets, breastplates, and uniforms of red and yellow, the colors of Castile. Around the vessel, on the representation of the shore, sat several maidens in skimpy tunics with feathered headdresses and carrying quivers full of arrows. The float told the story of male-conquerors and female-subordinates as the major tale of the discovery of the New World.

The second float, "The Allegory of Independence," displayed two images of the world, labeled Europe and Mexico, with a broken chain between them. The centerpiece was a woman identified as America, dressed in a white tunic with a red cloak and wearing a grand crown of feathers, pearls, and gold. This allegorical figure had been used since the colonial era for America, in general, and for New Spain or Mexico, in particular. After Independence, Mexico's tricolors often appeared on her headdress, sash, or staff.

A widely known and popular version of this image appeared in the painting, *Allegory of the Constitution of 1857*. The artist, Petronilo Monroy, had entered it in the Academy of San Carlos's 1869 exhibition. He painted the female figure in a wind-blown tunic, wearing a crown and carrying a laurel wreath in one upraised hand and in the other a stone tablet engraved with the words, "Constitution of 1857." Monroy's *Allegory* was an extremely popular and highly praised painting that today is in the National Palace.[14] For many spectators, then, the float carrying the image of America resonated with thoughts that she was heralding in a progressive Mexico under the reforms of the 1857 Constitution.

At the feet of America was a figure of a large alligator, an image that served the Aztec culture as the symbol of Earth. Above America presided the Mexican eagle, also drawn from Aztec symbolism. Thus, America, particularly Mexico, towered over the rest of the world in this representation. This float was sponsored by the Gran Círculo de Obreros, the mutualist worker organization.

The other allegorical floats in the parade, in sequence, had the following titles: "The Apotheosis of Hidalgo"; "The Republic"; "The Arms of Mexico City"; "Charity"; "The Fountain," the float of the water carriers; "Commerce"; "Fortune"; "Water"; "Aurora"; "Minerva —Public Instruction"; "Float of the Carriage Drivers"; "Progress— Industry and Peace." Here, many of the concerns of Mexicans received attention, such as potable water, civil order, secular education, and successful business.

The float sponsored by the Public Instruction Commission featured Minerva, the Roman goddess of wisdom, technical skill, and invention. While clearly an appropriate symbol for education, to some spectators the image had more specific significance. This same icon served as the focal point in the mural at the top of the main staircase landing at the National Preparatory School, the center of positivism. Juan Cordero intended his work, *Knowledge and Labor Triumph over Sloth and Ignorance*, to affirm the themes prominent in the philosophy of Auguste Comte. He unveiled his mural in tempera on November 29, 1874, to great fanfare. This allegory pictured Minerva enthroned with two figures representing steam and electricity placed below her. In the background, sailors unload a boat in front of a Parthenon-like structure, with Clio (the Greek Muse of history) writing, Envy fleeing, and in the distance a railroad train.[15] Seeing this float, anyone associated with the National Preparatory School —faculty, alumni, students, and visitors—knew that Minerva represented the values of Comte and the lessons of positivism in Mexican *cientificismo*.

The last float, "Progress," carried the slogan "Industry and Peace." Sponsored by the railroads of the Federal District, this float had gold and silver wheels as well as a gold and silver pedestal on which a carved wooden statue stood. The allegory represented "Industry" and "Progress" crowned by "Peace," embodied in a beautiful woman who was reaching out to crown a railroad locomotive as it emerged from a tunnel. The float also had railroad items such as track, wheels, and sledgehammers heaped upon it. At the front was the image of the Mexican eagle, with its wings unfolded as in flight, holding chains in its claws as though pulling the float. Six black draft horses, each decked out in black cloth bordered in gold and with tricolor plumes, were hitched to the float. The horses were ridden by three postilions dressed elegantly in the eighteenth-century Spanish style, with three-cornered black felt hats trimmed with white plumes, red and blue velvet jackets with silver and gold trim, knee-length breeches, low shoes, silk stockings, and gloves.

The steam locomotive, here emerging into the Mexican sunlight from the darkness of the tunnel, served as the international symbol of modernity and industry. The railroad, with its speed and power and its smoke and noise, meant that Mexico had arrived, while the float, actually drawn by horses, clearly linked old-style transportation to the old Spanish colonial society while the eagle of Mexico soared with its connection to steel rails and steam locomotion. No wonder this float was acclaimed the most popular in the procession.[16]

Some twenty-seven years later, while attending the Congress of Americanists held in conjunction with the centennial of Mexican Independence in 1910, University of Chicago anthropologist Frederick Starr considered the cost and purpose of the Centennial: "If the celebration embodied appreciation of the principles for which the fathers fought, if it emphasized the blessings of freedom, if it increased respect for the national constitution and kindled sound patriotism—

it was cheap at that price. But if it was simply the opportunity to make a grand display, to give gay pleasure and enjoyment to a rich few, it was a grievous burden."[17] His observation serves as a measure for all the Independence Day celebrations. In the parades and floats of these patriotic festivals, the governors, politicians, civic-minded individuals, occupational groups (for example, mutualist organizations), and industrial enterprises (especially the railroad companies) expressed their support for the nation. In examining these festivals we can discover what constituted the public spirit in 1869 and 1883.

Notes

1. Walter Satterthwait, *Accustomed to the Dark* (Toronto: Worldwide, 1998), 163–64.
2. For a persuasive argument for shifting analysis from text to performance, see Joséph Roach, *Cities of the Dead: Circum-Atlantic Performance* (New York: Columbia University Press, 1996).
3. This discussion relies on Benedict Anderson, *Imagined Communities* (New York: Verso, 1991; rev. ed.)
4. See Miguel Soto, "The Monarchist Conspiracy in Mexico, 1845–1846" (Ph.D. diss., University of Texas, 1983).
5. See Chapter Two, this volume.
6. See the unpublished paper by Erika Pani, " 'Nunca hasta ahora se había celebrado . . . con pompa tan razonada': Vida cortesana y ceremonial público durante el Segundo Emperio"; and her essay, "El proyecto de Estado de Maximiliano a través de la vida cortesana y del ceremonial público," *Historia Mexicana* 45, no. 2 (October–December 1995): 423–61.
7. Ignacio Manuel Altamirano's "Cronica de las Fiestas de Septiembre en México y Puebla" was first published in the literary journal, *El Renacimiento*. It was reissued by Puebla's Secretaria de Cultura in 1987 as *Lecturas Historicas de Puebla, #6.*
8. Susan G. Davis provides a helpful guide to parades and processions as social and historical texts in *Parades and Power: Street Theater in Nineteenth-Century Philadelphia* (Philadelphia: Temple University Press, 1986). Also see Mary Ryan, "The American Parade: Representations of the Nineteenth-Century Social Order," in Lynn Hunt, ed., *The New Cultural History* (Berkeley: University of California Press, 1990), 131–53.
9. Morales also wrote the music for "Las Flores. Inspiración à la Schottische," published in 1880. Roberto L. Mayer, Antonio Rubial García, and Guadalupe Jiménez Codinanch, *México Ilustrado. Mapas, Planos, Grabados e Ilustraciones de Los Siglos XVI al XIX* (Mexico: Fomento Cultural Banamex, 1994), 46, 155, and 250.
10. On the militia, see Guy P. C. Thomson, "Bulwarks of Patriotic Liberalism: The National Guard, Philharmonic Corps, and Patriotic Juntas in Mexico, 1847–1888," *Journal of Latin American Studies* 22 (1990): 31–68; and "Popular Aspects of Liberalism in Mexico, 1848–1888," *Bulletin of Latin American Research* 10, no. 3 (1991): 265–92. On popular liberalism, see Thomson's *Patriotism, Politics, and Popular Liberalism in Nineteenth-Century Mexico: Juan Francisco Lucas and*

the *Puebla Sierra* (Wilmington, DE: Scholarly Resources, 1999); and Alan Knight, "El liberalismo mexicano desde la Reforma hasta la Revolución. Una interpretación," *Historia Mexicana* 35 (1985): 59–85.

11. See the biographical entry on Zaragoza in *Diccionario Porrua: Historia, biografía y geografía de México* (3d ed.; Mexico: Editorial Porrua, S.A., 1971), 2:2337.

12. Aída Mostkoff-Linares, "From Early Travel to Modern Tourism: International Visitors to Mexico since 1821" (Ph.D. diss., UCLA, 1998), chapter 3.

13. Linda Curcio-Nagy, "Giants and Gypsies: Corpus Christi in Colonial Mexico City," in William H. Beezley, Cheryl English Martin, and William E. French, eds., *Rituals of Rule, Rituals of Resistance: Public Celebrations and Popular Culture in Mexico* (Wilmington, DE: Scholarly Resources, 1994), 1–26.

14. Monroy (1836–1882) is best known for his work *Isaac*, praised as a synthesis of academic ideals. Stacie G. Widdifield, *The Embodiment of the National in Late Nineteenth-Century Mexican Painting* (Tucson: University of Arizona Press, 1996).

15. Ibid., 193–94.

16. Clementina Díaz de Ovando, *Las Fiestas Patrias en el México de hace un siglo, 1883* (Mexico: Centro de Estudios de Historia de México, CONDUMEX, 1984).

17. Frederick Starr Collection, Special Collections, University of Chicago, Box 19, folder 8.

CHAPTER SEVEN

The Capital Commemorates Independence at the Turn of the Century*

NORA PÉREZ-RAYÓN E.

With the immense joy that the sacred memory of the country awakens in all the people, the nation celebrated the ninetieth anniversary of its birth to independent life.[1]

The consolidation of national states in Latin America in the nineteenth century involved profound transformations in economic and political domains, accompanied by fundamental cultural changes. Cultural change implied the configuration of new moral regimes and new social regulations as well as a modified or renewed cosmology and the construction of national identities capable of integrating old and new values.[2] The analysis of commemorative speeches, civic and popular celebrations, patriotic monuments, and public inaugurations during a given historic period contributes to the understanding of changing cultural definitions and political practices. These expressions help describe and explain the ways in which a civic culture validating and re-creating myths and symbols are put forth by the state and how they are experienced and internalized by members of society.

*Modified and enlarged version of the article, "La sociología de lo cotidiano. Discursos y fiestas cívicas en el México de 1900. La historia en la conformación de la identidad nacional," published in *Revista Sociológica*, UAMA (September–December 1993). I want to express my gratitude to Jorge Torres Romero for his help in gathering the material for this article.

In reflecting upon the civic rituals and historical contexts, this essay attempts to analyze the coverage of the key festival that commemorates independence from Spain, as published in Mexico City's newspapers in the year 1900. In addition, it deals with the background and the popular fiestas that marked the event. The aim here is to highlight the explanatory power of these viewpoints in order to understand political and cultural processes of a more general nature.

Civic Rituals: Mirrors of a Place and a Time

> Just as they need food and drink, security and freedom of movement, people also require membership in a group. . . . Cultural life is shaped from the interior of a particular flow of tradition that comes from the collective historical experience shared only by the members of a group.[3]

The nation, "that strongly integrated and cohesive society, patiently knitted by states through long historical gestations," is built, according to Edgar Morin, through institutional, administrative, and coercive procedures but also through the articulation of local particularities and regional identities in a community unified by language and culture.[4] In states, power (understood as the capacity of individuals, collectivities, or institutions to control the behavior and ideas of other individuals, collectivities, or institutions) is present in all personal or social relationships. Importantly, it is also expressed through the appropriation of collective memory of a community through the projection of a discourse that privileges certain facts and idealizes the heroes and values that it finds useful.[5]

In national states, everyday life is an organized, regulated territory that includes both voluntary and imposed self-regulation of values. Agnes Heller defines history as the process whereby these values are built. Values, as she understands them, are all those things that pertain to human beings specifically—work, sociability, universality, consciousness, or freedom—and contribute to their development. Thus, from Heller's perspective, daily life, far from being extraneous to history, is its center. She holds that every great concrete historical deed becomes exceptional and historic precisely because of its effect in daily life.[6]

The forms and times through which what is social is internalized in every individual constitute a complex process that eventually becomes crystallized in a balance between outside and inside worlds.[7] This is what Pierre Bordieu describes as "habitus." If there is a balance between the social order and the practices of individuals, Bordieu says, it is not due to the power of political messages. Those actions insert themselves beyond the intellectual conscience in a system of habits, most of them acquired from infancy.

The most decisive ideological action toward constituting symbolic power does not take place on the battlefield of ideas or in anything that an individual can conceptualize. It happens in those unconscious associations of meaning that make up the habitus and that are accessible to us only through it. Habitus, generated by objective structures such as family, school, and social regulations, gives origin to individual practices and provides behavior with basic patterns of perception, thought, and action.[8] It is through these patterns that ritual acts and their manifestations in both civic and religious domains are developed, expressed, heard, felt, and experienced.[9]

In daily life such patterns are expressed and evinced in specific actions. Bordieu's habitus tends to reproduce the objective conditions that engendered it. Nevertheless, these patterns are not immutable. A new context or the availability of historic options allows the reorganization of acquired dispositions and the generation of transforming practices.[10] Through commemorative functions and speeches, civic rituals project representations of reality where social relations appear idealized and functional from the perspective of power. In daily life itself there is an abundance of ritual acts that reinforce social hierarchies and provide escape valves to potentially upsetting impulses of subordinate groups.[11]

The construction of the national state in Mexico and the consolidation of a national identity has been a long process—in fact, it is still unfinished. One reason that the process takes so long is the large imaginary content of nationalism.[12] The formula for the constitution of modern Mexico required, among other elements, the capacity to elaborate and disseminate a historical discourse that would homogenize the vision of the past and create a unifying set of myths and symbols and justify the requirements of the national modernizing project promoted from the center.

Porfirian Mexico projected an image of economic growth and modernity. In Mexico City, in particular, "order and progress" appeared to prevail, with electricity, electric trams, movie theaters, telephones, and cars. Mansions and public buildings, wide avenues, and roundabouts followed the architectonic styles and urban models fashionable in Europe and the United States. Porfirian elites thought themselves to be the creators of peace and economic prosperity as well as the promoters and embodiments of the nation's future. If the fruits of prosperity necessarily associated with progress had not yet reached down to the rest of society, it was, according to them, a matter of time, on the one hand, and of genetic limitations inherent to certain individuals or even certain groups, on the other.[13]

Mexico City and the year 1900 have been chosen as the space-time coordinates for this article for several reasons. The capital was the most important political, economic, administrative, and cultural nucleus in the country, the heart of the Porfirian process of centralization and "modernity." The year 1900 marked one of the moments of greatest popularity of the fin-de-siècle approach to modernity and the peak of Porfirio Díaz's dictatorship. The year also marked the end of a century—a psychological more than a historical phenomenon, of course, but one that promoted reflections on both the past and the future—as well as a year of elections where the aging don Porfirio was voted in office for the fifth time. It was also the year when *México y su evolución social*, a project coordinated by Justo Sierra, a masterpiece of Porfirian historiography as well as a monument to the regime's achievements, was published and when, simultaneously, criticism and unrest from the opposition began, foreshadowing future problems. The newspaper *Regeneración* appeared, and the initiative to organize Liberal clubs in different parts of the country was launched from San Luis Potosí.[14]

The Mexican middle and upper classes were by 1900 the beneficiaries—although in quite different degrees—of the process of economic transformation. Having access to information and education, these elite groups, especially the urban elites, constituted "public opinion." As their principal means of expression, they utilized the press which, more than a mere channel of political expression, became "the protagonist of cultural life." The numerous newspapers of the time mirrored their particular and oftentimes competitive interpretations of reality and their attempts to spread them at least to the more "conscious or potentially conscious" segments of the population.[15]

Toward the end of the last century, the press was the principal means of mass communication. Although for the country at large illiteracy extended to more than 80 percent of the population, in Mexico City the figure was 40 percent. Due to strong socializing traditions and the exchange of oral information, the scope of the written press was not limited to the number of actual readers.[16] Mexico City offered the largest number of periodicals. The dailies were sold at an average of three *centavos*.[17]

Public festivals of a civic or religious nature constituted another fundamental arena for social communication:

> Public festivities must have been a delightful experience in the Porfirian city . . . (they were) . . . found everywhere: outside churches after Mass; on Sundays in the parks; on national holidays; during unexpected events; at indoor and public parties at the plazas. Religious festivities deserve whole chapters; and the dead, mothers, and those who have fallen already have had a glimpse of their special days; and then, there are also the birthdays and other "particular joys."[18]

Official speeches, holidays, and openings helped to entertain the capital's residents during their spare time; and given the technological and financial means at the disposal of the 400,000 citizens of Mexico City to amuse themselves, people from all social classes attended events spontaneously.

We know that the population observed many religious celebrations throughout the year.[19] Neither the Reform Laws, nor Porfirian modernization, nor the influence of positivism with its cult for science and reason diminished in any significant way either popular devotion or the Catholicism practiced by most of the oligarchy and the middle classes. The policy of conciliation between Díaz's regime and the Catholic Church was the expression of a political, social, and cultural reality recognized by the state and adopted to obtain consensus and legitimacy.

Emanating from the state, an official history started taking shape during the last century that was manifested in speeches, mementos, sculptures, and the naming of streets and squares as well as in textbooks and books in general. The official history of the Porfirian regime presents a very broad vision of the past that goes back to pre-Hispanic Mexico as the starting point of the collective memory of the nation. This past was viewed as a glorious one over which the Conquest and three centuries of Spanish domination were superimposed. Independence broke with Spanish oppression; and, after years of struggling against conservative forces, the Liberals emerged victorious over internal and external enemies in the movement of the Reform and placed the country on the road to order, progress, and modernity.[20]

This interpretation of history was teleological and lineal, strongly influenced by positivist ideology, in which the nation marched forward on a single road—tripping on occasions but always completing stages in its journey toward the promising future. Finally, according to this vision, during the Porfirian years the expected positive stage was achieved, the stage of "order and progress."

During Díaz's time, history was more than an instrument of power and a tool for building a nation; "it had a global influence on the way of thinking." On expressions of the most diverse nature, a new sense of temporality was becoming apparent: "the belief in the novelty of the times," the "acceleration of time," and the availability of history (inasmuch as history is made). This sense was reinforced by Herbert Spencer's social Darwinism, which championed the view that the fittest would be the victors of history. All commemorations and manifestations of identity were animated by a tension between the desire to utilize the past and the aspiration to be modern.[21]

By championing positivism, according to Leopoldo Zea, Porfirians tried to achieve the mental revolution described years before by the ideologue of liberalism, José María Luis Mora. This revolution implied the homogenization of opinion in order that all Mexicans conform to what Gabino Barreda called "a common fund of truths." The instrument to attain such uniformity was not to be violence but rather persuasion, the effects of which, argued Mora, would come slowly but surely.[22] In this sense, as in others, positivism did not imply any radical break with Liberal thought.

The transition from the creation of a discourse with hegemonic pretensions to its assimilation by the individuals to whom it is directed, however, is not automatic. The internalizing process involves multiple factors that promote the integration of concrete practices where these discourses crystallize. Family, school, traditional religious and patriotic celebrations, reading materials, and oral tales are the vehicles whereby the discourse of identity is internalized and of which the state can take advantage.[23] At the end of the nineteenth century, when the development of mass media and universal education were still incipient, civic commemorations played an important role in these processes.

The civic festivities that awakened the most enthusiasm were those related to the celebration of Independence. These were civic holidays of the most popular nature. Facing a deeply unequal society in socioeconomic and cultural terms and a plan of development that entailed high social costs, the Porfirian regime must have imagined and constructed all symbolic referents through which the different ethnic and social groups would be identified; in other words, a collective redefinition. The commemoration of the beginning of the Independence movement on September 15 and 16, which was already traditionally and popularly celebrated, was the perfect occasion to confirm and consolidate these preoccupations.

Debates over Independence in the Year 1900

> Welcome, month of September, month of national glories that evoke so many memories in the hearts of the Mexicans! Your dates hold sublime pages of the history of the country. And Heaven doubtless destined your name to be perpetuated in the annals of all Latin America.[24]

Rituals of a civic nature are the basic means through which the state presents itself to society. Authority is embodied in concrete individuals associated with the state and its project that speak directly to the people through speeches given at public squares or through texts in newspapers directed to more exclusive social groups who create and spread public opinion and try to legitimize the status quo. "Public politics is synonymous with festivity or commemoration, not action: one celebrates, one does not act."[25]

Symbols evoke a response from the senses as well as from the intellect. Rites relate the individual to the collectivity tying up ideology and emotion. Social norms and values are greatly strengthened when enveloped by emotion, while basic emotions are ennobled through the association with social values.[26] The quest is the construction of a sole truth to read into the past, accept the present, and imagine the future.

In all its varieties, the Porfirian press perceived the month of September as a time consecrated to the country, of remembering the great founding processes of the nation: the ten-year struggle for its independence from Spain (1810–1821). In September also, in 1847, important battles were fought in Mexico City during the war with the United States: on September 8, in the place known as Molino de las Flores; and on the 13th, at Chapultepec Castle.

The struggle for Independence had produced a Manichaen conception of history, in which Liberal and Conservative elites built their vision of the past by choosing their own heroes and antiheroes. But, thanks to the Porfirian policies of conciliation, both elites would share a project of development and benefit from stability. This state of affairs was exemplified in Justo Sierra's book, *La evolución política de México*, published at the turn of the century. Nevertheless, the fact that the animosity between Liberals and Conservatives was still alive is reflected in the way that the press dealt with the commemorative rituals associated with the struggle for Independence. Three journalistic views allow us to observe the ideological debate over the meanings of Independence from the official perspective, the liberal viewpoint, and the Catholic perspective.

The Official Press: El Imparcial

> Hidalgo has the right to immortality because as a man he planted the soil and promoted industry; as a priest he preached the religion of love and brotherhood; as a Mexican he acquired the conviction of his rights and by transmitting them to his brothers he turned an enslaved people into an independent, free nation.[27]

In 1900, President Díaz sent this "Message to Hidalgo" on the front page of *El Imparcial*, praising the priest's virtues as a workingman in the first place and then as a devotee of fraternity, justice, and peace. A few months earlier, the president had made reference to the heroic Wars of Independence as entailing horrendous civil and international conflicts, as a bloody and devastating time, yet decisive in the long and painful period of political and social gestation that was to nurture and make Mexico's autonomy and national powers viable. Thus, he integrated Independence into a staged conception of history.[28]

In the commemorative editorial of September 16, *El Imparcial* praised Miguel Hidalgo as destined by Providence to be Chief of the Revolution and paladin of the sanctified cause of liberty. The allusion to Providence in a context supposedly permeated by the spirit of positivism and science surprises us. But in a country with a profoundly religious culture originating in a double legacy of pre-Hispanic and Spanish roots, the construction of a civic culture includes a language, a symbolism, and a ceremonial culture that made constant reference to religious experience. The people, the editorial continues, responded to the summons to engage in the titanic struggle to defend sacred rights: "That army of patriots, lacking organization and discipline, went through towns and cities . . . while looking at death closely, they could also see a smiling future of happiness for the beloved country."[29]

An editorial of September 17, "El principio de la gran lucha. ¿Cómo nació la patria?" (The beginning of the great struggle. How was the country born?) praises love for the country as well as men's heroism and disposition to martyrdom for the sake of liberty: "The nation stood up: peasants, artisans, students, priests . . . some were conscious, others did not comprehend, but all felt impelled by incontestable forces." Independence is seen and portrayed as a popular uprising.[30] The newspaper published several essays on the same subject by eminent writers of the Reform period and the Porfiriato. Luis González Obregón, for example, outlined the origins and history of the celebrations associated with Independence.

The author of the editorial reviewed the official history of the celebration. The Congress had established this civic commemoration in 1822, with the first important popular celebration taking place in 1825 during the time of President Guadalupe Victoria. From then on, it would be celebrated year in and year out, with the exception of 1847, when it was canceled in Mexico City due to the American invasion. Those first anniversaries were, according to Obregón, of a civic as well as a religious nature, as apparent in the decorative lighting of both public buildings and churches. After 1857 they would adopt a lay character; and, as years went by, he suggests, the celebrations started to decline. But, as of 1883, the author declared, youths, workers, foreign communities, and the people in general participated in the festivities, thus bringing on their complete rebirth. Every year they were observed with more enthusiasm and splendor. "Today it is celebrated in the midst of peace and progress."[31]

Ignacio Ramírez offered a quick historic panorama: the Aztec nation succumbed in its struggle against Cortés. Three centuries elapsed before the wound healed. During the colonial period, the atmosphere was disastrous for the conquistadors. The class in power, the privileged race on the European peninsula, renounced its intelligence in America and abandoned itself to "automatic movements dictated by the parish church clocks." That assessment applied to the nobility only, as the masses suffered from lack of work: the ports were closed due to prohibitive systems; the vineyards, tobacco fields, and berry fields were burnt by the monopoly; and the positions of power were occupied by foreigners and the intelligentsia in the hands of the Inquisition. The ideal of life was the convent.[32] Manuel Gutiérrez Nájera wrote an homage to the hero of Independence, stating that Hidalgo will not have a heroic poem—"History is his own poem"—that he does not need one as his existence depends on his own strength. "The projection of his spirit happens in history," and "history never finishes, does not stop or end."[33]

By the fortuitous coincidence that Díaz's name day coincided with Independence Day, many birthday congratulations to don Porfirio appeared in *El Imparcial*. Among others, the Circle of Friends of the President praised the services rendered the country by him whom they called the best friend of the Mexicans and of all cultivated nations. The students of the National Preparatory School congratulated Díaz on the faith that he inspired in young people, claiming themselves to be representatives of the new generation, free of all passion, devoid of any spirit of *bandería* (factionalism), and "estranged from anything other than Union, Peace, and Progress."

Worthy of notice among the congratulatory messages is the panegyric addressed by the recently appointed minister of defense, General Bernardo Reyes, to his president and old army buddy. Reyes extolled Díaz's military feats aimed at change and the reform of the institutions as well as his efforts toward peace and his having smashed the monster of anarchy. He praised the president's talent as a statesman and finished by stating that Díaz's birth will be seen by history as "one of the occurrences that saved modern Mexico."[34] The diplomatic corps also expressed its congratulations and acknowledgments to Díaz for the peace and prosperity enjoyed by the country.

The Liberal Press: Diario del Hogar

> The *Diario del Hogar* . . . has been working on rekindling the civic cult to the country's heroes, the true saints among Mexican martyrs, entitled to veneration and respect from all the citizens.[35]

By the end of the nineteenth century the Liberal press championed a vision of history that served mainly political purposes. The Liberals were the new saints, and the clergy the new demons. Building the cult to national heroes became a duty, part of shaping the makeup of the citizen and forging a new basis for Mexican patriotism. Editorials and articles were dedicated to recounting the feats of the heroes of Independence, the struggle against the United States during the war of 1846–1848, the time of the Constitutional Congress and the Reform, the fight against the French intervention, and the rebellion of Tuxtepec. The discourse, images, and rituals implemented in order to extol historical memory and its protagonists paradoxically reverted to language of a religious nature.

The need to educate all Mexicans from an early age in the love of the heroes and the duty to honor and glorify them was seen as a fundamental aim of building the cult of heroes. Toward this end during 1900, the *Diario del Hogar* endorsed proposals and actions conducive to gathering together the remains of all eminent men who had brought brilliance and honor to Mexico and placing them in one site, the temple of the country:

> There, the people will come together on a given day consecrated to the heroes and water the flowers of memory and gratitude. There, the speakers will tell of the great deeds of our history, and children will become used to paying reverence to the names of those who gave us country and freedom . . . A dignified and fitting place where the people can go freely to present their offerings of gratitude and acknowledgment.[36]

For the *Diario del Hogar* (as for *El Imparcial*) the Father of the Country, and thus the most important foundational hero, was Miguel Hidalgo. In the words of the daily, "to the entreaties of his prophetic voice battalions of admirable men rose up, and after eleven years of superhuman toils delivered Mexico from the yoke of oppression and servility that had lasted for three centuries."[37]

The Liberal daily defined three glorious stages of the Independence movement: the onset, with Hidalgo, Ignacio Allende, and Juan Aldama, who awakened a sleepy people and placed them on the road to glory and immortality; the period of organization, with José María Morelos, Hermenegildo Galeana, Francisco Javier Mina, Mariano Abasolo, and Mariano Matamoros, who, encouraged by the example of the first stage, overpowered the royalist forces everywhere they went and gave shape to the conflict; the consummation of Independence, with the heroic and invincible Vicente Guerrero, the Rayón brothers, Pedro Ascencio, and others, who, after long years of persevering, attained freedom from Spanish domination.

The Liberals of the nineteenth century and those of 1900 presented themselves time and again as followers in the footsteps of Hidalgo. With freedom and independence ensured and the greedy chastised, "the consolidation of peace as well as the development of all public riches in their diverse manifestations had to come." Benito Juárez and Miguel Lerdo de Tejada were key ingredients in the achievement of public tranquility: "The country entered an era of absolute tranquility that it had looked forward to during two-thirds of a century of autonomy and, leaving the shotgun in the cupboard, grabbed the tools of labor, the song of peace."[38]

Worthy of notice in the liberal interpretation of the meaning of Independence is the omission of Agustín de Iturbide, whose role was fundamental in the consummation of Independence. Because he was identified with the Conservatives and their causes, he was erased from the process.

> Once out of the hands of the Spaniards, the country was left at the mercy of circumstantial politicians led by Iturbide. By way of his ambition he appropriated the spurs of the conquistador. Such an insult triggered the birth of the Liberal Party, and in the tug of war the reign of the "presidents for a minute" thrived . . . until the arrival of [Antonio López de] Santa Anna and his absolutist tendencies and cruelty. The tyrant, that vulgar, ambitious man, was overthrown, and the robust plant of liberalism blossomed infiltrating everything in a moment; penetrating even the hearth of the family where the fecund seeds of progress, dignity, freedom, and fraternity were planted. Its magnificent task was sealed with the admirable law of February 5, 1857.[39]

The need to find continuity agreeable to the Liberal logic was thus manifested in the reinterpretations of history.

Independence, according to the Liberal mindset, was followed by disorder brought about by "that depraved farrago composed by a fanatic and riotous clergy, a corrupt army, and a worthless nobility with its privileges and depravities that comprised the monstrous trinity that constantly threatened the future of the Republic."[40] The fruitful days of reconstruction arrived after the first half of the century with the men from Ayutla, the wise men of the Constitution—Juárez, Lerdo, Ocampo, Doblado, "and that whole constellation of suns that lit the skies of our Country with the clarity of an aurora borealis brought about the real and magnificent independence of the people dissociating their minds from error and fanaticism."[41]

Thus, in this vision, the aims of the heroes of Independence were fundamentally the same as those of their colleagues of the Reform. Freeing New Spain had not been the only objective of Hidalgo's Revolution. His goals included the sovereignty of the people as the basis of all rights, fraternity, and freedom, and the construction of a nation of free workers with liberty of conscience and thought. This movement nurtured and shaped the Ayutla Revolution.

A related touchstone of the Liberal vision was the defense of the 1857 Constitution as a banner of democracy and social well-being.

The Constitution was dealt with as some kind of sacred book, the civic Bible, the "great book of the salvation of the Country, a blessed palladin."[42] At the end of the century, the *Diario del Hogar* denounced the policy of conciliation between the government and the Church, attacking the Church on a daily basis as covering with a shroud the great conquests derived from the Plan de Ayutla. "Liberty is adhered; the Constitution, frozen," exclaimed an editorial which nevertheless closed on an optimistic note: "In the religion of Country and Humanity the heroes, turned into gods by the cult of a grateful people, want as an offering civic virtues, respect for the rights of others, political probity and honesty, and a constant and resolute effort toward progress."[43]

History is brought up constantly in the Liberal press in order to emphasize the disastrous and retarding role that the Catholic Church signified for the development of the people in Mexico and in the world. The commemoration of Independence was an opportunity to reiterate this discourse: "With the cross as a banner, they have spilled rivers of blood when revolt and disturbance have been at hand; in the name of God they have ravaged the country whenever possible, and he who takes pride in violating the law will not hesitate to preach the killing and extermination of that which does not belong to the Spanish race."[44] Taking these principles as a point of departure, Liberals denounced a priest from San Luis Potosí as abject, despicable scum, "a miscarriage of ignorance and stupidity" for insulting the memory of the illustrious dead. On September 16 this person had insulted the memory of Hidalgo and of all persons who had contributed to Independence: "I am puzzled at seeing the house of God so full; but I am not ignorant. I know that if you have come here, it is not for the sake of devotion, but to celebrate the so-called national festivities. But let it be known that Hidalgo and all of those whom you call heroes are burning in Hell."[45]

Enraged, the *Diario del Hogar* responded: "The memories come to mind of those mournful times when the clergy exerted its influence over the fanatical masses and, with the Christ in one hand and the incendiary torch in the other, went through the Republic inducing revolt, instigating murder and extermination, and being the constant obstacle to all progress."[46] In championing its vision of Independence and related historical movements in Mexico—the holy code of the Constitution of 1857, the Reform as the splendid light that leads the country toward true redemption—Liberals developed a religious vocabulary that evoked ancestral images and symbols. In so doing, they revamped their discourse in order to legitimize new ideals and values and claim a substantial part in the construction of the utopia of progress and modernity.

The Catholic Press: El Tiempo *and* El País

The Catholic attitude and its published discourse on Independence had specific characteristics. While accepting the fact of Independence and celebrating it, Catholics took a defensive stand: "we feel no hate or cruelty toward the great country that, through the first saintly and virtuous missionaries, brought us their rich language and the most precious gift to man, that of the religion of the Crucified, the only One who opens the doors of Heaven to mortals."[47] From the standpoint of *El País*, countries as well as individuals reach adulthood dependent on others. There is a clock, it is said, that marks the time of emancipation.[48] Again and again, both in *El Tiempo* and in *El País*, it was remembered that the banner that led the insurgent forces was the image of the Virgin of Guadalupe.

In the discourse and in the official Liberal press the heroes of Independence are Hidalgo and Morelos, followed by Guerrero, Rayón, and Matamoros; but, as it has been pointed out, the great absentee is Agustín de Iturbide. The Catholic press vindicated him. Three colossal heroes were found in this crossroads: Hidalgo at the inception, Morelos as continuator, and Iturbide in its consummation.

On the 27th of September—the date that marked the entry of Trigarante (Three Guarantees) Army into Mexico City after the signing of the Plan de Iguala—*El País* dedicated the whole issue to Iturbide's memory demanding, in the spirit of peace and conciliation, congruence with history. Thus, it asserted: "eleven years later, when only the ashes covering the dormant fire remained, the idea of independence embodied in the noble shape of a caudillo reappears; it is Agustín de Iturbide who, together with Guerrero . . . consummated the feat."[49] It was Iturbide who proclaimed the Plan de Iguala, who signed the Treaties of Córdoba, who entered the capital at the head of the Trigarante Army, and who, for the first time, raised the tricolor banner that symbolized the purity of religion, the treasure of Independence, and the inestimable value of union.

The Sociedad Patriótica Agustín de Iturbide asked for a reprinting of 30,000 copies of that issue of *El País* and published an invitation to a solemn Mass and a Te Deum to be celebrated on the 27th in the Church of La Profesa, "to express gratitude for the National Independence consummated by the Illustrious Liberator, don Agustín de Iturbide."[50]

The Catholic Church would insist repeatedly that Independence was announced and acclaimed by Spaniards and Creoles who lived in New Spain. Hidalgo never thought of the restoration of Cuitlahuac's dynasty; he was the son of two Spaniards and his lieutenant was Allende; his main co-conspirators—Aldama, Abasolo, and doña Josefa Ortiz de Domínguez—were either Spanish or Creole. All of them grouped around the same ambition: "Long live Fernando VII!" They even aspired to the continuation of the same political sovereignty, and their "Death to the gachupines!" referred to the abolition of the privileges held by the Spaniards in the peninsula. "Long live the Virgin of Guadalupe!" they exclaimed in veneration of the religious ideals of Catholicism. But, stimulated by pillage, the Revolution grew in unintended ways. When Spain recovered from the Napoleonic Wars, the popular struggle in the New World was over. And it was over thanks to Iturbide.

The Festivities of Independence

> It should not be forgotten that the "only mass communication media" in the nineteenth century were the press and the speeches given at the square. To communicate means to find each other face to face at the esplanade where those who listen are part of the spectacle. . . . Publicly, politics is synonymous with celebration or commemoration, not with action . . . Politics meant having a good time at patriotic rituals or solemn openings.[51]

Public festivities go beyond the authorities and their efforts to intimidate, instruct, and form their subordinates. People are not only witnesses but also actors in public festivities—celebrating being one of the few real rights through which they express their values, aspirations, and resentments. Moreover, celebrations strengthen social solidarity, expressing not only consensual and supporting relations but also contestation and conflict. They can both reinforce and threaten the relations between elites and subordinates. Love for the country, for the Mexican people, for peace, order, progress, and work, for prosperity and modernity may originate from the state but then become part of daily life through festivities that are anticipated year after year.

For the celebrations of the 15th and 16th of September 1900 the government of Mexico City authorized 6,000 pesos.[52] Additionally, the celebrations committee asked the executive power to "kindly manifest the amount that it will contribute, as in years past, to the festivities of September 15 and 16."[53] The secretary of the interior pointed out to the secretary of the treasury that the president had given an order to provide the government of Mexico City with 5,000 pesos as the federal government's contribution toward the expenses incurred by the celebrations.[54]

Downtown Mexico City dressed up for the festivities that commemorated Independence—with national and foreign flags flying on public buildings, stores, and embassies. Tricolor bunting and floral decorations abounded on the streets of Plateros and San Francisco—the best streets of the city. The Singer and Boker stores, the Flammand salon, Siemens and Halske, Loeb Glass, the Droguería Belga, the Casino Español, and the French, German, British, and American stores all displayed dazzling decorations. In embassies and foreign delegations of the United States, France, England, Germany, Belgium, Russia, Spain, China, Guatemala, Argentina, and Japan, bunting in the colors of their flags as well as those of the Mexican flag were hung.

At Droguería Labadie three portraits stood out: Hidalgo's, with the legend "Independence"; Juárez's, with the legend "Constitution"; Porfirio Díaz's, with the legend "Peace and Progress." On some balconies General Díaz's monogram appeared, crowned by a large eagle of gilded wood. Over one door there hung a large oil painting "by the renowned scene painter S. Mendoza," an allegory of Independence—depicted as a bell—from which the people of Mexico converged, breaking their chains while being illuminated by the torch of Liberty. At the bottom of the picture, a chained Indian was awakened by the echoes of the bell. At the sides, also painted in oil, were portrayed the heads of Hidalgo, Juárez, and Díaz.[55]

Electric lighting stunned a society that was only just becoming familiar with this technical innovation. "Electric bulbs simulated long, white, shining threads that embroidered the center of the streets and avenues in the capital, . . . Plateros . . . San Francisco . . . Paseo de la Reforma; the abundance of lights and multicolored decorations was enough to blur the eyesight."[56] The downtown areas were the best lit, but all over the city, on the night of the 15th, there was a profusion of luminous decorations. One building that stood out in newspaper accounts was located at the corner of Cinco de Mayo and San José del Real streets. Displayed in the center of the decoration and bathed in the white light of innumerable lightbulbs were the figures of Hidalgo and President Díaz.

September 15

The explosion of firecrackers, the tolling of bells, and the imposing firing of the artillery in the Ciudadela awakened, on the morning of the 15th, the residents of the capital with "a smiling and magnificent sight." The first rays of the sun lit the bunting, streamers, and huge hangings displayed on the public buildings, on all downtown stores, and, in general, on all the streets of the city. The great hullabaloo and enthusiasm that grew throughout the morning and early afternoon were extensively covered in newspaper accounts. In every public place, there was an incessant parade of carriages, and people came and went in what seemed to observers to be veritable waves. Electric tramcars full of passengers ran along the streets "like lightning bolts," and even at 7 P.M. "innumerable visitors disembarked at every station," most of them having to spend the night walking the streets because hotels and inns had no vacancies.[57]

El Tiempo described the Plaza de Armas at 8 P.M. as "most resplendent . . . like an immense fountain of multicolored lights; in the Cathedral's atrium a profusion of fireworks became rain of gold, and shooting stars."[58] Angel del Campo Micros left a rich description of those hours and the celebrations that were repeated year after year:

> Vendors install their intricate stands under the red flash of the fireworks. The seller of "oven roasted" displays his fistful of peanuts; sugarcane and oranges are piled together; plump ladies in purple skirts, the *rebozo* [shawl] hanging, wearing patent leather shoes with pewter buckles and silver hoops, eat up, using both hands, spicy *enchiladas* or drink up huge pitchers of lemonade. . . . And thus, more and more groups of *ensabanados*, vegetable vendors, and honest carpenters with their children perched on their shoulders . . . while the wife tries to put the baby to sleep keep on arriving. . . . Somewhat farther along, people are toasting . . . "friendship" and the "compadres." The crowd gets bigger. . . . The guitars are being played and the voices of the drunks start singing, "Tuli, tuli, pan."[59]

The fireworks, according to *El País,* were vastly superior in 1900 to those of previous years. Eight huge fireworks constructions were burnt. At the end of the show, the image of the head of General Díaz, formed by white lights, appeared while the people cheered. Afterward, ninety musicians from the High Command Staff of the Artillery and Sappers, organized by the Circle of Friends of the President, serenaded General Díaz from a platform in front of the National Palace.[60]

When the representatives of the Demarcation Police flowed into the square with their torches ablaze, the enthusiasm grew. Micros described the scene: "The crowd trembles. The hand of the clock on the [National] Palace has only one minute to go; the last drink of moonshine is consumed . . . the *charros* [cowboys] shoot at the sky with their guns; the embers that the kids will use to light the firecrackers are rekindled. The bells in the towers of the Cathedral toll; the glass door of the Palace balcony now opens."[61] Finally, the president emerged and rang the historic bell of Independence while cheering its heroes. According to *El Tiempo*, "the enthusiasm and the joy of the people had no limits": "The sparklers are on fire . . . eyes well up and an indescribable chill runs down the spine. A deep desire to yell, to cry, to applaud is felt. With teary eyes, the serene image of Hidalgo is beheld, and with the words 'Long live freedom!' one's soul is cast to him in an expression of gratitude."[62]

The plan of the city certainly worked to heighten the experience of enjoying oneself during these patriotic rituals. The trees in the Zócalo (main square) created more of a secular space than a locale for the masses in the European style. In the public space, Porfirio Díaz played the role of "pastor" as much as of accomplished leader.[63] The Plaza de la Constitución was teeming, according to the dailies, with tricolor flags waving in every hand: policemen, the working class, construction workers, *charros*, and firemen. The newspapers also reported hard rains on both Saturday night and Sunday. Even though the festivities were not interrupted on Saturday night, on Sunday, due to a storm that flooded the downtown area in twenty minutes, all acrobatics, greased pole games, and sack races were postponed. But *El Universal* related that in spite of the foul weather, the populace filled the air with patriotic expressions. "It was observed that in comparison to previous years, the disagreeable, hateful screams that sanction neither the culture nor our historic present, diminished in such a way that the few that were heard should be considered exceptional."[64]

In the Alameda, popular speakers delivered speeches that, in the words of *El Imparcial*, were "more or less correct" and full of patriotic expressions.[65] Only a few bars remained open during the rest of the night, but the crowds walked the streets of the capital singing patriotic songs to the music of guitars far into the night. Students formed *estudiantinas* (musical groups) and played popular music in public places and downtown promenades.[66]

In the different municipalities around Mexico City, the night of the *grito* was also celebrated, and the festivities included bullfights in improvised bullrings. In Mixcoac, the bullring collapsed half an hour before the spectacle began, "crushing some prominent citizens, although without serious consequences, with the exception of two dead children, three or four people with broken bones, and ten or twelve bruised."[67] According to *El Imparcial*, even at four in the morning, the populace, in animated groups, was still on the streets.[68]

In the Catholic press in particular—even though not exclusively— another face of the commemorative celebrations was recorded. For example, in order to reduce the innumerable thefts that visitors had to endure year after year during the national holidays, the governor of the Federal District ruled that all thieves known by their constant incarcerations should be detained in the headquarters of the eight precincts for a period of three days.[69] For the sake of order and tranquility, spontaneous popular events were limited or confined to the periphery and replaced by controlled functions and parades organized in pre-established parks and avenues.[70]

As was the case every year, the dailies from the opposition emphasized that there were a number of disturbances. On Juárez avenue, one hundred individuals armed with sticks and stones gathered to block the transit of carriages. A shower of stones fell over the "América" restaurant, and over the "Número Uno" and "El Club" bars: "The group expanded in an extraordinary way to the point that the mounted police were forced to use their sabers. It was only by way of a belting that the mob was dispersed only to gather again after half an hour on Juárez avenue."[71] The leaders went to the Alameda where the crowd danced joyfully to the tunes of street organists. Another group proceeded to Dolores street where they destroyed the glass door to the "El Bosque" restaurant and stoned some houses.

The newspapers also described a squabble in a bar close to Tabacaleros alley between a group of drunks and some Spaniards where several were wounded before the police could intervene. A large group stoned a house in El Buen Tono. Indicating that it all had happened without any previous attacks from the police or any firing of workers or labor conflicts, *El País* deemed the disturbances the consequence of subversive atheist theories: "These are at the core of the attacks launched against the capital and the authorities, and constitute the first examples of the socialist venom produced by anti-Christian preaching, atheist education, and all the efforts to inculcate immorality." A police headquarters in the Sixth Precinct was stoned, something that according to *El País* had never happened before.[72]

Disturbances in the provinces during the patriotic celebrations were also documented by Mexico City newspapers. In Jalapa, for example, on the night of the 15th the populace insulted Spaniards and stoned their homes, without any reaction from the police. *El Universal* pleaded for the authorities to punish this behavior.[73] On the same night, *El Tiempo*, in an editorial entitled "The Unruliness of the Populace," offered a radically different view of the festivities from the one presented by *El Imparcial*. This newspaper pointed out that during that night the populace in the capital was intent on creating a disturbance by breaking store windows, destroying and stealing plants, stoning carriages, and even stabbing people.[74]

Moisés González Navarro states that during the ceremony of the *grito*, the riffraff and others who did not belong among them were expected to insult the gachupines and cheer the Virgin of Guadalupe.[75] The year 1900 was no exception. To the exclamation of "Death to the gachupines!" the shout of "Death to the riffraff!" was added to symbolize, according to the editorial in *El Tiempo*, the hatred that the *pelado* (uncouth persons) felt for everything associated with cleanliness, beauty, and decency. It also implied the *pelado*'s abhorrence of the landowner and his "idolatry for the rabble": "the lowlife of the capital is one of the most obscene in the world and as dirty as it is brazen; unable to improve its condition, it can't be civilized . . . it should be kept restrained so that it doesn't create any disturbances."[76] Fueled by drink, this segment of the populace stoned carriages, ran over the police, and destroyed the windows of several establishments, "thus casting an ugly stain on our stage of civilization through the display of such beastly savagery."[77]

September 16

The 16th of September in 1900 was commemorated with a series of military maneuvers and parades, the awarding of medals, and the pledge to the flag in the periphery of the city. These commemorations were conducted in the presence of the president and his cabinet as well as of the diplomatic corps and a distinguished audience. Beginning in the early hours of the morning, large numbers of people formed an endless line along the Paseo de la Reforma in order to see the troops, the president, and the members of his cabinet on their way toward the hills of Anzures, with Chapultepec Castle in the background. Some grandstands holding 1,500 to 2,000 people had been set up in empty lots, and yet they were inadequate for the public who walked, drove their cars, took taxis, or came down by train to attend the ceremonies. At 8 A.M. the troops started occupying the field, and by 8:30 they had taken their places. At 10 A.M. a trumpet announced the arrival of the president and his entourage, their entrance accompanied by the national anthem. An official speech given by Lic. Rafael Lozano Saldaña was "concise, full of deep concepts," and followed the modern style in its brevity.

The military display began with the awarding of medals to the most distinguished men for their services to the Republic. The first person called was General Bernardo Reyes, recently appointed minister of war, who was followed by several soldiers among whom a group of twelve Indians, dressed in the humble attire of the common people, were decorated by the president for their bravery during the siege of Querétaro. They were warmly acclaimed by the thousands of spectators.[78]

El Universal presented a summary of the national holidays. It emphasized the organizational efforts of the Patriotic Committees that overdid themselves that year, remarking that the entertainment and public festivities had multiplied while the private parties for the "wealthy classes" had been limited.[79] According to *El País*, the festivities had not been as brilliant as the previous year's, and they hoped that this was not due to a decline in the patriotic spirit characteristic of the *científicos'* belief that patriotism was an abstraction and not a virtue of the Latin race.[80] Further, *El Universal* observed that the civic festivities of the year 1900 had dwindled in enthusiasm and grandeur: "May the adulation of the living not erase forever the memory of the illustrious dead." The same daily noticed in that year a certain decline in the floating population. This change, according to the newspaper, was not attributable to the "chilling of patriotic sentiment" but rather to the continuing poverty of the masses due to economic disparity.[81]

General Díaz, said *El Universal*, besides feeling proud, should take public acclaim as an incentive to continue his efforts toward national progress. The latter should be directed now toward granting the people and public opinion the freedom that they have only been able to taste, given that the administration has been fully dedicated, in logical gradation, first, to securing the peace; then, to cementing credit; and now, to organizing the administrative order.[82]

Conclusion

In *Ortografía de los sentimientos humanos*, published in 1907, Ramón García Trueba commented that the patriotic celebrations of September brought together "a continent of languages, races, and classes" like "islands under the shelter of patriotic symbols and rituals."[83] But, as Valenzuela Arce points out, national culture is also "the cloud of history" that covers up inequalities and forces a populace to celebrate the deeds that generated inequality.[84] Commemorative festivities on the 15th and 16th of September were eloquent examples of these processes. All the people—riffraff and dandies, rich and poor, famous and anonymous—celebrated under a unifying patriotic discourse. The festivity was at root related to a foreign conflict and thus contributed to secure a nationalism of the kind characterized, as Benedict Anderson has shown, by its power to mobilize multitudes and ignite patriotic passions in them.[85]

In 1900, Díaz joined the images of Miguel Hidalgo and Benito Juárez in the pantheon of Mexican heroes. In the commemorative symbolism that accompanied the September celebrations, Díaz became the equal of the great national heroes of Independence.[86] Public financing of the festivities of September 15 and 16 reinforced the paternalistic nature of the regime, emphasizing Díaz's role as direct sponsor and benefactor of the people's fiestas.

The media coverage of the 1900 events shows that the government elite was convinced of following the right path and of being at the cutting edge with modernity. It relished the material progress that it had achieved and the peace that it had conserved. The 1900 festivities also showed that Mexican society at the end of the century was, in greater part than ever before, permeated by a cosmology that was both traditional and religious. The chief administrator of religious symbolism, the Catholic Church, had recuperated from the losses brought by the Reform and recovered its strength. The Porfirian elite had succeeded in creating an alternative civic ritual expressed systematically in a language where religious categories were adopted and redeployed.

Although the people attended and enjoyed the parades, openings, fireworks, and music of the Independence Day celebrations of 1900, they did so on their own terms. There is much evidence of verbal and physical assaults against the "rich" and the "authorities" in the 1900 celebrations—symptoms of discontent that would become more evident in time.

Thus, the forms that constitute the civic culture of a state—how it is perceived, lived, and remembered; what it reflects and chooses to celebrate of the collectivity's past in speeches, in popular or exclusive festivities, in statues and monuments—all cast a light on the attitudes and behavior of social actors, including the state. All actors sent and received messages conditioned by their "habitus" in 1900, and they also influenced its configuration and reconfiguration.

Notes

1. *El Universal*, September 18, 1900.

2. For a more comprehensive study following this viewpoint see, as an example for the specific case of England, Philip Corrigan and Derek Sayer, *The Great Cultural Revolution* (Oxford, Eng.: Blackwell, 1985).

3. H. J. Herder quoted by Isaiah Berlin, "Nacionalismo bueno y malo," in *Vuelta* 183 (Mexico) (February 1992): 13.

4. See J. M. Valenzuela Arce, "Identidades culturales: Comunidades imaginarias y contingentes," in J. M. Valenzuela, comp., *Decadencia y auge de las identidades: Cultura nacional, identidad cultural y modernización* (Tijuana, Mexico: El Colegio de la Frontera Norte, Programa Cultural de las Fronteras, 1992), 52.

5. In his monumental work on the subject of power, Michel Foucault offers numerous examples. See also Lynn Hunt, *The New Cultural History* (Berkeley: University of California Press, 1989).

6. Agnes Heller, *Historia y vida cotidiana* (Mexico: Enlace-Grijalvo, 1985), 42.

7. See H. Lefevre, *La vida cotidiana en el mundo moderno* (Madrid: Editorial Alianza, 1972), 40–41.

8. See N. García Canclini, "Introducción" to *La sociología de la cultura de Pierre Bordieu* (Mexico: Sociología y Cultura, Conaculta-Grijalvo, 1984), 34.

9. At the same time that it organizes the distribution of material and symbolic assets, society—according to Bordieu—organizes, in groups and individuals, its subjective relationship with them, their aspirations, and the awareness of what it is that each can appropriate. In this orchestration of daily life, hegemony is rooted not in a set of ideas about the inferiority of the popular classes, for example, but in a mute internalization of social inequality under the shape of unconscious dispositions inscribed in the body, in the positioning of time and space, and in the consciousness of what is possible and what is unattainable. Ibid., 35.

10. Ibid., 35–36.

11. See the Introduction and series of essays in William H. Beezley, Cheryl English Martin, and William E. French, *Rituals of Rule, Rituals of Resistance:*

Public Celebrations and Popular Culture in Mexico (Wilmington, DE: Scholarly Resources, 1994).

12. For some studies done under this perspective for the Mexican case, see F. Escalante Gonzalvo, *Ciudadanos imaginarios* (Mexico: El Colegio de México, 1996); E. Semo, "La ciudad tentacular: Notas sobre el centralismo en el siglo XX," in *Macrópolis mexicana* (Mexico: UIA-CONACULTA, 1994); and C. Nava and A. Carrillo, *Mexico en el imaginario* (Mexico: Gresal-UAM-X, 1995).

13. The dominant ideological conceptions at the end of the nineteenth century were positivism and social Darwinism. For an analysis of its specific characteristics and the relation between liberalism and positivism in Mexico, see Ch. Hale, *El liberalismo en México a fines del siglo XIX* (Mexico: Vuelta, 1990). For a well-documented analysis on the development of the Porfirian regime and its political and social actors, see F. X. Guerra, *El Antiguo Régimen y la Revolución* (Mexico: Fondo de Cultura Económica, 1988).

14. The present essay is part of a broad research project, now in progress, by the author on mentality and culture in Mexico at the turn of the century—1900—and the articulation of tradition and modernity.

15. See Florence Toussaint, *Escenario de la prensa en el porfiriato* (Mexico: Fundación Manuel Buendía, 1989), 8ff. Also see Carmen Ruiz Castañeda, *El periodismo en México. 450 años de historia* (Mexico: UNAM, 1989), 135–74.

16. According to Toussaint's estimates, it is possible to speak of a newspaper-reading elite consisting of a mere 10 percent of the population. Toussaint, *Escenario*, 69.

16. Among the most important newspapers were *El Imparcial*, founded in 1896 with state-of-the-art technology and strongly subsidized by the government (an issue could be priced at one *centavo* and thus have a large edition); *Diario del Hogar*, printed by the Liberal opposition; and the Catholic dailies *El Tiempo* and *El País*.

18. Semo, "La ciudad tentacular," 50–51.

19. The religious holidays celebrated throughout the country were January 6 and 17 (the Three Kings and Saint Anthony); February 2, Candlemas; Mardi Gras; Ash Wednesday; Holy Week's Maundy Thursday, Good Friday, Holy Saturday, and Easter Sunday; May 3 (the Holy Cross); Corpus Christi Thursday; June 24 (Saint John the Baptist); June 29 (Saints Peter and Paul's Day); July 16 (El Carmen); July 31 (Saint Ignatius Loyola, founder of the Society of Jesus); August 15 (Assumption of the Virgin Mary); November 1 and 2 (All Saints' Day and Day of the Dead); December 12 (the Virgin of Guadalupe); the ten days of *posadas*; Christmas and New Year's Eve. See Moisés González Navarro, *El porfiriato vida social* (Mexico: De. Hermes, 1973), 458–68.

20. In his famous civic homily, Gabino Barreda would announce, already on September 16, 1867, the premises of that new conception of history. Gabino Barreda, "Oración Cívica pronunciada el 16 de septiembre de 1867," in *Estudios* (Mexico: UNAM, 1941), 71–110. In first place among the main examples of "official" history during the Porfiriato is the monumental publication coordinated by V. Riva Palacios, *México a través de los siglos. Historia general y completa del desenvolvimiento social político religioso, militar, artístico, científico y literario de México desde la Antigëdad más remota hasta la época actual, 1884–1889.* Justo Sierra was the coordinator, as well as a contributor, of the foremost title in Porfirian historiography of a thoroughly positivist nature: *La evolución social de México*, published between 1901 and 1902.

21. See Annick Lempérière, "Los dos centenarios de la Independencia," in *Historia Mexicana* (Mexico, El Colegio de México) 45, no. 2 (1995): 321–22.

22. Leopoldo Zea, *El positivismo en México* (Mexico: Fondo de Cultura Económica, 1981), 94–95.

23. See María García Castro, "Identidad nacional y nacionalismo en México," *Sociológica* 21 (Mexico, UAM-A) (1993), 35.

24. *El País*, September 16, 1900.

25. See Semo, "La ciudad tentacular," 52.

26. See Beezley et al., *Rituals of Rule.*

27. *El Imparcial*, September 16, 1900.

28. Ibid., March 8, 1900.

29. Ibid., September 16, 1900.

30. Ibid., September 17, 1900.

31. Luis González Obregón, "Los aniversarios de la Independencia," *El Imparcial*, September 16, 1900.

32. Ignacio Ramírez, "Grito de muerte," ibid.

33. Manuel Gutiérrez Nájera, "El poema de Hidalgo," ibid.

34. *El Imparcial*, August 16, 1900.

35. *Diario del Hogar*, July 4, 1900.

36. Ibid.

37. Ibid.

38. Ibid.

39. Iturbide's role in the achievement of Independence is a recent historiographic phenomenon, even though in his time he enjoyed wide consensus. See G. Jiménez Codenach, "El olvido de Iturbide," in Enfoque, México, *Diario Reforma*, September 22, 1996.

40. *Diario del Hogar*, October 12, 1900.

41. Ibid., June 24, 1900.

42. Ibid., February 3, 1900.

43. Ibid., June 24, 1900.

44. Ibid., September 22, 1900.

45. Ibid., September 27, 1900.

46. Ibid.

47. *El País*, September 16, 1900.

48. Ibid.

49. *El País*, September 26, 1900.

50. Ibid.

51. Semo, "La ciudad tentacular," 52.

52. Some 3,500 pesos destined to cover the expenses of the festivities were authorized and charged to entry 141, section 45 of the General Municipal Budget, Sala de Comisiones, July 1900. Archivo Histórico del Ex-Ayuntamiento de la Ciudad de México, Archivo de Festividades 16 y 27 de septiembre de 1895 a 1915 (Tomo V, expedientes No. 128 al 168).

53. Ibid., July 24, 1900.

54. Ibid., Secretaria de Gobernación, July 3, 1900.

55. *El Tiempo*, September 18, 1900.

56. Ibid.

57. *El Imparcial* and *El Tiempo*, September 17, 18, 1900.

58. *El Tiempo*, September 18, 1900.

59. Angel del Campo Micros, "El grito," in *El Imparcial*, September 16, 1900.

60. *El País*, September 1900.

61. Angel del Campo, Micros, "El grito," 2.

62. *El Tiempo*, September 18, 1900.

63. Semo, "La ciudad tentacular," 52.
64. *El Universal*, September 1900.
65. *El Imparcial*, September 16, 1900.
66. *El Tiempo*, September 18, 1900.
67. *Diario del Hogar*, September 18, 1900.
68. *El Imparcial*, September 16, 1900.
69. *El Universal*, September 16, 1900.
70. For example, the festivity of the burning of Judas is analyzed by William H. Beezley in *Judas at the Jockey Club and Other Episodes of Porfirian Mexico* (Lincoln: University of Nebraska Press, 1987).
71. *El Tiempo*, September 18, 1900.
72. *El País*, September 16, 1900.
73. *El Universal*, September 25, 1900.
74. *El Tiempo*, September 18, 1900.
75. Moisés González Navarro, *Documentos gráficos para la historia de México* (Mexico: Editora del Sureste, 1985).
76. *El Tiempo*, September 22, 1900.
77. *El Universal*, September 18, 1900.
78. *El Imparcial*, September 17, 1900; also in *El País*, September 18, 1900.
79. *El Universal*, September 18, 1900.
80. *El País*, September 17, 1900.
81. In "Crítica de Boccaccio," *El Universal*, September 9, 1900.
82. *El Universal*, September 18, 1900.
83. Quoted by Semo in "La ciudad tentacular."
84. Valenzuela Arce, "Identidades culturales."
85. See Benedict Anderson, *Imagined Communities* (London: Verso, 1985).
86. Annick Lempérière points out that the great national heroes are useful for the enlightenment of the citizens as well as for their glorification through a parallelism with the caudillo. In Hidalgo and the First Insurgents' case she maintains that "even if their valour in combat served their main objective, their ensuing failure and the destructive and anarchic nature of their historical deeds do not allow any identification with Díaz." Their memory, she concludes, was thus marginally honored by the regime. Lempérière, "Los dos centenarios," 328. Nevertheless, the evidence found in the present essay is directed to rescuing the hero Miguel Hidalgo from the image and the values dear to the regime's logic. Historic memory is, ultimately, selective and an object of manipulation: "Hidalgo is the father of all Mexicans and a worker who seeks the peace."

CHAPTER EIGHT

1910 Mexico City
Space and Nation in the
City of the *Centenario**

MAURICIO TENORIO TRILLO

The year 1910 is one of weighty historical connotations. It is the year, according to Virginia Woolf's well-known comment, in which "human character changed,"[1] and it is also the year of the Mexican revolution. This article seeks to understand the nature—and the particular Mexican version—of the culture that in 1910 was disappearing but still feeding new cultural forms. To do so, I consider Mexico's 1910 less as the year of the Revolution than as the year of the *Centenario*.

Specifically, I deal with the centennial celebration of Mexico's independence in 1910 and its materialisation in Mexico City. But what I aim to examine are the ideal views with which the *Centenario* was conceived. These views, though they never had a concrete realisation, furnished the parameters within which social, political, cultural and economic realities were discussed. I map this celebration not in order simply to confront false and true cultural geographies of Mexico City. Rather, my purpose is to demarcate how some cultural axioms—that is, nation, state, cosmopolitanism, national culture and national history—were envisaged at a specific historical moment.

*From *Journal of Latin American Studies* 28 (February 1996): 75–104. © 1996 Cambridge University Press. Reprinted with the permission of Cambridge University Press.

El Centenario: A Postcard

1910 saw the centennial anniversary of the beginning of Mexico's independence war. As such, the year was consciously planned to be the apotheosis of a nationalist consciousness; it was meant to be the climax of an era.[2] In many ways, it was. On the one hand, it constituted a testimony to the political and economic success of a regime. On the other, the *Centenario* documented Mexico's achievement of two supreme ideals: progress and modernity.

As early as 1907, the Porfirian government established the Comisión Nacional del Centenario, which was in charge of staging the luxurious and extravagant commemoration of the centennial year. From 1907 to 1910, this commission received thousands of proposals for different ways to honour the national past. A plethora of projects was proposed: changes in the names of streets, mountains, avenues; airplane shows, monuments, parks, changes in the national flag, anthem and symbols; freedom for political prisoners and a scheme for young daughters of the elite to educate their *criadas*.[3] The Comisión Nacional appointed subcommissions to evaluate such proposals, and those made by distinguished members of the elite were often accepted. Accordingly, September (the month in which Mexico's war of independence began in 1810) witnessed thirty days of inaugurations of monuments, official buildings, institutions and streets; days filled with countless speeches, parties, cocktails, receptions and dancing fiestas.[4] A national fund was created to collect the contributions of businessmen, financiers, professional organisations and mutualist societies.[5] By September of 1910, Mexico City had acquired visible and lasting symbols of nation, progress and modernity, notions that the *Centenario* had actualised and intermingled.

From 1 to 13 September, Mexico City saw the inaugurations of a new modern Mental Hospital; a popular Hygiene Exhibition; an exhibition of Spanish art and industry, of Japanese products, and of avant-garde Mexican art; a monument to Alexander von Humboldt at the National Library; an *estación sismológica*; a new Theatre in the Escuela Nacional Preparatoria; two primary schools in the Plaza de Villamil; a new building for the Ministry of Foreign Affairs; a new school for women teachers (Escuela Normal de Maestras); a new school for men teachers (Escuela Normal de Maestros); and a new building for the Ministry of Defence. This in addition to such events as laying the foundation stones of the planned National Penitentiary in San Jerónimo Atlixco (Calzada de la Coyuya). In addition, there were opening sessions of such congresses as the 17th International Congress of Americanists, the 4th National Medical Congress, and the Congreso Pedagógico de Instrucción Primaria. Yet these were only the first thirteen days of September.

On 16 September 1810, Father Miguel Hidalgo had begun the rebellion that led to independence. Consequently, days 14, 15 and 16 became the apotheosis of the entire celebration. On the 14th, the *Gran Procesión Cívica formada por todos los elementos de la sociedad mexicana* paraded from the Alameda to the Cathedral, depositing flowers at the graves of the national heroes, and then marching to the National Palace. On the 15th, as in a good dramatic play, the theatrical tension rose with the grand *Desfile Histórico*: the entire history of the nation on foot, episode after episode; this was a march of representations of the stages of Mexico's patriotic history as understood by the official ideologues of the Porfiriato. In effect, these were walking chapters of an official history that marched over the chapters of yet another history recorded in the city itself. Accordingly, the parade traversed the chapters of the city as a history textbook—it went from the Plaza de la Reforma, along the Avenida Juárez and finally to the Plaza de la Constitución. That evening, a number of parties and receptions took place; fireworks illuminated the skies of the city and at eleven o'clock at night, Porfirio Díaz rang the bell of independence at the Zócalo, in the midst of a popular gathering. For aristocratic observers, "la noche del grito" was a quasi-tourist portrait of Mexico's popular fiestas and joy. This was the exotic Mexico that intrigued the world—an exoticism that did not compromise Mexico's cosmopolitanism but rather made it distinctive: guitars, enchiladas, *pulque* . . . But that night also saw undesired and unplanned popular discontent.[6]

September 16, in turn, was the official day of commemoration of Independence and the long-planned monument *El Angel de la Independencia* was inaugurated in the Paseo de la Reforma. A military parade went from the Paseo de la Reforma to the National Palace; and at night, luxurious dancing parties took place in various official buildings.

The celebrations continued until the end of the month. During this time, a public park was inaugurated, in a workers' neighbourhood (Balbuena) as well as a grand monument to Juárez in the Alameda; a statue of San Jorge (donated by the Italian government), in addition to a gunpowder factory in Santa Fe; the hydraulic works of Mexico City; the National University; a livestock exhibition at Coyoacán; the

Gran Canal del Desagüe; and an extension of the national peniten-tiary. Furthermore, there were ceremonies to honour the beginning of construction of the planned enormous new Palacio Legislativo, and of a monument to Pasteur. Extravagant celebrations commemo-rated Spain's and France's diplomatic courtesies: the former returned the personal belongings of the national hero, José María Morelos; in turn, France returned the Keys to Mexico City—keys that had, pre-sumably, been stolen by the French invaders (1862) (although, as Federico Gamboa pointed out, Mexico City never had an entrance, let alone a key). Finally, there was the great Apotheosis of the Caudillos and Soldiers of the War of Independence: a giant altar con-structed at the main patio of the National Palace to honour these he-roes, to which the entire government, foreign missions and the elite as a whole paid their respects. Never before had the city been so radi-cally and profusely embellished and transformed in such a short span of time. The centenary was a fleeting show, but it made a lasting mark on the city and thus it can be seen as a segment of long-lasting world views.

Mapping the Celebration

In 1910 various ideal views of the city overlapped in a limited space and time: the capital city of a hundred-year-old nation that had struggled arduously for political stability, economic development and overall modernisation. First, the ideal view of modernity, understood as harmonious and peaceful economic development, progress and science. The best embodiment of this ideal was the modern city, which contained the proofs of the nation's pedigree—economic progress and cultural greatness—but which was also sanitary, comfortable and beautiful. Second, the ideal of a long-sought coherent and unified nationality; that is, the consolidation of a modern nation-state. The particular epitome of such an ideal view was the capital city under-stood as a textbook of a civic religion, a city of monuments and well-defined public and private spaces. Finally, the modern ideal view, inseparable from the other two, of a cosmopolitan style. The quintes-sential incarnation of this ideal of cosmopolitanism was Paris itself.

To examine these ideals, I undertake tours around the city of the *Centenario*. In doing so, I seek to reconstruct how ideally it was viewed and planned for the future. The first tour surveys the streets, avenues and neighbourhoods of celebration. A second journey involves walking the streets and visiting the monuments which were part of the national history textbook. This last tour also takes us to examine the history that supported the Porfirian ideal city.

Tour 1

Since the 1880s, Mexico City's urban planning and sanitary reforms had been linked to plans for the eventual centennial celebration. The economic, symbolic and political interests that supported urban transformation were associated with the centennial celebration in two respects: on the one hand, through the long-standing idea of staging a world's fair in Mexico City to celebrate the centennial; on the other hand, by using the organisation of the *Centenario* to achieve a fundamental acceleration in the development of an ideal city within the actual city.

As when the U.S.A. celebrated the centennial of American Independence, or as Paris did to commemorate the centenary of the French Revolution, in Mexico the idea took root of celebrating the *Centenario* with a world's fair staged in Mexico City.[7] This was but a natural conclusion for all good modern nations and cities; the project was debated throughout the Porfirian period, though it never materialised. World's fairs were expensive, and it was one thing to create an image picture of Mexico to be exhibited at fairs attended by all the world, and another to make the world come to an old city full of problems. Nonetheless, these unmaterialised projects expressed ideas about how the city ought to be transformed to favour modern urban planning, sanitation reforms, nationalist symbolism and, of course, the elite's economic interests.

As early as 1889, Antonio A. de Medina y Ormaechea, founder of the Sociedad Mexicana de Consumo, conceived the idea of a universal exhibition in Mexico for the year 1910. Inspired by the 1889 Paris exhibition, he claimed that, like France, Mexico ought to celebrate the centennial anniversary of its major historical event, that is, its independence, with the first Mexican universal exhibition.[8] Medina y Ormaechea argued that a Mexican world's fair would help to educate and modernise Indians, who "se conforman con una camisa y un calzón de manta para cubrir sus carnes, con unos guaraches para calzar sus pies . . . con una cazuela de chile, frijoles y tortillas y una medida de pulque." A Mexico City world's fair would also serve to show that Mexico had achieved international standards of comfort, sanitation and general progress. Armed with these arguments, Medina y Ormaechea persisted in advocating his project for the rest of the century, but it was never realised.[9]

From the 1890s to the 1910s, the idea of a universal exposition in Mexico City to celebrate Mexico's centennial of independence re-emerged with various sponsorships. The first such occasion was in the 1890s. By this date, companies—often funded by North American capital—that specialised in the management and organisation of world's fairs came together with Mexican and foreign private interests involved in Mexico City's profitable urban development, to envision a Mexican fair. For instance, a specialist at organising European exhibitions, René de Cornely, interested a group of Mexican politicians and industrialists in staging an international exhibition from September 1895 to April 1896 in Mexico City. This exhibition was publicised and indeed arranged almost to the last detail.[10] The former hacienda of Anzures, near the Paseo de la Reforma and Chapultepec Park, owned by the wealthy speculator Salvador Malo, was the proposed location for the fair.[11] Indeed, a Mexican, Ignacio Bejarano, served as front for an international concern involved with Mexico City real estate. In 1896, Bejarano informed Porfirio Díaz that the Land Company of New York had become the Mexican National Exposition and Land Company.[12] As such, it had bought all the Anzures lands. Subsequently, friction developed between the company and the Mexican government.[13] There the matter rested—yet another project for a Mexican world's fair that never materialised. The same occurred with the proposal by Fernando Pimentel y Fagoaga of the Banco Central Mexicano in 1908. In *The Mexican Financier*, Pimentel y Fagoaga offered to collect 2 to 3 million pesos among the Mexican financiers by coining five hundred commemorative coins. With this he proposed to organise a major world's fair around El Castillo de Chapultepec and on the grounds on both sides of the Paseo de la Reforma. The commission for the centenary responded negatively, arguing lack of time to organise such a fair.[14]

Another attempt to organise an exhibition led to the construction of the Mexican Crystal Palace. In 1895 the Compañía Mexicana de Exposiciones constructed a steel and crystal structure in Germany to serve as the Mexican Palace for permanent exhibitions in Mexico City. However, by 1903 the company was dissolved, and one of its wealthiest investors, José Landero y Cos, became the owner of the building. In 1910 the government decided to acquire the building and assembled it at the site known as El Chopo at Santa María la Ribera.

The Mexican Crystal Palace was then used to house the Japanese Exhibition during the centennial celebration and afterwards became the National Museum of Natural History.[15] In this way, after the many attempts to celebrate the centennial anniversary of independence with a world's fair, at last a Crystal Palace *à la Mexicaine* became part of the celebration.

Nevertheless, what these planned fairs included was the notion of developing the ideal city along the spinal column of the Paseo de la Reforma. Every plan involved the grounds surrounding the Paseo de la Reforma (whether at Chapultepec or at Anzures). This was but an echo of the process of urbanisation that Mexico City underwent beginning in 1890. The old colonial city was abandoned by the elite who moved to the new suburbs growing to the west of the city. In fact, the entire *Centenario* was an episode in the development of this ideal city.

One can clearly distinguish the borders of the ideal city—from the inside out—by mapping the celebration. Or, one could delimit the ideal city from the outside in: for instance, by following the geographical limits established by the Consejo Superior de Salubridad for the distribution and consumption of pulque in Mexico City.[16] The ideal city was a hybrid model derived from the ancient colonial Spanish urban tradition,[17] combined with the influence of nineteenth-century European urban planning.[18] Hence, the ancient (political, cultural and geographical) centre was extended through main avenues that linked the new comfortable modern suburbs with the old city. During the centennial celebration, all the monuments, events and parades appeared within (and were part of the making of) this ideal city.

Beginning in the 1880s, Mexico City experienced a selective and pragmatic urban transformation in part inspired by that made in Paris by Baron Georges-Eugène Haussmann, as well as in the British and American versions of garden cities. Thus, avenues were developed on the model of the Champs-Elysées, and suburbs that combined urban comfort with the beauty and health of gardens grew to the west of the city.[19] There, residences at the edges of Reforma were required to keep eight metres of garden on the front façade.[20]

Buenos Aires, which also experienced a centennial celebration in 1910, is a good parallel. It underwent a major Haussmann-like transformation and, like Mexico city, experienced its first radical reshaping from the 1880s to 1910s. In both cities the elites moved out from their traditional setting to the Casa Quinta (Buenos Aires) or to new elegant *colonias* (Mexico City).[21] Public space was reshaped and resegregated in order to accommodate the growing population of foreign immigrants in Buenos Aires, and of workers and internal immigrants in Mexico City. In addition, public space was reshaped according to new cosmopolitan fashions—required format for all modern capital cities.[22] Therefore, in Buenos Aires "se abandona la vieja ciudad y se recrea París,"[23] in Mexico "la ciudad multiplica prodigiosamente el número de sus barrios modernos . . . las clases acomodadas han construido una verdadera ciudad de atractivos chalets y residencias suntuosas al poniente de la población."[24]

In Mexico, most of the planned workers' *barrios* and wealthy neighbourhoods were developed in the 1900s.[25] To the north-east such *barrios* as Santa María and Guerrero housed middle-class workers and artisans, and the newly developed *colonias* Morelos, La Bolsa, Díaz de León. Rastro, Maza and Valle Gómez were Mexican versions of proletarian quarters.[26] For their part, Indian communities remained on neglected and impoverished sites at the edges of the city.[27] In contrast, the west was developed with two huge projects for the growing urban middle class, the *colonias* San Rafael and Limantour. Finally, during the 1900s the south-west became the city of wealth, style and power with such *colonias* as Juárez, Cuauhtémoc, Roma and Condesa. These last *colonias* were connected to the traditional city through the Paseo de la Reforma, Avenida Juárez, and such fashionable streets as San Francisco. In turn, Cinco de Mayo linked the old city to the not so new but still elegant San Cosme. Electrification and modern street planning accompanied these new urban developments.[28] These transformations followed the pace of consolidation of a relatively authoritarian and centralist national administration, which has proved to be a necessary component of this type of urban changes in Latin American and European cities as well.[29]

The *Centenario* could be seen as the final touch in the demarcation of the ideal city conceived by the Porfirian elite. This ideal encompassed the Zócalo and its surroundings, ran west to the Alameda and then along the Paseo de la Reforma as far as Chapultepec. On the south side of Reforma, the ideal city ended at the Río de la Piedad, and that border went from there to Niño Perdido and back to downtown. On the north side, the limit blurred into haciendas and countryside (especially Anzures and Los Morales).[30]

During the *Centenario*, the streets and avenues around the Paseo de la Reforma were embellished with commemorative posters, electric lights, flowers, medallions and the national colours—white, red and green.[31] The decoration constantly reiterated the Latin word *Pax*.

The ideal city combined Haussmann-like rebuilding with garden city elements, and this combination acquired an accelerated pace during the *Centenario*. In addition, the ideal city, as [John] Lear has argued, included the project of "ridding the centre of the poor . . . the Government wished to eliminate the presence of the poor so close to the corridors of power and wealth and feared the problems of health and morality."[32] In truth, the ideal city was developed apart from the rest of the city. By 1906 an architect clearly distinguished the existence of two cities within the city:

> Entre el México oriental y occidental hay una diferencia marcadísima; aquel vetusto, triste, angosto, a menudo tortuoso y siempre sucio, con callejas insignificantes, plazuelas desiertas y anticuadas, puentes ruinosos, depósitos de agua pantosa y casas insignificantes de adobe, donde se albergan gentes miserables; éste por su parte, moderno, alegre, amplio, trazado a cordel, limpio, con calles cuidadosamente pavimentadas, parques frondosos, jardines y alamedas, pasages en condiciones satisfactorias, y residencias confortables, elegantes, algunas del peor gusto pero ciertamente costosas, aseadas, importantes, y que llevan el sello indiscutible de influencia moderna.[33]

Mexico's Haussmanns laid out avenues and boulevards, but, unlike their European counterparts, they did not have to destroy urban sectors or to relocate large inhabited zones. Instead, they displaced *campesinos* and Indian communities from the nearby haciendas. Indeed, compared to Europe, where urban reform was considered a matter of social reform and internal security, or the product of "catastrophic change,"[34] in Mexico it was a manner of frontier expansion. The ideal city, therefore, was conceived as a conquest not only over tradition, chaos and backwardness but also over nature. What the Porfirian elite did was to blend, on the one hand, ancient urban planning, architecture and old symbols and forms of domination with, on the other, a new planned urban landscape and new social stratification. Therefore, the Zócalo remained the central point of departure, but the Paseo de la Reforma became the path of power, the representation of the course of the nation towards supreme order and progress: from the Plaza de la Reforma (with the statue of Carlos IV, *El Caballito*) to Columbus's monument, past Cuauhtémoc and the monument to Independence, arriving, finally, at the Castillo de Chapultepec (the Presidential residence).[35] According to an organic conception of the city, other parts of the city were developed to serve as providers, storage or a working complement for the ideal city.

As in Paris, parks were developed within the ideal city. Since the time of Maximilian, Chapultepec had become the prime example of Mexico's modern urban gardens. The new luxurious suburbs were demonstrations of the modern combination of urban comfort and green beauty. The development of parks in zones outside the limits of the ideal city was a matter of debate concerning the sanitary, moral and regenerating aspects of nature, especially in regard to their effects on Indians and the lower classes. Throughout the 1890s and 1900s, defenders of the ecological conservation of the city spoke out, but their opinions were ignored. In fact, the workers' park at Balbuena, constructed for the *Centenario*, was one of the very few parks developed outside the ideal city.[36]

As part of the events of the *Centenario*, Miguel Angel de Quevedo delivered a report, "Espacios libres en el interior de las ciudades, su adaptación en plazas monumentales, en jardínes, plazas con árboles o squares y terrenos de juego."[37] Quevedo explained how, as director of Mexico City's public works, he sought to shift the official preference for luxurious French-style gardens in favour of simple "squares" that could accommodate trees and provide healthy recreation for the lower classes. He therefore presented a project for a garden in the populous Calzada de la Viga. No grounds were available at La Viga, but an alternative location was the 96 hectares at Balbuena, and as a result the workers' park of Balbuena was created in order to make "nuestra querida capital como el París de América."[38]

Although for the current victims of Mexico City, the late twentieth-century *ville-monstre*,[39] a bucolic Mexico City would seem a part of a mythical past, there were in fact many forests near Mexico City, as Quevedo explained. However, deforestation meant that ample deserts extended between, for example, Mexico City and Tacubaya, Santa Fe and Santa Lucía. These broad tracts caused terrible duststorms and pollution. Despite these problems, it seems that the ideal city epitomised by the *Centenario* had no strong "bucolic" content. Historically the Mexican elites had had an urban attachment, though their fortunes often had rural origins. Since colonial times prestige and status were urban or nothing. But by the early twentieth century the model of the garden city and the planning of parks and gardens were cosmopolitan ideals that the Porfirian elite aimed to pursue. In Mexico, however, there were neither strong bourgeois "populist-rural" traditions, nor the contradictions commonly associated with "the machine in the garden." Unlike American Jeffersonians or those American urbanisers who sought a balance between city and countryside, Mexican elites (like most Latin American elites) regarded the city as the only form of true civilisation.[40]

In this sense, the ideal city consolidated by the Porfirians should be seen as a civilising process, as a frontier expansion. The civilising conquest began the slow physical blurring of the firm distinction between city and countryside. In an 1870s José María Velasco landscape canvas of the Valley of Mexico, we can clearly point out where the city ended and where the countryside began. By the 1910s, the Porfirian ideal city had reshaped the old city, but had also colonised (through *colonias*) what was believed the uncivilised "emptiness" of the countryside. Thereafter, the city gradually lost its firm physical borders. Nonetheless, socially and massively, as Alan Knight has observed, it was the revolution—which brought Indians and provincial elites to the capital—that began the merging of city and countryside.[41] By the 1940s, with rapid industrialisation, the uncivilised countryside could be found in Mexico City less in reality than in many popular nostalgic films of *charros* and haciendas.

The Mexican elite shared with their European and North American counterparts a belief in the evil and degenerating characteristics of cities. Agglomeration, pollution, lack of nature and industrialisation led to corruption, laziness and degeneration of races, as crystallised in Federico Gamboa's myth of Santa.[42] But the Mexicans had an almost blind confidence that upon achieving a modern city—and not a bucolic return to nature—those evil by-products of urban development would be overcome. In this sense, the achieved ideal city of the *Centenario* was both the climax of the city of wealth, and the main therapeutic measure for the poor.

In addition, the *Centenario* furnished and re-arranged the main *lieux de mémoire* of the nation.[43] The monument to Independence was placed along the Paseo de la Reforma. The old project of having monuments of distinguished citizens from every single state of the nation along the Paseo de la Reforma re-emerged.[44] In the Alameda, on Benito Juárez avenue, the elaborate monument to Juárez was constructed.[45]

The monument to Independence, designed by the architect Antonio Rivas Mercado, echoed the theme epitomised by the entire Paseo. Rivas Mercado feared that the column would be overshadowed by the size of nearby trees and houses, so he built a 35-metre column from which the entire city could be viewed: on one side, the Castillo de Chapultepec; on the other, the Alameda and the Zócalo. Between these two points along the Paseo, there were luxurious modern urban developments. The ancient and aristocratic old Mexico and the new ideal city were thus united in a single panorama from the standpoint of a towering monument, from a great historical moment (independence).[46] I will return to this monument later.

Other monuments were inaugurated, several of them gifts from foreign missions. For instance, in the sumptuous Colonia Roma, a statue of Garibaldi was erected, donated by Italy. In general, the avalanche of monuments fitted within the parameters of the ideal city. The same was true of all centennial parades which traversed the planned geography of the ideal city, whose avenues synthesised Mexican modernism and cosmopolitanism as well as national history. A parade of allegorical chariots rolled from the Plaza de la Reforma to the Plaza de la Constitución (Zócalo). A *Gran Procesión Cívica* went from the Glorieta de Colón to the Alameda. In turn, the military parade went from the monument to Independence to Avenida Juárez and then along Calle San Francisco to the National Palace. The Paseo de Antorchas followed the same path, as did the acclaimed *Desfile Histórico*. By traversing these streets and avenues, the parades occupied public space that was at the same time an urban utopia and a conceptualisation of the nation's history.

In addition the *Centenario*, as part of the world's cycle of centennial celebrations, included a number of diplomatic missions.[47] The city that hosted these envoys of the world was the city of *Centenario*, the ideal city. That could be easily observed in the way most of the diplomats were accommodated. Although there were comfortable and luxurious hotels in Mexico City, as well as many large diplomatic residences, the Ministry of Foreign Relations had since 1909 compiled a list of "casas que pudieran utilizarse para dar hospitalidad a las delegaciones que vengan del extranjero al Centenario."[48] Thus the ideal city welcomed the world, literally, at home, in the various houses of the small and tightly interrelated Porfirian elite. Most of the houses that were identified as potential accommodations were located along the Paseo de la Reforma and Avenida Juárez, and the environs of these avenues. The families that acted as hosts were wealthy and distinguished members of the Porfirian elite: Landero y Cos, Braniff, Landa y Escandón, Limantour, Scherer, Pasquel and Pearson, among others.[49]

The inaugurated and the planned new buildings were located either within or outside the ideal city of the centenary, depending on their function. There were buildings to house undesirables, and these were of course located outside the limits of the ideal city, as was the national mental hospital (at the Hacienda de la Castañeda), and the penitentiaries (San Lázaro and San Jacinto). In contrast, it was projected that the great new Palacio Legislativo would be an inherent part of the ideal city, a prolongation of Avenida Juárez. The same was true of the planned new Mexican Opera House, which was to be placed between the Alameda and the new luxurious Edificio de Correos, facing the replanned Avenida Cinco de Mayo. When the old National Theatre at the end of Cinco de Mayo was demolished, the avenues of the new ideal city were embellished. Therefore, when Cinco de Mayo became the direct link between the Zócalo, the Alameda and the new Opera House, a contest was held to select the most beautiful of the many new buildings that lined the street.[50]

These buildings and streets formed the desired core of the ideal city: instead of antiquated colonial buildings, the National Palace would form a straight line with the huge neoclassic republican parliamentary palace designed by a distinguished French engineer. This straight path included the luxurious San Francisco street and the Avenida Juárez, and along them the modern monument of Juárez, the Alameda park, and the new Art Nouveau marble white Opera House. This was indeed a cosmopolitan urban mirage.

The ideal city was also demarcated by a sort of *cordon sanitaire*. A city free of miasma and illness was a difficult achievement in the Valley of Mexico, with its long history of floods and epidemics. Nonetheless, the city of the *Centenario* saw the conclusion of the Desagüe works. It also hosted the first large popular hygienic exhibition, built a national penitentiary, opened a new modern mental hospital and forced Indians to shower and dress in trousers.

The organisers of the *Centenario* considered that the city needed to be whitened racially and culturally. During the centennial, pursuit of this goal reached extreme levels. As John Lear shows, there were various efforts to eradicate the presence of Indians and the lower classes from the ideal city. But the very functional needs of the ideal city required the presence of Indians and all kinds of servants and workers. To solve this dilemma during the *Centenario* a solution was found: if we cannot get rid of them, at least let us camouflage them.

Indians habitually wandered throughout the city in *calzón de manta* and *guaraches*. Therefore, during the *Centenario* influential Mexican diplomats proposed either prohibiting Indians from circulating in the city during the celebration, or dressing them properly: "Vistámosla [a la población indígena] y obligémosla a que use pantalones y blusa y calzado."[51] Not only because "¿qué dirán los extranjeros?" but because it was important to make the Indian population "tener necesidades," so that "para vivir tenga que trabajar." For Indians, it was argued in this kind of proposal, "para conseguir un cariño es casi fisiológico el procurar agradar. Nuestro pelado enamora y lo hace con la cabellera hirsuta y los pies descalzos. Aun entre salvajes cuando uno de ellos pretende a la hembra, se ponen sus collares más vistosos."[52]

These proposals were part of the hygienic needs of the ideal city. Since the 1880s, Mexican hygienists had been dealing with urban-planning theories and practices of the hygienic city. By the 1900s this manoeuvering was linked both to urban developers' interests and to the growing influence of positivist ideas. Consequently, to a certain extent the sanitary city was made possible at least within the limits of the ideal city. The team of doctors and engineers that since the 1880s had been in charge of Mexico's sanitation were all actively involved in the centennial celebration.[53]

In accordance with the hygienic focus, the national penitentiary was rebuilt for the centennial celebration, and the foundation stone of the new structure was laid on the grounds of San Jacinto Atlixco in the south-east of the city. Since the 1880s, a commission had been studying the possibility of establishing a modern national penitentiary.[54] Once it was established, the engineering problems proved to be many, and the space was inadequate for the needs of the city. At this point, a Mexican criminologist observed that a large penitentiary was especially needed because of Mexico's racial heterogeneity which, he believed, increased crime.[55] Therefore, a horizontal extension of the penitentiary was planned in 1908 and finished in time for the centennial.[56]

The same could be argued of the mental hospital of La Castañeda, one of the many public construction contracts granted to Porfirio Díaz Jr.[57] A special commission to plan a new mental hospital had been appointed in the 1890s. Distinguished hygienists and sanitary engineers were members of the commission. In 1906, at the Pan-American Medical Congress, the results were presented. The design for the new hospital was an immense complex of 24 buildings located in 141,600 square metres in the former Hacienda of La Castañeda, which was previously owned by Salvador Malo, the prominent urban real estate speculator. The hospital was, it was argued, "a la vanguardia del alienismo mundial."[58] Although outside the ideal city, the hospital assisted the needs of a city of modern times in which *fin-de-siècle surmenages* could drive anybody crazy.

An Hygienic Exhibition and a National Congress of Medicine completed the picture of a hygienic city. The Hygiene Exhibition was organised by the Consejo Superior de Salubridad, that is, by Eduardo Liceaga, who for decades had been in charge of Mexico's hygiene as permanent director of the Consejo Superior de Salubridad.[59] In fact, the exhibition was a copy of many of the kind that had been organised at European world's fairs during the late nineteenth century. The goal of these exhibitions was not only to display advances in hygiene, but, more importantly, to popularise basic notions of hygiene. The greatest advance of hygienic theory was to make hygiene a concern of the state, beyond the common distinction between the public and private realms. The Hygiene Exhibition was placed at a special site constructed on the avenue of Los Hombres Ilustres. It was a free show of hygiene that, like the famous exhibition at the 1889 Paris world's fair, included models of *la maison salubre* and of *la maison insalubre*, as well as models of water supply systems, pumps and a number of publications and statistics of the Consejo Superior de Salubridad. The paraphernalia of Mexican hygienists, which had been exhibited around the world to produce Mexico's modern image, were now displayed in Mexico City for the benefit of Mexicans.[60]

Tour 2

The city of the *centenario* was the city of written and re-written history, erected in monuments and piled over and over again on the same sites. In order to examine this history, let us limit our tour to four main vistas. That is, let us examine first the two principal monuments that were inaugurated in 1910 and the exercise of historical reconstruction represented by the *Desfile Histórico*. Second, the tour reviews the historiographical rewriting of the *Centenario*.

Since the Paseo de la Reforma was the spine of the ideal city, it was natural that the city as a textbook of national history should be written along this avenue and its surroundings. In the 1880s the Porfirian government pondered the plan to make the Paseo de la Reforma an exact chronological reconstruction of the nation's history, from its origins to its modern peace and progress. The Emperor Maximilian, a heterodox Haussmannian, and his architect Louis Bolland, originally designed the Paseo as a modern way to link the Castillo de Chapultepec with the Zócalo (1865).[61] Since 1852, the monument of

Carlos IV (known as *El Caballito*) had been placed at the Plaza de la Reforma, marking the beginning of the Paseo. This was also the case of the monument of Columbus, designed by the French sculptor Carlos Cordier, which was erected in the 1860s by Antonio Escandón, and placed at the next circle in the Paseo on the way from Juárez to Chapultepec.[62] Next came Cuauhtémoc, one of the most important products of Porfirian *indigenismo*, whose statue was inaugurated in 1886; it was the glorification of Mexico's great Indian past.[63] Following this sequence, it was thought that the Paseo could present a precise narration of Mexico's history: Spanish past (*El Caballito*), discovery (Columbus), Indian past (Cuauhtémoc), and the logical conclusion, the great monument to Independence. Hence, in 1910 the Angel of Independence was placed in the next circle after Cuauhtémoc. Plans existed to construct another monument at the last circle before Chapultepec: an Arch of Triumph that would celebrate the achievement of peace and its main hero, Porfirio Díaz.[64] The debate was intense, and financial problems limited the plans. Besides, it seems that Díaz hesitated to accept a monument to himself. Therefore, the *Centenario* limited the "monument fever" to two important pieces of history set in stone: the monument to Independence, and that to Juárez.

The monument to Independence has endured as Mexico City's symbol, and indeed was conceived as the universal symbol of Mexico's modernity and sovereignty. The designer, Antonio Rivas Mercado, was one of the few Mexican architects favoured with contracts for major national constructions. But Rivas Mercado was a French-trained architect, a follower of the Paris Beaux-Arts style, who had lived in London and Paris for many years.[65] After winning the contract for the monument to Independence in 1906, he was sent to Europe to study sculptural works in France and Italy.[66] Rivas Mercado decided to place a Winged Victory standing on a column rooted on a vast base that encompassed more symbols and made the column taller.[67] The Winged Victory, a half-naked Greek-like woman carrying laurels, was the quintessential representation of republican liberty throughout the nineteenth century.[68] In 1910, for the first time, Mexico obtained its own version of this classical symbol.

At the centre of the base, a bronze composition represented an enormous lion guided by a little boy, and in each corner of the lower base there were representations of Law, Justice, War and Peace. The lion and the boy, according to Rivas Mercado, depicted "el pueblo, fuerte en la guerra y dócil en la paz." The statue of Hidalgo was placed on the upper base, facing the city, "recibiendo el homenaje de la Patria y de la Historia." Also on the upper base, on either side of Hidalgo, were statues of Morelos, Guerrero Mina and Bravo. All the marble statues were designed by the sculptor Enrique Alciati and were made in Carrara; the bronze statues were made in Florence, and the decorations of the monument in Paris. The entire composition formed another *mélange* of republican neoclassic symbolism. There was nothing particularly Mexican about it, nor should there have been: republicanism and nationalism were regarded as universal values.[69]

The Juárez monument was located in the Alameda, along the avenue which carried his name. The monument was a fundamental icon of the Porfirian pantheon: Benito Juárez was the epitome of nineteenth-century liberalism which Porfirio Díaz constantly invoked, regardless of his own ideological transformations. Juárez was considered the provider of justice for the nation, in what was then called the second independence (*La Reforma*). He was the architect of modernising liberal reforms and the commander against the French invasion. What Juárez represented was the political and military background of Díaz's generation, which by 1910 was almost obsolete. But the monument was so important for the regime's symbolic purposes that originally it was intended to locate it just in front of the National Palace, in the Zócalo. The influential and "modern" urban-planning view of Finance Minister José Y. Limantour encouraged a change of plans, and thus the monument was located on Avenida Juárez on one side of the Alameda, even though this meant dismantling and relocating the Mexican Alhambra—Mexico's pavilion at the 1884 New Orleans world's fair.[70]

In the 1890s, a national commission for the construction of the monument of Juárez was created.[71] A contest for the model was organised, and the winner was Guillermo Heredia's design. His was a grand project for a marble monument weighing 1,625 tons and occupying 510 square metres. The monument represented Juárez seated on a regal throne with two allegoric women surrounding him and a gardenia on his head. As de la Barra described it, the monument had a "puro estilo helénico, divina mezcla de dulzura y fuerza, majestad y de gracia, evoca su contemplación el hermoso pensamiento de Hegel: 'la belleza es la identidad del pensamiento y de la forma.' "[72] Such a style suited Juárez as hero, because, it was argued during the inauguration, he was "firme ante el huracán desbordante de las pasiones." Two bronze lions, designed by the Mexican sculptor Guillermo Cárdenas, concluded the monument. All the marble and bronze works were contracted in Paris.[73]

Unlike the monument of Cuauhtémoc that was meant to honour a mythical Indian past, the monument of Juárez was dedicated to an Indian and sought to honour the present. Here was an Indian who responded to contemporary universal values—republicanism, liberty and justice—although Juárez's jacobinism was not mentioned in this selective Porfirian reappropriation of the *Benemérito de las Américas*. Juárez carried a message, as Carlos Robles eloquently argued during the inauguration of the monument, for Mexicans and foreigners alike: "¡He aquí la carne de mi carne, la sangre de mi sangre! Juárez es mío, pero también vuestro; pertenece a la Humanidad."[74] An Indian who belonged to humanity had to be represented in an Hellenic fashion and in white marble. There was a design for a Juárez monument in Zapoteco style, but the Juárez centennial commission judged it a "brave" but improper project.[75]

With both the Juárez and the Independence monuments, the ideal city acquired a coherent set of icons that made the idea of nation discursively, ideologically and physically real. This was a national history and a specific conception of a liberal and republican consensus that made the nation possible and durable. Whether read from the Zócalo to Chapultepec or from Chapultepec to the Zócalo, the Paseo de la Reforma told the same story, fulfilling the ideal of a patriotic history: to make history a perfect unmistakable palindrome, with no conflicts or contradictions.

In turn, the *Desfile Histórico* was the momentary reshaping of the public space to make it into a perfect simulacrum of the official past. Like the Paseo de la Reforma itself, the *Desfile* was divided into three great eras: Conquest, Spanish rule and Independence. Conquest was allegorised by a specific historical event that belonged to the chapter "Conquest." The selected event was acted out and turned into history-in-motion. This historical event was Moctezuma's meeting with Cortés outside Mexico City. The parade was composed of one thousand persons, mostly Indians, divided into warriors, priests, captains, virgins and kings. The Spanish group of the scene was constituted by a troop of men on horseback, by Cortés and doña Marina, as well as by a company of Tlaxcatecan Indians. The procession marched from the Plaza de la Reforma towards the Zócalo.

The scene selected to represent Spanish domination was *El Paseo del Pendón*—the colonial ceremony organised in Mexico City to commemorate the anniversary of Conquest (every 13 August). The scene was formed by 800 persons[76] dressed in colonial style and aligned according to colonial hierarchy (headed by the Viceroy and the members of the Ayuntamiento). The parade went from San Hipólito towards Calle San Diego, and from San Francisco towards the Zócalo.

Finally, the era of independence was originally planned to include more than ten different scenes.[77] But in the end the independence was represented only by the entrance into Mexico City of the Ejército Trigarante, headed by Iturbide. This was an inclusive depiction of the insurgent army including its commanders, Agustín de Iturbide, Vicente Guerrero, Manuel Mier y Terán, Guadalupe Victoria and Anastasio Bustamante. The procession was followed by many allegorical carriages, equipped by the various states, representing scenes of the War of Independence that took place in their particular territories.[78] It went from the Plaza de la Reforma (in *El Caballito*) towards the National Palace at the Zócalo.

It was estimated that more than fifty thousand people witnessed the entire *Desfile Histórico*. This was the first time that such a public lesson had taken place in Mexico City.[79] Indeed, the *Desfile Histórico* was from the outset thought to be a conscious pedagogic and visual nationalistic lecture, specifically meant to target the special needs of illiterate Mexicans, but in allegorical language understandable to the world at large. Such influential personalities as Guillermo de Landa y Escandón and José Casarín were the original choreographers of the *Desfile*.[80] And they aimed to make it a nationalistic lesson, but one that could be pedagogic (magnificent), historically accurate (scientific), multicomprehensive (to include all groups in the depiction of the nation); a lesson that was supported by, and paraphrased, the story told by the city.

The designers of the project emphasised the importance of authenticity and historical accuracy. All clothing "estará ajustada rigurosamente a la verdad histórica." Casarín sent envoys to such states as Oaxaca, San Luis Potosí, Tlaxcala, Morelos and Chiapas as well as to the National Penitentiary in search of Indians. For instance, he wrote to the governor of Tlaxcala, Próspero Cahuantzi, an Indian himself, requesting 110 Tlaxcalan Indians to join the representation of Cortés meeting Moctezuma. From the governor of San Luis Potosí, Manuel Sánchez Rivero, he requested 250 Indians, and, "si fuera posible," 20 Indian women "de las más hermosas."[81] In the same way, Spanish organisations were asked for "native" or native-looking Spaniards to represent *gachupines* in the various scenes of the *Desfile Histórico*.[82]

The emphasis on historical accuracy was but one of the echoes of a scientific era.

The emphasis was expressed not only in the historical accuracy of the *Desfile*, but more importantly in the many scientific events which had to do with Mexico's past. In these congresses, the themes of science, nation and race were discussed. The relationship between science and nation had as its pivotal topic the intricate interrelation between the conceptualisation of modern nation, cosmopolitan city and race. In the last analysis, what this interrelation showed (at least in its materialisation in the ideal city) was the insurmountable ambivalence of Porfirian scientists and thinkers in regard to race: while fostering the universal acceptance of a mestizo nation, they had to manipulate international and national sciences, and prejudices that were applied against Indians, in order to produce both modern science and a cosmopolitan nation.

As part of the *Centenario*, and for the second time in Mexico, the prestigious scientific Congress of Americanists was organised in Mexico City (it was simultaneously hosted in Buenos Aires, which was also celebrating Argentina's centennial).[83] The 17th Congress of Americanists was indeed of great significance for the history of Mexican anthropology and archaeology. The reconstruction of Teotihuacán was concluded and the celebration was a good excuse to publicise Mexico as the Egypt of America. In addition, as a result of the 17th Congress of Americanists, the International School of Anthropology was created in Mexico City, headed by Franz Boas, and sponsored by the Porfirian regime.[84] Simultaneously, the first *Indianista* Congress took place, as well as the Pedagogical Congress.

Together, these congresses in Mexico City displayed the several ambivalent approaches to Mexico's Indian reality. An ancient Las Casas type of paternalism combined with late nineteenth-century scientific racism and with innovative forms of culturalist anthropology and romantic *ateneismo*. By and large, there existed a consensus on the perfectibility of Indians through education. Moreover, by 1910 the celebration of a mestizo nation had already acquired importance, producing a scientific and ideological infrastructure that would survive for the rest of the century. In both, the *indianista* and the Americanists' congresses, the glorification of *mestizaje*—often considered a post-revolutionary accomplishment—was a fundamental ingredient.[85] No one better embodied the particularly ambivalent *indigenismo* and pro-*mestizaje* of the Porfiriato than Justo Sierra. He stated at the inauguration of the 17th Congress of Americanists: "Todo ese mundo pre-cortesiano . . . es nuestro, es nuestro pasado, nos lo hemos incorporado . . . [a] nuestra verdadera historia nacional, la que data de la unión de conquistados y conquistadores para fundar un pueblo mestizo que (permitidme esta muestra de patriótico orgullo) está adquiriendo el derecho de ser grande."[86]

However, the consensus on *mestizaje* contrasted with the many scientific evaluations of Indians as inferior, degenerative, and—for the national development—an obstructive race. The Congress of Americanists generated many papers dealing with the racial inferiority of Indians studied through bone measuring and the anthropometry of Indians' skulls.

Another view of Indians was expressed by the Congress of *Indianistas*.[87] Following both a Catholic and quasi-Lascasian approach and nineteenth-century biological thought, this Congress promoted the education and welfare of Indians in order to foster the achievement of a real and homogenous nation. Jesús Díaz de León, a member of the Sociedad Indianista Mexicana, observed that Mexico was constituted by some surviving indigenous kingdoms. One of these kingdoms dominated the rest, "los convirtió en elementos de nutrición para su desarrollo." In this sense, for Díaz de León, Mexico's war of independence was a sort of "incomplete" physiological revolution. *Indianismo* was not a utopian movement, but a biological trend that would select the best Indian attributes and project them towards a progressive future.[88]

Indianismo and pro-*mestizaje* contrasted with the revival of a deep-rooted pro-Hispanism on the part of the Porfirian elite. This renewed pro-Hispanism was particularly noticeable in the number of homages and speeches dedicated to Spain, *la madre patria*. Unlike previous decades, the official position was profoundly favourable to Spain, and Porfirio Díaz himself stated: "Si España ufánase de habernos dado vida, México se enorgullece de reconocerlo y proclamarlo."[89]

This official switch in the national history was made through a variety of diplomatic formalities as well as the natural tools of patriotic history: books, monuments, cities. As part of its homage to Mexico during the *Centenario*, Spain returned Morelos's possessions to Mexico, and granted the honorific Order of Carlos III to Porfirio Díaz. In return, Mexico inaugurated a monument for Isabel la Católica and splendidly honoured the Spanish envoy, the Marqués de Polavieja.

This pro-Hispanic switch was a result both of a generational change of the political elite (the old jacobin anti-Spanish liberals had been supplanted by the *cientificos*), and of a deliberate attempt to display reconciliation in the context of the 100th anniversary of the nation's birth. The new generation was strongly marked by a new modernist language, as Darío and Rodó had articulated it. In such a language, a quasi-racist Hispanism—mostly directed against the North American "lion"—was a fundamental component. In addition, within an organicist scheme, reconciliation was considered a sign of physical and cultural maturity. As Pimentel y Fagoaga, president of the Ayuntamiento of Mexico City, stated at the dedication of Calle Isabel la Católica: "Bien podemos decirlo hoy que la creciente cultura del pueblo mexicano ha borrado, con el agua lustral de un cosmopolitismo bien entendido y mejor practicado, los prejucios, los odios, y los rencores que impedían en no muy lejanos días el reconocer merecimientos como los que motivan la presente ceremonia."[90]

However strong this renewed Hispanism was, it had to be constantly adapted and accommodated to *indigenismo, indianismo* and pro-*mestizaje*. Nonetheless, the fact that in 1910 this sort of pro-Hispanism became so apparent helps to explain why the generation that was coming of age at this precise moment pushed these tendencies further: consider, for instance, the case of José Vasconcelos and the *Ateneo de la Juventud*. But it also helps to explain why the 1930s Indigenist reaction was so powerful.

These tendencies were part of the continual rewriting of the national history. Monuments, parades, streets and even modern movie pictures[91] were the pens with which the *Centenario* wrote the national history. New heroes were revindicated, or new virtues were found in the eternal heroes, all according to the context of the 1900s. With one last revealing example of implicit historical revisionism we conclude our visits to the centennial city. In 1910, Porfirio Parra accepted a proposal to alter stanzas of the national anthem. Accordingly, the fourth stanza was totally expunged, and the seventh was modified significantly. The fourth, a glorification of [General Antonio López de] Santa Ana, had remained unnoticed by official historians. The seventh stanza alluded to the problematic figure of the conservative Emperor, Agustín de Iturbide. The historiographical ambivalence towards the role of Iturbide in the war of independence was one thing, but it was quite a different matter to glorify him in the national anthem. Parra did not hesitate to change a verse so that instead of saying "de Iturbide la sacra bandera," it said "de la patria la sacra bandera."[92]

Conclusion

As I have shown, Mexico City was not only the scenario, but itself the main target of the Porfirian elites' ideals, which receives resplendent expression in 1910. But this was a city that already had stacked various cities in itself. There were many sanitary, social, urban and even cultural anti-ideals. After all, the ideal views epitomised by the *Centenario* were only a simulacrum; "reality" did not match with these ideals, yet that fact neither hindered the celebration nor terminated the ideals. If anything, it made them more alluring for the elite. Nonetheless, only a month after the great celebration, the cultural fabric I have here surveyed seemed to be radically contested. The democratic revolution headed by the wealthy and cosmopolitan landowner Francisco I. Madero unlocked a Pandora's box of injustice and violence. By 1914 the Porfirian city was taken over by Indians and *campesinos*, and by the 1940s the ideal city seemed to be uncovered, almost in an archaeological fashion, by Carlos Obregón Santacilia, the official post-revolutionary architect who transformed the ruins of the Porfirian Palacio Legislativo into an enormous fascist-like monument of revolution. Then, the foundation stone that Porfirio Díaz had laid during the 1910 celebration was uncovered, and its cargo of newspapers, coins and documents of the time was stolen. These objects, Obregón Santacilia observed, disappeared, and with them "desapareció hasta el último vestigio del edificio porfiriano, como debía desaparecer para dejar paso a otra época, la que sobre sus despojos, estábamos levantando."[93]

   In truth, the post-revolutionary city eventually appropriated and redirected the essential ideals of the Porfirian ideal city, though radically departing from the Porfirian style. For, in fact, the culture that the centennial city epitomised was superseded not only because of Mexico's revolution; the revolution was a part of a wider demise: the nineteenth century itself had come to an end. Mexico City began to pile a new "modern" city over the remains of the Porfirian ideal city. And yet, this article does not try to suggest that the "real" Mexico City has been, as Italo Calvino's imaginary Berenice, "a temporal succession of different cities, alternatively just and unjust"; in fact, it may very well be that the 1910 Mexico City already included, as Calvino's imaginary city, all the future Mexicos: "all the future Berenices are already present in this instant, wrapped one within the other, confined, crammed, inextricable."[94] The essential ideals—conclusive nationalism, cosmopolitanism, urban speculation and modernisation—that inspired the centennial city are still today's goals. Whatever a late twentieth-century *ville-monstre* does with those ideals will be a lesson—alas, devastating and heartless—for the world that for so long has asserted them.

Notes

1. Virginia Woolf, "Mr. Bennet and Mrs. Brown" (1924), reprinted in *Collected Essays*, vol. 1 (London, 1966), p. 320.

2. See the "Programa definitivo de las ceremonias y fiestas oficiales para la celebración del Primer Centenario de la Independencia en la Ciudad de México (acordado el 28 de Julio de 1910)"; see also the same document but annotated at the margins by the Ministry of Foreign Relations, explaining special diplomatic events and type of formalities to follow (Archivo Histórico Genaro Estrada, Secretaría de Relaciones Exteriores, Tlatelolco, Mexico City—hence SRE, Le. 101). Genaro García, Nemesio García Naranjo, Alfonso Teja Zabre, Rubén Valenti, Manuel H. San Juan, Ignacio B. del Castillo were appointed official historians of the celebration, see García's *Crónica Oficial de las Fiestas del Centenario de la Independencia de México* (Mexico, 1911); see also E. Barros, *Album gráfico de la república mexicana* (Mexico, 1910). Regarding this book and the propaganda efforts of the Porfirian regime during the centennial celebration, see Archivo General de la Nación, Mexico City: Secretaría de Gobernación, Porfiriato, Cententrio—hence AGN GOB 909-3-1. American and French newspapers offered their pages for Mexican propaganda (AGN GOB 920-3-1). My main sources of data are the AGN, Ramo Gobernación, SCOP Obras Públicas, and the Archivo del Ayuntamiento. However, the Genaro García collection at the Benson Library, University of Texas–Austin, includes an impressive collection of pamphlets, paraphernalia and photographs of the centenary. About this collection, see Thomas F. Reese and Carol McMichael Reese, "Revolutionary Urban Legacies." The Archive of the Ministry of Foreign Relations includes rich information on the invitation and correspondence with invited foreign missions. For the general cost of the many events of the commemorations, see approvals by Limantour in AGN GOB 910-2-5. The estimated total budget was 317,000 pesos.

3. The last proposal was submitted by the little girl María de la Luz Islas, to whom Casarín, director of the centennial commission, responded, June 1910, AGN GOB 910-3-1.

4. Many of these *Iniciativas* can be found in AGN GOB Centenario.

5. For examples, see AGN GOB 910-3-1 (for architects and merchants).

6. Federico Gamboa, for instance, described the popular celebrations but also the Maderista protests that took place that night, and how he himself concealed those expressions of opposition from the attention of foreign observers. Federico

Gamboa, *Mi diario. Mucho de mi vida y algo de la de otros*, segunda serie, vol. II (Mexico, 1938), pp. 181–93.

7. Part of this analysis is developed in Mauricio Tenorio, *Mexico at World's Fairs: Crafting a Modern Nation* (Berkeley, CA, 1996).

8. *El Faro*, 19 March 1889. Reprinted by the author in *Iniciativa para celebrar el Primer Centenario de la Independencia de México con una Exposición Universal* (Mexico, 1893), pp. 15–19, 25–51. Medina y Ormaechea continued pushing for the celebration of such a world's fair in Mexico City, and printed the pamphlet *La Exposición Universal del Primer Centenario Mexicano* (Mexico, 1894).

9. By 1900, *El Diario del Hogar* was advocating Medina's idea, but on 5 May it announced the death of Antonio Medina y Ormaechea.

10. *Gran Exposición Internacional de México que se abrirá el día 15 de septiembre de 1895 y que se clausurará el día 3 de abril de 1896* (Mexico, 1894), pp. 3–10.

11. Salvador Malo was in fact one of the most important urban developers of the time He developed the Hacienda de la Teja, the Hacienda de Anzures, and the Hacienda de la Castañeda. He was a member of the Mexico City Improvement Company, and an admirer of, and participant in, world's fairs and modern urban planning. In fact, he proposed a Barcelona-like *Ensanche* for Mexico City, to gentrify the grounds surrounding the Paseo de la Reforma. In this regard, the most complete study of the subject is Jorge H. Jiménez Muñoz, *La traza del poder. Historia de la política y los negocios urbanos en el Distrito Federal* (Mexico, 1993); a reproduction of Malo's *Ensanche* for Mexico City can be found in Fernando Benítez, *La Ciudad de México* (Mexico, 1984), vol. 6 (there is no reference on the original location of the map).

12. *Agreement made between Mr. John R. Dos Passos, as legal representative of the Mexican National Exposition and Land Company, and Vicomte R. de Cornely, in San Francisco, México*, 22 April 1896. See AGN, Ramo Fomento, Exposiciones Internacionales—hence EXP, Box 99, Exp. 22.

13. Mexico, Secretaría de Fomento, *Memoria de la Secretaría de Fomento, 1897–1900* (Mexico, 1908).

14. AGN GOB 909–3–1.

15. The data regarding the building known today as El Museo del Chopo were furnished to me by the Department of Architecture at the Museo Nacional de la Arquitectura, at the Palacio de Bellas Artes. They possess data and pictures of the building until the 1960s, when it was abandoned after the Museum of Natural History was moved to Chapultepec. Later, it was remodelled by the National University, and still stands as one of the university's exhibition sites.

16. In this regard, see Luis G. Ortiz, *Prontuario . . . de acuerdos, bandos, circulares, decretos, leyes, reglamentos y demás disposiciones vigentes de la Secretaría de Gobernación y sus despachos* (Mexico, 1980–10). This document can be found in Archivo Histórico, Secretaría de Salubridad y Asistencia, Mexico City—hence SSA, Salud Pública, Impresos, and it includes those aspects related to sanitation. Another interesting contrast for the map of the ideal city is the mapping of prostitution in Porfirian Mexico City. In this regard see the insightful, though preliminary, maps and argument of I. Delgado Jordá, "Prostitución, sífiles y moralidad sexual en la ciudad de México a fines del siglo XIX," unpubl. Tesis de Licenciatura, Escuela Nacional de Antropología e Historia, Antropología Social, Mexico 1993.

17. For the cultural and urbanist analysis of this tradition, see Santiago Quesada, *La ciudad en la cultura hispana de la Edad Moderna* (Barcelona, 1992).

18. See Jorge Hardoy, "Theory and Practice of Urban Planning in Europe, 1850–1930: Its Transfer to Latin America," in J. Hardoy and R. Morse (editors), *Rethinking the Latin American City* (Baltimore, 1992), pp. 20–49. For Mexico, see Jérôme Monnet, *La ville et son double. Images et usages du centre: La parabole de Mexico* (Paris, 1993), pp. 19–36.

19. Regarding the development of the Paseo following the style of the Champs-Elysées, see Salvador Novo, *Los Paseos de la Ciudad de México* (Mexico, 1980). See also Barbara Tenenbaum, "Streetwise History—The Paseo de la Reforma and the Porfirian State," unpubl. manuscript, p. 5.

20. See *Archivo Histórico del Ayuntamiento*, 3583, Exp. 17, 1889–1993.

21. In this regard, see what John Lear calls "segregation of wealth," Ch. 3, "Space and Class in the Centennial Capital," in John Lear, "Workers, Vecinos, and Citizens: The Revolution in Mexico City, 1909–1917," unpubl. Ph.D. Diss., University of California, Berkeley, 1993, especially pp. 106ff. For a summary of this phenomenon in European cities, see Michael Wagenaar, "Conquest of the Center or Flight to the Suburbs? Divergent Metropolitan Strategies in Europe, 1850–1914," *Journal of Urban History*, vol. 19, no. 1 (November 1992), pp. 60–83.

22. For Buenos Aires, see the various essays included in José Luis Romero and Luis Alberto Romero, *Buenos Aires, historia de cuatro siglos*, vol. I (Buenos Aires, 1983), especially James R. Scobie and Aurora Ravina de Luzzi, "El centro, los barrios y los suburbios," and Francisco J. Bullrich, "La arquitectura: el eclecticismo"; for the transformation of Buenos Aires during the 1910 centenary of Argentina's independence, see Jorge Hardoy and Margarita Gutman, *Buenos Aires* (Madrid, 1992), pp. 113–62. For Mexico, see Hira de Gortari and Regina Hernández, *La ciudad de México y el Distrito Federal. Una historia compartida* (Mexico, 1988); María Dolores Morales, "La expansión de la Ciudad de México en el siglo XIX. El caso de los fraccionamientos," *Investigaciones sobre la historia de la Ciudad de México*, vol. I (Mexico, 1974); the various essays and maps included in Gustavo de la Garza (ed.), *Atlas de la Ciudad de México* (Mexico, 1987); Jorge H. Jiménez Muñoz, *La traza del poder*; Hira de Gortari, "¿Un modelo de urbanización? La ciudad de México de finales del Siglo XIX," *Secuencia*, no. 8 (1987); Erika Barra Stoppa, *La expansión de la ciudad de México y los conflictos urbanos (1900–1930)* (Mexico, 1982).

23. Francisco J. Bullrich, "La arquitectura: el eclecticismo," in Romero and Romero, *Buenos Aires*, vol. I, pp. 173–200.

24. Barros, *Album gráfico*, p. 11.

25. Jiménez Muñoz presents the most complete panorama of *colonias*. Jiménez Muñoz, *La traza del poder*.

26. See ibid.; and María Dolores Morales, "La Expansión de la Ciudad de México"; for the workers' *barrios* see John Lear, "Workers, Vecinos and Citizens," pp. 91–143.

27. See Andrés Lira; *Comunidades indígenas frente a la ciudad de México* (Mexico, 1983).

28. See Carlos Sierra, *Historia de los transportes eléctricos de México* (Mexico, 1976); Manuel Vidrio, "Sistemas de transporte y expansión urbana: los tranvías," in A. Moreno Toscano (ed.), *Ciudad de México. Ensayo de construcción de una historia* (Mexico, 1978), pp. 201–17.

29. For the relation between authoritarian and centralist government and inner-city interventions in Paris, Brussels, and Rome, see Michael Wagenaar, "Conquest of the Center," pp. 63–71.

30. For the clear mapping of this area, see the various maps of *colonias* and *nomenclatura* included in *Archivo Histórico del Ayuntamiento*, 4765. Especially, see the map titled "Comisión permanente de nomenclatura de la ciudad de México, cuarteles V, VI, VII, VIII," 1908.

31. See AGN GOB 909–10–4–3. The document included expenses reported by Manuel Escalante in the decoration of avenues and streets such as Cinco de Mayo, San Francisco, Juárez, 16 de Septiembre. It includes descriptions of those decorations and their cost. For colour sketches of this decoration see *Archivo Histórico del Ayuntamiento*, 4753, "Postes para Avenida Juárez," "Postes que van de la estatua de Carlos IV al Portal de Mercaderes y San Fernando."

32. J. Lear, "Workers, Vecinos and Citizens," p. 130.

33. Architect Manuel Torres Torrija, in Francisco Trentini, *Patria. El floreci-miento de México (The Prosperity of Mexico)* (Mexico, 1906), p. 64. Torres Torrija made the first report of the status of *colonias* in Mexico City. For that report, see Jiménez Muñoz, *La traza del poder*, pp. 24–44.

34. In this regard, see the summary of M. R. G. Conzen's contributions to the study of urban change in Western Europe (as the product of gradual change or catastrophic change) in Peter Larkham, "Constraints of Urban History and Form Upon Redevelopment," *Geography*, vol. 80, no. 2 (April 1995), pp. 111–24.

35. Most of the elite resided within the limits of the new ideal city. However, since the 1870s Porfirio Díaz had owned a house in Cadena street (in the old part of the city, today Venustiano Carranza). For a detailed description of the origins and characteristics of this house, see Carlos Tello, *El exilio. Un retrato de familia* (Mexico, 1993).

36. Regarding this park, see *Archivo Histórico del Ayuntamiento*, Legajo 603, Exp. 6.

37. Presented to Porfirio Díaz and Eduardo Liceaga, SSA Box 6, Exp. 33.

38. Loc. cit. Quevedo argued that the total cost of the Balbuena park was 100,000 pesos. The park was also harmonious with the profits of high authorities. John Lear has shown that, according to workers' publications, in 1912 José Y. Limantour came under congressional investigation for having profited from construction of the park. See Lear, "Workers, Vecinos and Citizens," p. 145.

39. See Jérôme Monnet's analysis of Mexico City as the prototype postmodern metropolis; Monnet, *La ville et son double*.

40. See the classic works on American cities: Thomas Bender, *Toward an Urban Vision. Ideas and Institutions in Nineteenth-Century America* (Lexington, Kty, 1978), and Leo Marx, *The Machine and the Garden* (New York, 1964). For an interesting view of the different cultural considerations of urbanisation, see Kenneth T. Jackson, *Crabgrass Frontier: The Suburbanization of the United States* (New York, 1985), especially pp. 287ff.

41. Alan Knight, "Revolutionary Project, Recalcitrant People: Mexico, 1910–1940," in Jaime Rodríguez (ed.), *The Revolutionary Process in Mexico. Essays on Political and Social Change, 1880–1940* (Los Angeles, 1990), pp. 233–35.

42. See Federico Gamboa's novel, *Santa*: the story of a country girl who migrates to the city and is corrupted by the city's evil, becoming a prostitute.

43. See Pierre Nora's introduction to the collection he edited, *Les lieux de mémoire*, vol. I (Paris, 1989), English version as "Between Memory and History: Les Lieux de Mémoire," *Representations*, no. 26 (Spring, 1989), pp. 7–25.

44. See letter by secretary of the Centennial Commission, J. Casarín, to Juan Bibriesca, secretary of the Ayuntamiento of Mexico City, in which he accepted the

194 *¡Viva México! ¡Viva la Independencia!*

proposal by the influential sanitary doctor Luis E. Ruiz (Feb. 1910). Ruiz proposed to revive the old project in which each state would send statues of *hijos distinguidos*; according to Ruiz, by 1910 very few states had sent their statues. Throughout 1910, many states responded to the request arguing financial difficulties. See AGN GOB 910–3–1; see also *Archivo Histórico del Ayuntamiento*, Legajo 2276, Exp. 36–38, and 61. In this regard, see Joe Nash, *El Paseo de la Reforma* (Mexico, 1959); the re-publishing of Francisco Sosa, *Las estatuas de la Reforma* (Mexico, 1974). For the origins and early development of the Paseo, see Tenenbaum, "Streetwise History— The Paseo de la Reforma and the Porfirian State."

45. Regarding this monument, see *Archivo Histórico del Ayuntamiento*, Legajo 60, Exp. 1; Legajo 2276, Exp. 58; and regarding the origins of a national fund for the construction of the monument, see Legajo 2276, Exp. 35.

46. See AGN GOB 909–10–4–3. About the monument, see Legajos 1166 and 1667 of the *Archivo Histórico del Ayuntamiento*. See also José de Jesús Núñez Domínguez, *El monumento a la independencia. Bosquejo Histórico* (Mexico, 1930); and Samuel Ruiz García, *Monografía de la columna de la independencia, 1910–1958* (Mexico, 1958).

47. There were 28 "civilised" countries that attended: six as special diplomatic missions (Italy, Japan, the U.S.A., Germany, Spain and France); 18 with special envoys (Honduras, Bolivia, Austria, Cuba, Costa Rica, Russia, Portugal, Holland, Guatemala, El Salvador, Peru, Panama, Brazil, Belgium, Chile, Argentina, Norway and Uruguay); and three countries commissioned residents in Mexico to represent them (Switzerland, Colombia and Venezuela). Great Britain could not attend due to the death of King Edward VII and Nicaragua due to a coup d'état, though the Nicaraguan poet, Rubén Darío, who was appointed envoy of Nicaragua before the political turmoil, was treated as a national "Guest of Honour" by Mexico's intelligentsia and government. See Genaro García, *Crónica*, and SRE LE 101.

48. SRE LE 101, 117.

49. The actual distribution was as follows: Japan, Viuda de Braniff's house (Reforma 27); Germany, Hugo Scherer's house (Reforma 3); Spain at Guillermo de Anda y Escandón (Artes 31); the U.S.A. at the Palacio Cobián in Bucareli, which was acquired by the Ministry of the Interior to house its new offices; part of France's delegation was accommodated at Tomás Braniff's house (Ribera de San Cosme 15); Italy at de la Torre y Mier's house (Plaza Reforma). Other houses mentioned were: Landero y Cos, Sebastián Mier, Santiago Méndez, Viuda de Martínez del Río, J. Y. Limantour, Coronel Pablo Escandón, W. Pearson, Romualdo Pasquel, Manuel Buch, Viuda de Romero Rubio and Lorenzo Elizaga. See loc. cit. and Génaro García, *Crónica*, pp. 25ff.

50. See *Archivo Histórico del Ayuntamiento*, Legajo 594, Exp. 4.

51. This proposal was made by E. Lozano, R. Nervo, Carlos Lazo de la Vega and R. Riveroll del Prado, AGN GOB 910–6–1.

52. AGN GOB 907–3–1.

53. See also "Resumen de la historia de los trabajos de la penitenciaría de San Lázaro, leido por Angel Zimbrón secretario del gobierno del Distrito Federal," 1900, SSA Impresos Box 2 Exp. 2/61.

54. See José María Romero, *La penitenciaría* (Mexico, 1886).

55. See "Resumen de la historia de los trabajos de la penitenciaría de San Lázaro, leido por Angel Zimbrón secretario del gobierno del Distrito Federal," 1900 inauguration of the penitentiary, SSA Impresos Box 2 Exp. 2/61. See also Miguel Macedo, *La criminalidad en México* (Mexico, 1897).

56. "Informe leido por el señor Licenciado don Agustín M. Lazo, miembro del Consejo de Dirección de la penitenciaría del Distrito Federal, en el acto de la inauguración de las obras de ampliación de aquella, el 29 de septembre de 1910"; reproduced in G. García, *Crónica,* pp. 114–16.

57. Porfirio Díaz Jr. was often favoured with contracts. He published a handsome book of pictures of the works of the *manicomio.* See Echegaray's 1906 *informe* to the Ministry of the Interior regarding the design for the mental hospital, SSA Benéfica Pública, Manicomio general, Legajo 1, Exp. 10. This document includes a detailed account of the amendments made in the project by the special commission of public works. See also Congreso Médico Pan-Americano, "Exposición y proyecto para construir un manicomio en el Distrito Federal que presenta a la junta nombrada por el C. Ministro de Gobernación la comisión especial encargada de formarla."

58. G. García, *Crónica,* p. 109; and also Ramón Ramírez, *El manicomio* (Mexico, 1884).

59. On the Hygienic Exhibit see *La salubridad e higiene pública en los Estados Unidos Mexicanos. Brevísima reseña de los progresos alcanzados desde 1810 hasta 1910* (Mexico, 1910); and SSA, Salubridad Pública, Congresos y Convenciones, Box 10, Exp. 1–19.

60. Among other things, the famous study by Dr. Orvañanos, *Geografía médica y climatología* (1889); studies on the eradication of yellow fever in Mexico by Dr. Liceaga. See "Obras que remita la secretaría del Consejo a la sección de exposición de higiene y Conferencias Relativas . . ." in SSA, Box 10, Exp. 11.

61. Mauricio Gómez Mayorga, "La influencia francesa en la arquitectura y el urbanismo en México," in Arturo Arnaiz y Freg (ed.), *La intervención francesa y el imperio de Maximiliano cien años después, 1862–1962* (Mexico, 1962).

62. On the Columbus monument, see Luis García Pimentel, *El monumento elevado en la ciudad de México a Cristóbal Colón* (Mexico, 1889).

63. See Tenorio, *Mexico at World's Fairs,* chs. VI and VII; Nash, *El Paseo de la Reforma;* José de Jesús Nuñez Domínguez, *El monumento a la independencia. Bosquejo histórico* (Mexico, 1930); Samuel Ruiz García, *Monografía de la columna de la independencia, 1910–1958* (Mexico, 1958); Francisco Sosa, *Las estatuas de la Reforma* (Mexico, 1974); and Alan Knight, "Racism, Revolution, and *Indigenismo*: 1910–1940," in R. Graham (ed.), *Race in Latin America* (Austin, 1990), pp. 71–114. Barbara Tenenbaum has also dealt with the subject, especially in regard to the first stages of the planning of the Paseo de la Reforma and the inauguration of the Cuauhtémoc monument. See "Murals in Stone—The Paseo de la Reforma and Porfirian Mexico, 1873–1910," in *La ciudad y el campo en la historia de México. Papers presented at the VII Conference of Mexican and United States Historians, Oaxaca, Mexico, October 1985* (Mexico, 1992), pp. 369–81.

64. For examples of this type of arch, see sketches found in *Archivo Histórico del Ayuntamiento,* 4753, arches for the Paseo de la Reforma, Juárez avenue, and Independencia street.

65. For data on Rivas Mercado, see the biography of his daughter, F. Bradu, *Antonieta* (Mexico, 1991). That Rivas Mercado's daughter became José Vasconcelos's mistress, and that she was a patron of bohemian artists, and that she killed herself in Notre Dame in Paris, gave don Antonio some historical visibility.

66. See *Archivo Histórico del Ayuntamiento,* Legajo 116, Exp. 9, 13, and Legajo 1167, Exp. 24.

67. "Informe leído por el señor Ingeniero don Antonio Rivas Mercado, Director de la Escuela Nacional de Bellas Artes, en el acto de inauguración de la

Columna de la Independenca, el 16 de septiembre de 1910," reproduced in G. García, *Crónica*, p. 74.

68. For an insightful analysis of the history and meaning of this symbol, see, for France, the collection of essays in P. Nora (ed.), *Les lieux de mémoire* (Paris, 1984), first two vols.; for Brazil, José Murilho de Carvalho made an important analysis of the symbols of the republic in *A formação das Almas. O imaginário da República no Brasil* (São Paulo, 1990).

69. For the understanding of republicanism as a universal value, see C. Nicolet, *L'idée républicaine en France (1789–1924). Essai d'histoire critique* (Paris, 1982).

70. Regarding this relocation, see *Archivo Histórico del Ayuntamiento,* Legajo 3603. As in many other aspects during the 1890s and 1900s, Limantour was extremely influential in the entire organisation of the centennial celebration. All expenditures had to be approved by him, and often he returned the approvals with many comments that he directly expressed to the president. Thus, often his suggestions were law. See, for instance, AGN GOB 910–2–5, in which Limantour acknowledges having received the final version of the programme for the *Centenario*, and he returned it with the budget approved but with many comments. For instance: "La exposición de flora y fauna nacionales del día 1 de septiembre, ¿no estaría mejor el día 2 que tiene libre la mañana?" "Me parece conveniente que el presidente de la república sea quien presida la inauguración del anfiteatro de la escuela preparatoria, por tratarse de una obra que habrá costado más de un millón de pesos . . ." Small wonder, when Ministers proposed projects for the celebration, they often said, as Justo Sierra did, "¿qué le parece a nuestro amigo Limantour? Al Sr. Presidente le gusta la idea." See Sierra's letter to Corral, 25 Feb. 1910, making some amendments to the original plan of the Ministry of Public Education, AGN GOB 910–2–5. In this regard see also Marta Baranda, "José Yves Limantour juzgado por figuras claves del porfiriato," *Estudios de Historia Moderna y Contemporánea de México,* no. 9 (1983), pp. 97–136.

71. Formed by distinguished and wealthy members of the Porfirian elite, José Landero y Cos, Gabriel Mancera, Carlos Rivas, Carlos Herrera, Genaro García (the only historian of the team), and Ignacio de la Barra. See "Informe al presidente de la república respecto al monumento a Juárez," by de la Barra, June 1910, AGN GOB 906–4–2.

72. Loc. cit.

73. Total cost: 299,438 pesos.

74. "Discurso pronunciado por el señor Licenciado don Carlos Robles en el acto de inauguración del monumento a Benito Juárez, el 18 de septiembre de 1910," reproduced in G. García, *Crónica*, p. 80.

75. See results of the 1906 contest for a Juárez monument; especially, see the project in Zapoteco style (including illustration). See Antonio Rivas Mercado, Nicolas Mariscal, Velázquez de León, in *El Arte y la Ciencia*, vol. 7, no. 11 (May 1906), pp. 281–89.

76. This is the figure given by the original plan, though García mentioned that only 280 persons participated.

77. See original AGN GOB 909–3–1.

78. See approval of this proposal in AGN GOB 910–3–1, proposed by J. Schafer.

79. Genaro García, *Crónica*, pp. 148–52.

80. See original plan in AGN GOB 909–3–1.

81. The state of Morelos was asked for 250 Indians. The governor decided to send them, but then he wrote to Casarín explaining that the Indians decided not to

travel to Mexico City, because "ha corrido el rumor que de México los mandarían a San Luis Potosí donde hay Guerra, por lo que se niegan a ir." AGN GOB 909–3–1.

82. There are letters to the Centro Vasco, Asturiano and Castellano, Loc. cit.

83. For an analysis of scientific politics, see Charles Hale, *The Transformation of Liberalism* (Princeton, 1989).

84. See *Actas del XVII Congreso Internacional de Americanistas*, Sección México (Mexico, 1910). The president of the Mexican section of the Congress was Justo Sierra, and it was attended by mainstream scholars on anthropology and archaeology (among them, Edward Seler, Franz Boas). For the history of these congresses see Juan Comas, *Cien años de congresos internacionales de americanistas* (Mexico, 1974); and for the history of the international school of anthropology see Ricardo Godoy, "Franz Boas and his Plans for an International School of American Archaeology and Ethnology in Mexico," *Journal of the History of Behavioral Sciences*, vol. 13 (1977), pp. 228–42.

85. In this regard, see Alan Knight, "Racism, Revolution, and *Indigenismo.*"

86. *XVII Congreso Internacional de Americanistas,* p. 8.

87. In this regard, see Jesús Díaz de León, "Concepto del indianismo en México," in *Concurso científico y artístico del Centenario* (Mexico, 1911), p. 23.

88. Jesús Díaz de León, "Concepto del indianismo," p. 23. Along these lines, see also "Propuesta de una exposición etnográfica durante las fiestas del centenario de la independencia nacional," AGN GOB 909–3–1.

89. "Discurso pronunciado por el señor General don Porfirio Díaz, presidente de la república, al recibir del Excelentísimo señor Embajador de España las reliquias de José María Morelos, el 17 de septiembre de 1910," reproduced by G. García, *Crónica*, p. 23.

90. "Discurso pronunciado por el señor don Fernando Pimentel y Fagoaga, presidente del Ayuntamiento Constitucional de la ciudad de México, en el acto de dedicación de la Av. Isabel la Católica, el 31 de agosto de 1910," reproduced by G. García, *Crónica*, p. 45.

91. For example, Eduardo Fernández Guerra proposed to make a film that would be exhibited at municipal palaces to make the history of Mexico's independence enjoyable and communicable to all people. AGN GOB 909–3–1. There is no direct response to this initiative, but popular performances of movies took place on 15 and 16 September in all the city theatres. See AGN GOB 910–3–1. Out of the many films that were made during the *Centenario*, very few survived. For a detailed explanation of these films, see Juan Felipe Leal, Eduardo Barraza and Alejandro Jablonska, *Vistas que no se ven. Filmografía mexicana, 1896–1910* (Mexico, 1993).

92. The proposal was sent from Veracruz by Huerta Vargaz. Parra completely agreed with the amends. The fourth stanza was as follows: "Del guerrero inmortal de Zempoala/te defiende la espada terrible/tu sagrado pendón tricolor/y será del feliz mexicano/en la paz y en la guerra el caudillo/porque el supo sus armas de brillo/cincundar en los campos de honor." The seventh went as follows: "Si a la lid contra huestes enemiga/los convoca la tropa guerrera/de Iturbide la sacra bandera/ Mexicanos valientes seguid." AGN GOB 907–3–1.

93. Carlos Obregón Santacilia, *El Monumento a la Revolución* (Mexico, 1940).

94. Italo Calvino, *Invisible Cities*, translated by William Weaver (New York, 1972), p. 163.

CHAPTER NINE

The 1921 Centennial Celebration of Mexico's Independence
State Building and Popular Negotiation

ELAINE C. LACY

In the summer of 1921, Mexico's new president, Alvaro Obregón Salido, received an anonymous letter from the state of Chihuahua suggesting that a "fitting and noble" addition to the centennial celebration of Independence, which was being planned by the federal government at the time, would be the return and burial with honor of the remains of former dictator Porfirio Díaz. Mexicans should learn to forgive Díaz, argued the writer. "To be human is to have defects: and who does not have them?" Obregón did not grant the request.[1]

This plea to forgive the dictator illustrates the diversity of mindset, emotion, and meaning that surfaced on the occasion of the Centennial of 1921. Mexicans celebrated the 100th anniversary of their achievement of independence from Spain with ceremonies and galas that touched a broad spectrum of society. Although similar in many ways to the extravagant celebration of 1910, that of 1921 was far more extensive and inclusive in scope, and the objectives of its planners and many of its participants differed from those involved in the commemoration of 1910. This observance of the consummation of Independence, held for the first time since the midnineteenth century, is notable for many reasons, not the least of which is the fact that the Liberal nemesis Agustín de Iturbide was venerated even as the dust of the Revolution settled. The commemoration was appropriated by federal officials, the social elite, middle-sector groups, and workers as a means of achieving their various objectives. Moreover, the celebration acted as an arena where public memory as well as Mexican national culture and identity were debated.[2]

For Mexico's new postrevolutionary government, the Centennial became a state-building enterprise. The role of popular celebrations in the state formation process is generally recognized by historians.[3] A number of recent studies have demonstrated the function of patriotic rituals and their associated myths and symbols in enhancing state power by, for example, engendering civic loyalty and social unity. Political leaders have employed patriotic displays to foster social control, for such displays may act, as one scholar noted, as a "crucial dimension of that power that represents itself as 'the state' and us as members of a 'body politic.' "[4] Further, the nineteenth-century notion that political and cultural unity were or should be functionally related has contributed to state efforts at "cultural engineering," an attempt to shape a common national culture and identity.

However, this "cultural revolution," as scholars have pointed out, takes place not only through "state activities, forms, routines and rituals . . . for the constitution and regulation of social identities" but also "in the way subjects of the state elaborate their experience."[5] In other words, public rituals may act as arenas of negotiation where various groups dispute the events and meaning of the past as well as the properties of a common culture. In this regard, dominant groups may seize such occasions to confirm their social positions, to vie for authority, and/or to "reiterate . . . the moral values on which their authority rests."[6] For subordinate groups, celebrations can serve to challenge authority and to articulate group consciousness. Official agendas may be undermined as these groups use "public ritual time for recreational purposes or patriotic symbols to demand political rights."[7] The September 1921 commemoration, heretofore neglected in studies of popular rituals and/or state building in Mexico, acted as such an arena. This essay will examine the month-long celebration in September 1921 of Mexico's achievement of Independence, with the aim of characterizing its function in postrevolutionary state building and cultural engineering, and as a site where public memory and notions of national culture and identity were negotiated. It will also emphasize the manner in which various constituencies appropriated the affair for their own purposes. While the Centennial was celebrated in most of the Mexican states, the focus here will be on events in the capital, given the more elaborate and extensive nature of the festivities there.[8] The elite played an important role in shaping the centennial celebration, but the new government was not incapable of enhancing its power or shaping national culture through the 1921 commemoration. The manner in which events unfolded illustrates that the formation of a strong, centralized postrevolutionary state was a process begun under Obregón's predecessor, Venustiano Carranza (and not, as historians of Mexico have long contended, with the origin of the Revolutionary Party in 1929), and that the elaboration of Mexican national culture and identity is a complex and prolonged procedure to which numerous constituencies have contributed.

The Centennial as a State-Building Project

The new, relatively weak regime headed by General Alvaro Obregón dominated the official celebration of the consummation of Independence. Federal planners incorporated into the affair traditional rituals as well as new rites, all of which would act, the Sonorans anticipated, to meet their own state-building objectives, which included enhancing state power, uniting the country's disparate elements, and forging a common national culture and identity.

The notion of celebrating the milestone emerged in various regions of Mexico in late 1920 and early 1921.[9] Among those who suggested the idea was Conservative *capitaleño* José de Jesús Núñez y Dominguez, who proposed that the memory of Agustín de Iturbide be honored with a "grand ball" on September 27, the anniversary of his 1821 triumphal entry into Mexico City. Núñez y Dominguez's suggestion, published in the newspaper *Excelsior* in early January, was well received by the old wealth of the capital, in particular the descendants of Iturbide himself.[10] From outside the capital, businessman Tomás Medellín of San Luis Potosí wrote to President Obregón in early 1921 asking to be designated the person in charge of any national centennial commemoration that might take place.[11] Félix Palavicini, editor of *Excelsior*'s rival *El Universal*, also proposed a national observance early in the year, but the most elaborate plan was devised by the Mexico City Ayuntamiento (Municipal Council). Members of that body began in January 1921 to plan a month-long commemoration of Independence, and Municipal President Herminio Pérez Abreu sent a copy of the proposal to Obregón in early February with a note urging that the occasion be elaborately observed not only because the centennial of El Grito had been lavishly celebrated in 1910, but also because with the end of the "glorious Revolution" and the beginning of national reconstruction such festivities would demonstrate that "peace is firmly reestablished in the country."[12]

The Ayuntamiento's planned celebration closely resembled the Porfirian government's centennial extravaganza of 1910. It called for extensive involvement on the part of the federal government; hence, Abreu needed Obregón's approval and assistance. Relations between the Ayuntamiento and the federal government, which were already strained, worsened as a result of the commemorative plans. A struggle over control of the affair began immediately. Despite Abreu's repeated efforts to gain federal support, Obregón did not respond in writing to Abreu until early April, when he informed him that the federal government would oversee the festivities. After several attempts to maintain oversight, Abreu eventually backed down and on April 14 sent Minister Alberto Paní a copy of the Ayuntamiento's proposed program.[13] In an April 16 cabinet meeting, Obregón designated ministers Paní, Plutarco Calles, and Adolfo de la Huerta as the official Centennial Commission. They later invited the Ayuntamiento to name a representative to sit on the commission.[14] In late April, public announcements appeared saying that the federal government would host a national, month-long extravaganza in celebration of the achievement of Independence.

In early May the Centennial Commission appointed an Executive Committee, comprised of three governmental bureaucrats and a prominent intellectual, and it charged the men with planning and executing the commemorative program. Indicating his intention that federal officials dominate the September events, Obregón ordered his ministers to bring to the mid-May cabinet meeting suggestions for celebratory events.[15]

Given that Obregón commandeered the centennial commemoration in order to enhance state power and prestige, the federal government would maintain strict oversight of the planned program. Private citizens, civic groups, and other organizations could devise public celebrations subject to official approval. Considering the government's economic woes, privately funded public events were welcome. Officials also aimed at making the events inclusive, thus enhancing national unity and loyalty to the regime.[16] The primary audience for federally planned events were *capitaleños* (residents of the capital), but 100,000 visitors of different social classes from across the nation streamed into Mexico City for the festivities.[17]

It comes as no surprise that a majority of activities included in the official 1921 commemoration were state efforts aimed at meeting the government's political and economic objectives.[18] Despite assertions that with the Revolution, Mexico had embarked on a new path of nationalism and egalitarianism that would be reflected in the commemoration, officials borrowed heavily from past celebrations, including the 1910 affair, incorporating a number of traditional patriotic rituals that had been a part of state celebrations since Independence. Many of these rituals were to "inculcate appropriate allegiances."[19] Some of the regime's new additions were inspired by a desire to assume a "revolutionary" posture; and in this regard the 1921 commemoration represents a state-building project in which new myths, symbols, and meanings were attached to older patriotic rituals in order to encourage a spirit of revolutionary nationalism among Mexicans.

The Sonoran state faced rigorous challenges in 1921, not the least of which was the maintenance of political peace. Sporadic rebellions had characterized the first six months of Obregón's tenure. The decade of violence just ended, in which one in every thirteen Mexicans was killed, had left the country divided. Within the capital itself political intrigues and social unrest threatened stability. The new government was also strapped economically. The Revolution had devastated the country's economy and left the majority of its people in poverty. In order to survive, the Obregón administration needed the support of foreign powers, especially the United States, but Obregón had to put the country on the road to economic recovery, which for him meant the rehabilitation of the poor, uneducated, and diseased masses. His priorities in 1921 therefore included securing the allegiance of diverse political and social constituencies, which meant presenting his government as the legitimate heir to the revolutionary struggle as well as preparing the nation for modernization and economic growth and development.

Among the groups whose allegiance was most sought in 1921 was the military. Obregón used the Centennial to placate that potentially rebellious group and to flaunt state power. Despite budgetary limitations, the government spruced up the army for the occasion by spending 400,000 pesos (or 15 percent of the total federal centennial expenditures) on new uniforms and "military equipment," and another 3,000 pesos on horses. During September a military band and orchestra played at various festivities; troops marched in military parades and engaged in a spectacular ceremony in which thirty battalions swore allegiance to the flag; and, on the 27th, the army performed what would have been considered unthinkable in past Independence observances—a reenactment of Iturbide's triumphal entry into Mexico City. Several events were included in the centennial program specifically for the military: sports competitions, a special luncheon with Obregón, an operatic performance, and a *velada* (musical review). Late in the month, the government inaugurated a new charitable institution to aid military invalids.

Obregón had good reason to encourage the military's loyalty and support in the fall of 1921. Faced with widespread insurrections, he had ordered executed or had killed in combat a number of army officers between February and June, and he had relocated scores of others from active duty posts to minor government jobs in the capital (in order to keep a watchful eye on them). Obregón had also begun a drastic reduction in military budgets and personnel after taking office.[20] The grand military exhibitions and the special treatment afforded its members during the Centennial were no doubt aimed at appeasing and maintaining the loyalty of this constituency. The show of military might and the pledge of military allegiance to the state were designed to enhance the strength and legitimacy of the Obregón regime in the eyes of the general public and of the foreign dignitaries who came to Mexico for the celebration.[21]

As had Porfirio Díaz in 1910, federal officials sought to enhance national legitimacy and prestige by inviting representatives from foreign countries to Mexico City to participate in the 1921 commemoration. Twenty-two European, Asian, and Latin American emissaries arrived in the capital in early September.[22] Obregón treated the visitors to ceremonies honoring the Independence heroes as well as to gala receptions, state dinners, entertainment in the best theaters, concerts, a luncheon at the newly uncovered Ciudadela at the Aztec ruins at Teotihuacán, parades, airplane and dirigible rides over the volcanoes, industrial and artistic exhibitions, and other functions designed not only to solemnly commemorate Mexico's freedom but also to demonstrate the country's new-found peace, prosperity, and progress. To prepare the capital for the visiting dignitaries, a massive refurbishing and beautification project, much of which involved the repair of damages associated with the war, began in late spring. Crews worked overtime to repair the National Palace and to clean and refurbish the central part of the city. As part of this process, officials again emulated Díaz and removed beggars from the streets. Obregón asked Calles in late August to round up the destitute and put them in asylums.[23] Again following Díaz's lead, Obregón ordered a film made of the month's events and sent copies to the various foreign ambassadors in Mexico.[24]

Like the centennial program of 1910, that of 1921 included several activities aimed at demonstrating to foreigners as well as to residents that Mexico was on the road to material recovery and technological progress. Officials dedicated new hospitals, roads, and public facilities. In early September the Executive Committee announced that new "government schools" (*escuelas de centenario*) would open in each of the capital's twelve municipalities.[25] A federally funded National School of Agriculture was established on the grounds of the old hacienda at Chapingo. Air shows and dirigible and airplane rides over the Valley of Mexico illustrated Mexican modernization. After weeks of delays, a grand commercial exposition opened in the old Legislative Palace, which had been remodeled for the event.[26]

The 1921 celebration, like those of past years, included patriotic spectacles such as military parades, flag ceremonies, entertainment with patriotic themes, fireworks displays, and tributes to the Independence heroes, the Niños Héroes, and the unknown Insurgent soldier in the Independence Monument.[27] As always, such patriotic rites promoted an official version of the past and were aimed at engendering allegiance and promoting state legitimacy.

The Mexican flag was everywhere during September. In a carefully orchestrated gesture, the Executive Committee arranged for thousands of schoolchildren from Mexico City and the surrounding municipalities to line the Paseo de la Reforma from the Plaza de la Constitución to Chapultepec Park on September 15 and to wave flags and sing the *himno nacional* as Obregón passed in review.[28] Flags appeared in theaters, at parades, on balconies, and at virtually all festivities and ceremonies that took place during the Centennial. The Executive Committee even presented women who gave birth during September with a Mexican flag.

Patriotic dramas and allegories appeared on the stages of Mexico City's theaters throughout September—dramas such as *El Grito* and *La Conjuración de México*.[29] At the close of these and other public events during September, audiences ended the evening by singing the national anthem. The public entertainment usually took place before packed houses, in part because the Executive Committee subsidized admission for workers.[30]

Official efforts to engender national unity also included solemn ceremonies honoring the men most closely associated with the achievement of Independence. Clearly, the very decision to observe the consummation of Mexico's independence implied homage to

Agustín de Iturbide, the general who had, at the order of the creole elites, forged an agreement with rebels and led the Army of the Three Guarantees into the capital city on September 27, 1821, thus officially separating Mexico from Spanish domination. The ritual of commemorating El Grito took place as usual;[31] and on the following day, in a solemn ceremony in the Cathedral (in which clerics were forbidden to participate), the urn containing the remains of Hidalgo and Morelos was brought from the Capilla de San José. The president, his cabinet, various ministers, foreign dignitaries, and others honored all the heroes of Independence (including Iturbide) with music and speeches.[32] The rebel Vicente Guerrero was remembered in a public ceremony on September 27. Again following tradition, the names of several Mexico City streets were changed to honor Hidalgo and another insurgent, Ignacio Allende.

In keeping with past traditions, federal officials also sought to engender loyalty and demonstrate state power by engaging in acts of benevolence as part of the centennial commemoration. The government provided daily meals to the poor in each of the city's districts during the last two weeks of September and also to inmates in prisons, jails, and charity wards.[33] Free clothing was distributed through police stations in each of the eight districts after mid-month and to prisoners on several occasions.[34] New mothers received infants' clothes during the month, and several thousand poor children were transported via automobiles to Chapultepec Park and given toys and sweets on September 23. Following a practice dating to the colonial era, the government also freed hundreds of prisoners in honor of the Centennial.[35]

From the outset the Centennial Committee contrasted the 1921 festivities to those of 1910, proclaiming that the 1921 events were for the people rather than for the elite.[36] While a large percentage of the official functions that made up the celebratory calendar were clearly planned for foreign dignitaries and the well-to-do of the capital, some functions were designed for the general public, such as theatrical and musical productions, dances, sporting events, parades, and fairs. General-turned-politician Obregón, maneuvering to secure the support of diverse factions, wooed groups, according to one historian, "ranging from Casa [del Obrero Mundial] radicals and elements of the Yaqui Indians to intellectuals and aspiring government functionaries."[37] During September 1921, Obregón partied with the elite while publicly identifying his regime with the urban and rural lower classes, sometimes presenting himself as the champion of the workers, at other times of the campesinos. Demonstrating that he was a man of the people, the president and his wife mingled with the masses at bullfights, sports competitions, and social affairs without official protection.[38]

Workers were targets of government populist activities during the Centennial, a factor that sets the 1921 events apart from those of 1910. In the early 1920s workers in the capital were an active, relatively literate group interested in national affairs. According to historian Alan Knight, they "read the newspapers, including the new penny press, and attended *veladas*. . . . They also shared with the urban middle class a series of cultural concerns: national politics, education, nationalism, often anti-clericalism."[39] The Obregón government and Mexico City's workers had an "uneasy alliance" in 1921. After siding with the Constitutionalists during the Revolution, organized labor in the capital had fallen increasingly under governmental domination. Obregón had enjoyed the support of labor since the early days of the Carranza occupation of the capital, and the fact that Luis Morones acted as head of the Congreso Regional Obrera Mundial, the syndicate that replaced the more radical Casa del Obrero Mundial in influence and strength, while occupying a post in the Obregón government, assured a more cooperative working class by 1921. But while radical labor elements were in decline, they still disrupted the peace. Workers throughout Mexico threatened a general work stoppage in December 1920 in sympathy with a strike in Veracruz.[40] Worker's Day was celebrated with noise and violence on May 1, 1921, and demonstrations and strikes led by the Federación de Sindicatos Obreros occurred sporadically during the first half of 1921. In an effort to avoid the street violence that had been a problem in the past, government officials called on the Federación de Sindicatos de Obreros to police the public events held for the lower classes during September and to monitor the distribution of food and clothing to the poor. The syndicate complied.[41]

With the assistance of Morones, the Executive Committee staged events strictly for workers and their families such as sports competitions, fairs, dances, concerts, bullfights, and a special performance of the opera, *Samson and Delilah*. The committee subsidized their admission to films, plays, and circus performances, and city and federal employees were allowed time off to attend. Workers were also given free clothing by federal officials. Workers' representatives were invited to participate in the ceremonies honoring the Independence heroes on September 16 and 27.[42]

Among the sports events for workers and other popular groups during the 1921 commemoration were horse and auto races, individual and team sports competitions, and a baseball exhibition in which the Sonoran state team played U.S. teams from Dallas and San Antonio. Recent scholarship examining the role of sports in the immediate postrevolutionary era emphasizes the anticlerical nature of spectator sports and views participatory sports as an official tool to inculcate "Protestant" values.[43] While it is possible that officials deliberately used sporting events for these purposes in 1921, more likely objectives were to generate goodwill toward the Obregón government and to expend popular energies on organized events rather than risking misconduct in the streets.

The Centennial provided the Obregón government with an opportunity to engage in cultural engineering. From the beginning, officials publicly stated that all celebrations would be entirely "Mexican." Again attempting to distinguish the commemoration from that of 1910, when emulation of foreign culture was the norm, Obregón said that all aspects of the 1921 version, including "ideas and details, have been given an orientation essentially national."[44] In this manner the new regime moved to unite the country's culturally diverse populations and to instill a sense of cultural nationalism by stressing a common national identity, a way in which all Mexicans were related. Planners eschewed foreign cultural elements in all state-sponsored celebrations and relied on music and food that was "Mexican," but they included indigenous dances, music, and crafts. Official *mestizaje* was the result, but the 1921 commemoration also incorporated the shadowy beginnings of official *indigenismo*.[45]

Many of the centennial celebrations incorporated Mexican music and dance. At every official public function in September 1921 one of the two special centennial orchestras, the Orquesta Típica, played only traditional Mexican music while its members were dressed in *charro* and *poblana* costumes. Distinct from the 1910 Centennial, this highly visible group performed Mexican songs for foreign visitors at official receptions, at a special luncheon at Teotihuacán, at bullfights, at *veladas*, and on occasions when the general public was treated to free diversions. A typical event for the middle and upper classes during the month was a *velada* on September 16 at the Teatro Iris, co-sponsored by the Centennial Committee. Those in attendance, including the president and some cabinet members, were entertained with Mexican operatic arias, *canciones mexicanos*, and *cantos populares* played by the Orquesta Típica as well as by indigenous dances from Oaxaca and Cuajimalpa, whose "exotic rhythms," a reviewer later said, "are generally unknown by the residents of the capital."[46]

The centennial organizers inserted Mexican songs into a program in honor of foreign dignitaries at the newly uncovered ruins of the pyramid of Quetzalcóatl at Teotihuacán, including "La Borrachita," "Paloma Blanca," "Adorable Eres, Morena" (a Yucatecan song), and other regional ballads. The Orquesta Típica also played a "Rapsodía Mexicana sobre Temas Revolucionarios." The menu consisted of *sopa de tortilla, arróz à la mexicana, tortilla de huevos, barbacoa*, and mole. The accompanying exaltation of the former inhabitants of those ruins where this very Mexican occasion took place points to the stirrings of official *indigenismo* during the Centennial.[47]

Among the more spectacular displays of the month was the "Noche Mexicana," a night of music, dance, and food in Chapultepec Park sponsored by the official organizers with the help of charitable groups. This event, said the organizers, was "essentially Mexican," put together "totally with Mexican elements of distinct national arts."[48] Those in attendance were initially asked to purchase tickets from one of several locations in the capital for the September 26 event. Conditions arose, however, that changed the nature of the evening. A local newspaper, *El Demócrata*, criticized the Executive Committee for selling tickets and thus denying access to the majority of those people living in the capital. Further, a heavy downpour led the committee to move the Noche Mexicana to the following night. Claiming that an insufficient number of tickets had been printed, the committee opened the September 27 event to anyone who wanted to attend.

Between 300,000 and 500,000 people, mostly from the working classes, descended on Chapultepec Park on the night of the 27th.[49] Entertainment included Yucatecan, Yaqui, and Tehuana dances (which newspaper reporters from two dailies termed monotonous and boring), other Mexican dances including the *jamaica* and *jarabe*, regional music played by several groups including the Orquesta Típica, and fireworks; in one of the lakes, a fake Popocatépetl "erupted." From female volunteers dressed in regional clothing, members of the public could purchase flowers and confetti, jugs of water from Lake Pátzcuaro, and *platos típicos* such as enchiladas, tamales, atole, and *buñuelos* served on regional pottery.

Given the fact that *el pueblo* was allowed access to the extravaganza on the 27th, the Executive Committee sold tickets to a repeat of the Noche Mexicana on the 28th, bringing to Chapultepec Park many people from the middle and upper classes. Entertainment remained much the same as that of the 27th, with the addition of a performance by the National Ballet. Among those in Chapultepec on the 28th were visiting dignitaries, "high functionaries," and the "*bellas damas y senoritas* of our highest levels of society."[50] So despite federal efforts to foster social harmony and unity, the issue of socioeconomic class kept groups distinct during the Noches Mexicana. Still, all those in attendance were exposed to roughly the same cultural activities.

An appropriation of indigenous culture, characteristic of postrevolutionary Mexican statecraft, was commonplace during the month-long Independence commemoration. Indigenous arts were on display in a special exhibition of crafts on Calle Balderas in September 1921. The Executive Committee, with the help of artist Gerardo Murillo (Dr. Atl), arranged a week-long exhibition of indigenous crafts beginning on September 19. The exhibition, which was open free of charge to the public, included indigenous pottery, baskets, rugs, and other examples of native handiwork from different regions of Mexico. During an opening reception, Obregón led visiting and local dignitaries through the display, the centennial orchestra played traditional Mexican music, the same Yucatecan dancers performed, and tamales and atole were served.[51]

In addition to public displays of indigenous music, dance, and crafts, the excavations at Teotihuacán continued; pre-Columbian achievements were touted, and the Aztec goddess Xochiquetzál, protector of artists, was honored at a rite in Xochimilco. But the vigorous *indigenismo* of the late 1920s and 1930s was not yet in evidence, and the government's overriding objective, like that of the intellectuals in 1921, was to integrate the indigenous population into mestizo culture. In that sense the influence of intellectuals such as Manuel Gamio was palpable. Official perceptions of the contemporary indigenous population in 1921 tended toward racism and paternalism. Plutarco Calles had written the state governor of Quintana Roo in midyear asking what could be done to "civilize" the local Maya population.[52] Obregón himself considered the indigenous population redeemable. Having taught among them and "studied their psychology," he considered the Indian capable of being made a "cultured man."[53] Yet as the centennial observance illustrates, at least a nominal *indigenismo* had moved from the realm of artists and intellectuals, where it

had been evident since the late nineteenth century, to official government programs by 1921.[54]

The Obregón administration also utilized the centennial celebration as an opportunity to engage in social engineering, a practice that
was a "revolutionary project" but which also had its roots in the pre-
1910 era. Before and after the Revolution, middle-class reformers
saw Mexican "vices" (such as abuse of alcohol, gambling, poor hygiene and disease, and lack of a work ethic) as hindrances to the
country's social and economic development. "Developmentalism"
took on new vigor after 1920; and its adherents, including the new
political leaders, viewed discipline, education, and instruction in moral
values as their proper role.[55] The Centennial provided an opportunity
to instruct and encourage the masses. Many of the didactic and de-
velopmental aspects of the Centennial took place during the Week of
the Child (Semana del Niño) on September 11–18, when the Department of Health on the Paseo de la Reforma was turned into an educational and health-care facility for the lower classes. Children and their
parents from the poorest sections of the capital were transported on
streetcars free of charge to the downtown facility, where the children
were given free vaccinations and saw plays staged by local teachers
on health and hygiene issues. They could stay in monitored playrooms
while their parents attended lectures and viewed exhibits.

During the Week of the Child, parents received instruction regarding their rights as citizens, but the bulk of instruction during the
week related to health and child care. Health Department representatives lectured on prenatal care and childhood diseases, eye and dental
issues, proper nutrition, sanitation, and how as adults to avoid their
"four terrible enemies"—syphilis, gonorrhea, mental degeneration,
and alcoholism—which, they warned, impeded the "improvement of
the race." Possibly because of the number of people coming into the
capital from the countryside for the Centennial, a special exhibit addressed the particular needs of children of campesinos, or rural peasants. Mothers could take sick children to the facility and receive free
health care during the week.[56]

The Centennial as a Public Arena

Even though the federal government appropriated and oversaw the
official commemoration of Independence, those participating in the

event interpreted and utilized it in a variety of ways. As John Bodnar puts it, "commemorative events . . . are inevitably multivocal," full of rituals and other expressions "that give meaning to competing interpretations of past and present reality."[57] For example, the commemoration in Mexico led to lively debates in several states and in the capital over the meaning of the past and the nature and identity of national heroes.

When José de Jesús Núñez y Dominguez and other *capitaleño* elites conceived of a commemoration of September 27, 1821, their objective was to honor Agustín de Iturbide. These Conservatives venerated Iturbide in public observances, private gatherings, newspaper spreads, and the like, and they praised the Obregón government's decision to pay homage to him through such activities as the reenactment of Iturbide's entry into the capital on the 27th. But many of these men were not willing to rehabilitate Iturbide. Liberals were horrified with the veneration of the "traitor," and the debate over his rehabilitation was waged in newspapers and journal articles in the capital, on the floor of the Chamber of Deputies, and at public functions such as the patriotic gala sponsored by the Asociación del Colegio Militar on September 4.[58]

As the centennial observance unfolded during September, it became apparent that insurgent Vicente Guerrero was being generally ignored by official commemorations. A Junta Patriótica Liberal "Vicente Guerrero" appeared, and its members wrote Obregón complaining that Guerrero had been forgotten.[59] Others upset by the veneration of Iturbide included organizations of workers and students. The Confederación Regional Obrera Mexicana (CROM) and the Partido Estudiantil Juventud Revolucionario joined forces to host a series of public meetings in Mexico City and various states beginning September 11, the purpose of which was to discern as nearly as possible the historical facts that resulted in the events of September 27, 1821. The central topic of discussion at these gatherings was the character and actions of Iturbide; and Luis Morones, one of the two speakers, stated that Iturbide was treacherous.[60]

Responding to public criticism, Obregón wrote the president of the Executive Committee on September 22 saying that he thought it fitting that the committee organize a "demonstration of gratitude" at Guerrero's tomb, and that a floral offering be made there in honor of his service.[61] The committee complied, and the newspapers carried an announcement on September 25 that Guerrero would be remembered in a public ceremony on September 27. All patriotic societies, mutual benefit organizations, labor organizations, and workers were urged to arrive with their banners to lay a wreath dedicated to Guerrero at the Independence Column on the Paseo de la Reforma. Government ministers, deputies, and senators participated in the rite in which a military band played and Obregón placed the wreath with an inscription naming Guerrero as the "Consummator of Independence." Thousands attended the ceremony, including representatives of workers' organizations.[62]

This official recognition of Guerrero's role was not sufficient for some in the capital, however. In early October 1921 another ceremony was held by the League of Ayuntamientos of the Federal District and various organized labor groups, who apparently wanted to hold a memorial separate from that of the federal government. Announcements on October 2 invited the public in general to attend but particularly urged "workers' groups, students, and professors" to participate in "a great civic demonstration pro-Vicente Guerrero."[63] Thousands of people, a large portion of whom were workers, returned to the Independence Monument on October 3 to pay homage to their hero. Members of workers' organizations carried banners and placards criticizing the Executive Committee for ignoring Guerrero. According to newspaper accounts, speakers at the ceremony cited the life and deeds of General Guerrero, "rudely attacked" Iturbide, and called members of the Executive Committee "official buffoons."[64]

The most incendiary arguments over the national heroes took place on the floor of the Chamber of Deputies in September and early October 1921.[65] Tensions between some deputies and the centennial planners surfaced early in September; deputies complained that they were being left out of the official events, and that rather than being a celebration for *el pueblo*, the Centennial once again catered to the elite.[66] But the recognition of Iturbide as a hero of Independence was the issue that most inflamed Liberal passions in the Chamber of Deputies. Voices of dissent were raised over the centennial organizers' expectation that deputies would attend the ceremony in the Cathedral on September 16. Deputy Carlos Argielles complained, "Now they invite us to a Mass or a Te Deum, and I don't know what they are doing in the Cathedral, in complicity with the clergy, who have always been enemies of freedom . . . [and the Te Deum] in honor of the traitor Agustín [de] Iturbide!"[67]

During the third week of September, deputies Octavio Paz and Antonio Díaz Soto y Gama proposed the removal of Iturbide's name from the Galería de Hombres Ilustres in the Chamber of Deputies, and the debates began. Liberal deputies cast the issue in a revolutionary light: why had the Revolution been fought, they asked, when everyone apparently thought the same as during the Porfiriato? They were supported by the Partido Juventud Revolucionario, which formally endorsed the proposal. No doubt influenced by their ill will toward the Executive Committee, deputies voted 125 to 11 to remove Iturbide's name in early October 1921.[68]

In addition to acting as a site of contestation over the meaning of the past, the centennial observance brought out differing notions of national culture and identity. While the Obregón government touted *mestizaje*, the elites of the capital, who were major participants, used the commemoration to reinforce their own notions of national identity. The makeup of Mexico City's elites differed in 1921 from what it had been before the Revolution; it now included remnants of the old Porfirian aristocracy who maintained a social and economic position of some importance, newly influential intellectuals, and those of the middle class who had advanced economically and/or politically during the revolutionary years. That diversity is illustrated by the variety of ways in which the elites chose to reinforce their notions of self and national identity.[69]

For the "old elite," those who had enjoyed privileged positions both before and after the Revolution, the Centennial was an opportunity to glorify Mexico's European heritage. Dressed in their finery, they honored Iturbide's achievement by attending *veladas* and concerts dominated by European artists and music, Italian and French operas, and *juegos florales*, literary contests modeled on French competitions dating from the fourteenth century. At these events, Mexico City's upper classes listened to poetry, classical music, and speeches extolling their Spanish ancestry. On one such occasion, a "queen," chosen from among local society women, reigned over the evening wearing Empress Carlota's crown and sitting in one of Cortés's chairs.[70] Many in high society combined celebrations of the Centennial with an observance of Covadonga, a commemoration of a thirteenth-century Spanish victory over the Moors, which they celebrated with grand displays of Spanish finery and traditions that included a special Mass. María Tapia de Obregón, the president's wife, attended some of these fiestas wearing typical Spanish dress.[71] The local newspapers included pages of information about Spain: its history, culture, and activities in Mexico over time. Several newspapers published special centennial editions in early September that focused on Iturbide, his family, the colonial past, and Mexico's Spanish heritage.[72]

Also eager to accent Mexico's Spanish heritage during the Centennial was the Mexico City Ayuntamiento. In spite of the federal government's appropriation of that body's centennial project, the Ayuntamiento proceeded with some of its own activities, including the inauguration of a new park, the Parque España, on September 21. Municipal President Abreu placed the first stone in a monument to Isabel la Católica at the park. An editorial in the Conservative newspaper *El Universal* reported that the purpose of the park was to illustrate the goodwill between Mexico and the "Mother Country" as well as to "repudiate the old and unjustified prejudices that formerly separated" the two nations.[73]

Another component of the *capitaleño* elite, the intellectuals, also demonstrated their esteem for Mexico's Hispanic heritage during the Independence celebration, but it was in the context of a nationalistic exaltation of mestizo culture, which also contained strong elements of *indigenismo*.[74] Many intellectuals in 1921, inspired by the Revolution, engaged in what later became a cult of *mestizaje*. But as certain aspects of the centennial celebration demonstrate, the capital's intellectuals were still "kindling the fires of Hispanic reintegration" into Mexican culture in 1921.[75]

Among the most vocal of this group, thanks largely to his position as editor of one of Mexico City's most widely circulated newspapers (and the unofficial government mouthpiece), *El Universal*, was Félix Palavicini. A "petit bourgeois intellectual," Palavicini was an ardent Maderista, and his sentiments regarding national culture reflected the paternalistic reformist mentality typical of the Maderistas.[76] He considered Mexican culture essentially mestizo but greatly indebted to its Hispanic roots. During September 1921, *El Universal* focused on those events sponsored by the elite and the government. In its pages, Iturbide's role in Independence was emphasized, and in various ways Palavicini used the celebrations as an opportunity to exalt the country's Spanish heritage.[77]

An emphasis on the indigenous component of Mexican culture gained impetus among Liberal intellectuals after the Revolution.[78] Anthropologist Manuel Gamio, among others, published a number of works on indigenous history and culture in the early 1920s, and Mexican artists began to incorporate Indian themes into visual art. Gamio was instrumental in "reinstating Anahuác as the glorious foundation of Mexican history and culture."[79] But Gamio, who desired a homogenized nation with a unified language and culture, therefore considered it essential to incorporate the Indian into national life. Like many other intellectuals, Gamio "stressed the role of *mestizaje* in shaping the popular acceptance of Mexican identity."[80] Further, in spite of this new interest in indigenous culture, there continued a tendency among intellectuals as well as others in 1921 to emphasize "exotic" aspects of the Indian population. This tendency was illustrated during the Centennial by the case of "La India Bonita."

Several months before the centennial commemoration began, *El Universal* began a national search for a beautiful "racially pure" indigenous woman, "La India Bonita." She would participate in the Independence observances to illustrate the "union of the races" in postrevolutionary Mexico. The winner, selected by a panel of judges who included Gamio, was a sixteen-year-old from Puebla, María Bibiana Uribe, who was described as "Azteca" in the press. Uribe was chosen for her beauty and demeanor, which was described by *El Universal* as an almost "priestly attitude of Indian silence."[81] She was awarded 3,000 pesos, and a local businessman agreed to act as her *padrino*.

Uribe actively participated in Centennial events—something that would have been unheard of in the 1910 commemoration—but she was treated as the exotic "other" by high society and as a charity case by the middle-class reformers. The society women of the capital stared (in admiration, according to the press) at La India Bonita's costume, dark features, and delicate hands and feet as she was displayed at social and official functions.[82] She and her court received a percentage of house receipts at public events (where she was "wildly applauded" by those in attendance) as well as numerous gifts from Obregón and private individuals.[83] She also joined in the Independence celebration by riding a parade float that had been decorated as an Aztec war canoe. At the Cathedral she placed flowers before the remains of the Independence heroes while in the company of representatives from nearby "Indian" villages and participated in the *fiesta de Juil* in the village of Santa Anita.

Maria Bibiana Uribe's selection and treatment underscores the paternalist-reformist attitudes of many among the elite in 1921. Palavicini said that his desire to select a representative of the "indigenous race" to take part in the Centennial was prompted by a desire "to do something for the Indian," given the fact that they were ignored, indifferent, lacked will power, and "no one had offered them a hand to improve their social standing."[84] But at the same time, the contest was intended to symbolize *mestizaje*. When Palavicini presented Uribe with her cash prize, he said that her selection symbolized "the union of the Mexican race with Spanish blood, of which all of us present are children."[85]

After a month of hobnobbing with the big shots in the capital, Uribe was transformed, according to *El Universal*. No longer shy and retiring, she now possessed a glowing personality and much more money. Similarities to *Pygmalion* end here, however. Several months after the events of the Independence commemoration, *El Universal*'s rival *Excelsior* sent a reporter to Puebla to find Uribe to see how she was faring. The reporter discovered that she was not only a mestiza, which had made all the fuss in the capital over her "racial purity" a joking matter in Huachinango, but she was also a single mother. *Excelsior* took great delight, of course, in publishing this information.[86]

The centennial observance also illustrates the fact that participants in civic ceremonies often utilize such events to serve their own purposes, thus demonstrating more interest in individual or group needs than in reifying the aims of the dominant power. In September 1921, *capitaleños* from the working classes to the very wealthy used the occasion to confirm their social positions and to satisfy individual or group economic and social needs.

The wealthy engaged in lavish rituals that excluded the masses, and their positions were further secured by a fawning press that chronicled their every activity. For this group, the Centennial afforded a means of affirming the social hierarchy and instructing in "proper" values. In their centennial observances they attempted to restore the formal splendor of the Porfiriato with parades, "flowery wars," lavish balls, and other private affairs.[87] They reopened Mexico City's country club with great flourish in honor of the Centennial. Further, the upper classes sought to demonstrate proper values through charity work during September 1921. Like their counterparts in the Porfirian era, they distributed toys and candy to poor children, sold food and beverages at government-sponsored events for the popular groups, helped to distribute food and clothing to the poor, and aided in the week-long exposition on health and hygiene that was part of the centennial events. Works of charity had accompanied Independence commemorations in Mexico since the 1820s as organizers actively demonstrated "the meaning of Independence," but women's participation in such activities increased after 1890, when they became "icons who represented national unity . . . and liberty."[88]

Many Mexico City intellectuals also saw the centennial observance as an opportunity to cultivate and improve the masses, further evidence that, as Aurelio de los Reyes asserts, "moral-paternalistic messianism resurfaced in the Obregón years."[89] Among the events planned by this group was the series of public lectures on art and architecture organized by José Vasconcelos, additional lectures on Mexican art by Dr. Atl, exhibits at the Academy of Fine Arts, poetry contests, essay contests, and musical reviews. Some of the activities that intellectuals sponsored also revealed their notions of the past. For example, the music faculty of the National University gave a concert on September 25 in one of the capital's theaters for which the stage was decorated with scenes from Mexico's history. Students in costume depicted Spanish conquistadors burning the soles of the feet of Cuauhtémoc and the king of Texcoco to learn where the Aztec king's treasures were hidden.[90]

Neighborhood associations and municipalities utilized the commemoration to honor their own choice of Independence heroes, raise funds, make local improvements, hold parties and dances, and in other ways to take care of local needs. Funds were usually raised with a fair or, in the case of wealthier neighborhoods, with theatrical benefits. Improvements included street paving, bridges, parks, tree planting, and construction of pavilions and new markets. In several areas, funds went also to helping the poor. Concerts, parades, fireworks, children's festivities, *gallos* (street parties), and dances were the most common form of public celebrations at the local level, with the latter taking place especially in workers' neighborhoods. Many, but not all, local celebrations included at least some form of patriotic rite. Among heroes remembered were the Niños Heroes, the *insurgente anónimo*, Hidalgo, Morelos, Iturbide, and Guerrero. In the populous 7th District, a photo album would commemorate the events shared by the residents. Such activities not only helped these local groups to advance their own causes but also strengthened local customs and neighborhood bonds.[91]

Diversity also characterized Mexico City's lower classes in 1921, a factor that explains their varied reactions to the Centennial. *El Demócrata* ran a series of articles near the end of September relating the sentiments of several labor organizations. The paper reported that four manifestos had been circulated in the *centros obreros* criticizing the affair because, while the government claimed that the centennial observation was for the people, in effect it was for the bourgeoisie. Soldiers, workers, and the poor, complained those interviewed, were kept out of theaters, parades, and other public events by the middle and upper classes. In response to questions regarding acts of official benevolence, workers said that they did not need 10-*centavo* movie tickets or clothes as much as they needed a means to improve their circumstances.[92]

Yet many people from the working class gladly accepted free clothing and other government handouts; newspapers reported that in one district alone on September 10, between 1,200 and 1,300 men each received free pants, a shirt, a pair of shoes, and a hat. Many immediately put their new clothes on over their old clothes.[93] They turned out in large numbers for neighborhood dances, free musical performances in public spaces, including the Noche Mexicana, and for sports events. At a minimum, workers appropriated the commemoration for its entertainment value.

On patriotic occasions such as El Grito the lower classes celebrated according to their particular rituals. Their traditional propensity to commemorate Independence with revelries of their own design created annual problems for city officials, as some among them drank to excess and resorted to acts of public disorder. In 1921 workers loudly protested official efforts to name Iturbide a national hero, and they chose instead General Guerrero as the man most responsible for Independence. They also rejected the official recognition of Guerrero, preferring to honor him with their own commemoration. The workers' homage to Guerrero on October 3 demonstrates that some members of the lower classes maintained their own perception of the national past.

The lower classes also used the 1921 commemoration to meet their collective needs. The volunteerism of syndicate members in helping to distribute clothes and food to the poor and in helping to maintain public order strengthened their bonds, emphasized their solidarity, and signified a social hierarchy within the working class. The participation of union members in officially sponsored sports events for workers also solidified group ties.

The diverse populations of the capital responded differently to the Centennial as a whole. Near the end of the commemoration the pro-government *El Universal* once again contrasted the current observance to that of 1910 and attacked Díaz for using public monies to entertain the aristocracy and foreigners while excluding the masses, and for making that event totally foreign and omitting everything Mexican. Luckily, wrote Palavicini, times had changed, and the recent "social revolution" had given Mexicans pride in what was theirs. There existed a new appreciation of everything Mexican, including art, music, and literature. These changes were reflected in the 1921 centennial observance, he said, in that "all the fiestas have been for the people." No longer did the government cater to the aristocracy and foreigners; sombreros and *rebozos* (shawls) had taken the place of Parisian styles during the celebration. "We joyfully salute," concluded the editorial, this "nationalist sentiment" fostered by the Centennial Committee.[94]

Many people in the capital, however, took the opportunity to criticize the Obregón government for once again turning the centennial observance into a grand party for the elite. Much of the criticism could have been no more than political and class bickering over the meaning of the event. *El Demócrata* reported receiving numerous complaints, saying the festivities were for the pseudoaristocrats. "Ten years of revolution were fought to destroy unmerited privilege," yet the Centennial demonstrated that nothing had changed. "The revolutionary element is profoundly disgusted," claimed the editor.[95] Three Mexico City newspapers—*El Demócrata, Excelsior,* and *Omega*— carried editorial cartoons depicting the people's contempt for the centennial planners. Said the editor of *Omega*: "The masses have been greatly entertained . . . they didn't eat but they watched others eating."[96]

Conclusion

In this manner the 1921 Centennial of Mexico's achievement of Independence acted as a public space in which various groups contested public memory, the meaning of the past, national culture and identity, and, to a certain extent, the legitimacy of the state. For political leaders, it acted as a government "project" to enhance state power and legitimacy, promote national unity, instruct and improve the masses, and demonstrate to foreigners and citizens alike Mexico's natural wealth and material progress. For the elite, the affair served as a means of affirming their position in the social hierarchy, instructing others in appropriate values, and elaborating their diverse notions of authentic Mexican culture and identity. Popular groups appropriated the Centennial to affirm local and cultural ties and to meet material and social needs. Finally, the overall meaning of the commemoration was publicly debated as the state touted the popular character of the affair while critics of the Obregón government lamented its elitist nature.

Public memory was contested and negotiated as *políticos*, intellectuals and aristocrats, and workers challenged one another over the identity of the Mexican heroes, with some accusing others of not knowing their own history. Public memory of the Revolution thus became another issue debated during the commemoration. There was a general lack of consensus in 1921 regarding the nature and meaning of the Revolution. Some revolutionaries, including Deputy Díaz Soto y Gama, who had been pressuring Obregón to move quickly in agrarian and labor reform, challenged the official use of the Cathedral in public rituals. The Conservatives' labeling of the Liberal faction as Jacobins illustrates a competing version of events just past.[97] This lack of consensus enabled the Obregón government to formulate an "official" concept of the Revolution, glimpses of which emerged in the Centennial—for example, through reformist and populist activities.[98]

The various notions of national identity that emerged during the commemoration underscore the identity crisis plaguing Mexico in 1921. The old elite hung on tenaciously to their Hispanic roots. Their notions of true *mexicanidad* were bolstered by Conservative elements among the new elite who may have been influenced by their eagerness to be included in the inner circles of high society or by the depravity and violence of the previous decade, which they associated with the savage and poverty-stricken masses of the countryside. The trickle of *indigenismo* visible in the early part of the century had swelled to a steady stream after the Revolution, but many of those observers who extolled the indigenous aspects of Mexican culture were not yet certain how that component fit into the whole. *Mestizaje* was seized upon as the defining national characteristic, but definitions of the term fluctuated. The cult of *mestizaje* was in its formative stage in 1921, thanks in part to official support. The Obregón regime promoted that concept of national identity during the Centennial in its efforts to unite the country's diverse populations.

An examination of the 1921 centennial commemoration reveals a great deal not only about the state-building process in Mexico after the Revolution but also about the relative strength and consciousness of the new Sonoran state. Ever the pragmatists, the middle-class leaders relied on older, proven traditions to solidify and consolidate their power base during the Centennial. Even though federal officials attempted to make the observance a popular affair, the elite were allowed to shape the commemoration as well. Without the backing of a strong, unified class the new government was forced to cater to constituencies that could promote or pose a threat to national peace and development. Still, governmental control of the commemoration and the official "spin" given the affair's meaning demonstrate a conscious effort at statecraft. Elements of the revolutionary state that emerged throughout the 1920s were discernable in official mythmaking, cultural engineering, and the co-optation that took place during the 1921 centennial celebration. Above all, what we learn from the 1921 observance of Mexico's consummation of Independence is that state formation and the articulation of national identity are complex processes, and that those processes were well under way in Mexico in 1921.

Notes

1. Letter to Alvaro Obregón, June 1921, Archivo General de la Nación de México (AGN), ramo Obregón/Calles, vol. 312, leg. 711, exp. C-41.

2. In 1821 the Congress had designated September 27, the day on which Iturbide's army entered the capital to proclaim Mexican independence, as the date that would be officially celebrated. In 1823, after Iturbide's fall, new legislators changed the official holiday to September 16 to mark El Grito, Hidalgo's initiation of the independence struggle. Among the many issues under dispute by Mexican Liberals and Conservatives in the nineteenth century was which of the two events should be commemorated, for the conflict was in part over royalist versus criollo authority. The midcentury Liberal victory and, ironically, Maximilian's selection of September 16 as the official holiday, settled the dispute. See William H. Beezley, "Amending Memories: The Nimble Mnemonics of Nineteenth-Century Celebrations of Independence," unpublished paper presented to the seminar at the Latin American Centre, Cambridge University, 1995. Still, according to the records of the Ayuntamiento of Mexico City, September 27 was officially celebrated during the following years: 1838, 1841, 1844, 1849, and 1858.

September 27 was not commemorated in 1920 nor was it recognized in 1922 or thereafter. See National Archives of the United States, Record Group 59, Records of the Department of State, 812.407.

3. See, for example, William H. Beezley, Cheryl E. Martin, and William E. French, *Rituals of Rule, Rituals of Resistance* (Wilmington, DE, 1994); John Bodnar, *Remaking America: Public Memory, Commemoration, and Patriotism in the Twentieth Century* (Princeton, 1991); Alessandro Falassi, ed., *Time Out of Time: Essays on the Festival* (Albuquerque, 1987); Gilbert Joseph and Daniel Nugent, eds., *Everyday Forms of State Formation: Revolution and the Negotiation of Rule in Modern Mexico* (Durham, 1994).

4. Derek Sayer, "Dissident Remarks on Hegemony," in Joseph and Nugent, *Everyday Forms of State Formation*, 375.

5. Joseph and Nugent, *Everyday Forms of State Formation*, 13, quoting Phililp Corrigan and Derek Sayer's *The Great Arch*. For more on nineteenth-century ideas regarding cultural and political unity see, for example, Herman Lebovics, *True France: The Wars over Cultural Identity, 1900–1945* (Ithaca, 1992). A stream of recent literature treats the notion of contested national culture and identity. A common theme is reliance on the ideas of Antonio Gramsci, which may be found in part in "Notes on Italian History," from *Selections from the Prison Notebooks*, Quintin

Hoare and Geoffrey Smith, eds. (New York, 1971); Philip Schlesinger, "On National Identity: Some Conceptions and Misconceptions Criticized," *Social Science Information* 26 (1987): 219–64; Lebovics, *True France*; Lawrence Levine, "The Folklore of Industrial Society: Popular Culture and Its Audience," *American Historical Review* (December 1992): 1369ff.; Jack A. Goldstone, *Revolution and Rebellion in the Early Modern World* (Berkeley, 1990); Philip Corrigan and Derek Sayer, *The Great Arch* (Oxford, 1985).

6. Beezley, Martin, and French, *Rituals of Rule*, xiii.

7. Bodnar, *Remaking America*, 15. See also William H. Beezley, *Judas at the Jockey Club and Other Episodes of Porfirian Mexico* (Lincoln, NE, 1989), 129.

8. An account by this author of the manner in which the Centennial of 1921 was observed in the Mexican states is forthcoming.

9. Unless otherwise noted, information reported in this essay about events during the Independence observance was gathered from the newspapers *El Universal*, *Excelsior*, *El Demócrata*, *El Heraldo*, and *Omega* during the month of September 1921.

10. Aurelio de los Reyes, *Cine y sociedad en México, 1896–1930: Bajo el cielo de México, 1920–1924* (Mexico, 1993), 110–11.

11. Obregón responded that it was not at all certain that the federal government would participate in any such celebration, so he could not appoint Medellín to such a post. See correspondence between Medellín and Obregón, AGN, ramo Obregón/Calles, vol. 312, leg. 816, exp. C-65.

12. Letter dated February 9, 1921, from Municipal President Abreu to Obregón, AGN, ramo Obregón/Calles, vol. 312, leg. 104, exp. C-5. Abreu conceded that municipal and federal funds were scarce, but he suggested to the president that the commemoration be financed in part by charging admission to many of the patriotic events, which he predicted would not only pay for the affair but would also yield a profit of roughly 20,000 pesos. He later suggested another option: that Mexican industrial and commercial interests be asked to contribute to the costs. He also thought that perhaps foreign investors, including U.S. bankers, might wish to contribute financially. Their involvement, posited Abreu, would encourage them to attend the celebration, which would bring in foreign capital and enable the visitors to see firsthand that Mexico was on the road to recovery.

A printed program for the Ayuntamiento's proposed centennial celebration, "Proyecto de Festejos Conmemorativos del 1er. Aniversario de la Consumación de la Independencia Nacional Propuesto al H. Ayuntamiento de la Ciudad de México, por los Sres. F. Gamoneda & Arqto. Luis R. Ruíz," dated January 23, 1921, includes the Ayuntamiento's entire plan and may be found in the Archivo Historico de la Ciudad de México (AHCM), vol. 4006, leg. 5. For information on Palavicini's proposal of early January, see *El Universal*, September 10, 1921.

13. Correspondence between Abreu and Obregón may be found in AHCM, vol. 4006, leg. 5.

14. Archivo Fideicomiso Plutarco Elias Calles–Fernando Torreblanca (ACT), fondo Calles, gav. 1, exp. 9, inv. 9.

15. The Executive Committee was headed by Emilio López Figueroa, a former military officer and bureaucrat who had served as Inspector General of Police under Francisco Madero; two *diputados*, Juan de Díos Bojorquez and Carlos Argulles; and Martín Luis Guzmán, a Liberal intellectual who was selected to serve on the committee by his friend Alberto Paní. Handling publicity for the centennial program were the intellectual Manuel J. Sierra, son of Justo Sierra, and Luis G. Malvaez, referred to in the press as *un periodista revolucionario* and *diputado*.

16. The minutes of a Council of Ministers meeting in April 1921 recorded Obregón and the ministers' desire that the commemorative affair be kept simple in order to keep costs low. ACT, fondo Obregón, vol. 11040200, exp. 2, leg. 5/19, inv. 4796, p. 196. By July, when the program was complete, Obregón budgeted 500,000 pesos to cover federal expenses during the festivities. AGN, ramo Obregón/Calles, vol. 312, leg. 104, exp. C-5.

The government funded the centennial events with taxes on oil revenues and donations from private individuals and enterprises. Estimates were that total expenditures on the celebration were roughly 6 million pesos, which included food and clothing for the poor, military equipment, and the adaptation of the Hacienda of Chapingo into a School of Agriculture. See AGN, ramo Obregón/Calles, vol. 312; El Demócrata, September 14, 1921, September 9, 1921; Excelsior, September 14, 1921.

17. El Heraldo, September 15, 1921; El Demócrata, September 11, 1921, September 15, 1921. According to newspapers, not since 1910 had so many outsiders been in the capital. The hotels were full, as were all public venues associated with the centennial celebration. Many of these visitors came to Mexico City by train, and additional first- and second-class cars and even extra trains could not accommodate all the travelers, according to the newspapers. Even the worst hotel rooms commanded as much as 20 pesos per day, and private citizens rented out rooms in their homes to the visitors.

18. Events of the 1921 Centennial are listed in the capital's newspapers in September 1921 and may be found also in Programa Oficial para la Celebración del Primer Centenario de la Independencia en la Ciudad de México, National Archives of the United States, Record Group 59, 812.

19. See Alan Knight, "Popular Culture and the Revolutionary State in Mexico, 1910–1940," Hispanic American Historical Review 74, no. 3 (August 1994): 406.

20. Luis Garfias M., El triúnfo de la Revolución Mexicana (Mexico, 1994), 38–39.

21. Information regarding the military's place in the centennial observance comes from the pages of capital newspapers including El Heraldo, El Demócrata, El Universal, Excelsior and others, and from Gustavo Casasola, Histórica gráfica de la Revolución Mexicana, 1900–1960 (Mexico, 1964).

22. Among the delegates were representatives of Argentina, Chile, Brazil, Peru, Bolivia, Uruguay, Paraguay, Venezuela, Costa Rica, Nicaragua, El Salvador, Honduras, Guatemala, France, Spain, Italy, Belgium, Germany, Sweden, Norway, China, and Japan. The United States did not send an official representative, but the U.S. chargé d'affaires, George Summerlin, was in contact with the Obregón government as the events took place and reported centennial activities to the secretary of state. Summerlin wrote the State Department on September 24 that official entertainment of foreign dignitaries was "most elaborate and expensive."

Even though U.S. representatives did not participate in the commemoration, they could not resist interfering. Late in September, Summerlin reported that the rules of precedence prescribed by the Obregón government "to obtain among foreign missions . . . appear to be directly opposed to the provisions of Articles 3 and 4 of the Rules of the Vienna Congress of 1815, and one against which the Department may possibly feel disposed to protest." The U.S. government subsequently filed a protest with the Mexican government. National Archives of the United States, Record Group 59, 812.415/27; 812.415/28.

23. AGN, ramo Obregón/Calles, vol. 312, leg. 104, exp. C-5. The president issued a memo to the press on September 1, 1921, saying that he had given the

order to collect the street people and "*asilarlos*" (asylum inmates) in order to improve their conditions."

24. Despite his emulation of Díaz's actions of 1910, Obregón emphasized time and again the new path that Mexico had taken with the Revolution. In speeches to the foreign visitors, Obregón claimed that Mexico was beginning a new chapter in its history, but he also repeatedly stressed the need for a strong central government in order to maintain peace and promote prosperity. ACT, fondo Obregón, vol. 402, leg. 13/19, exp. 4796.

25. *El Heraldo* reported in late September 1921 that the municipalities of Guadalupe Hidalgo and Tacubaya had not designated land for the new schools, so there would be none built there. See September 20, 1921.

26. The federal government provided 500,000 pesos for the remodeling of the building, which had an iron framework that government officials considered worth preserving. Private investors who incorporated as the Exposición Comercial Internacional del Centenario raised additional funds. The exhibition hall included nine galleries with space for roughly 450 exhibitors, a theater that would seat 2,500 people, a restaurant, a room to show films, another to display machinery, an art gallery and concert hall, and rooms to entertain children. The exhibition, which was to display Mexican industrial and agricultural products, was designed to attract foreign commercial interests. In a pitch to Obregón for additional funding, the private investors claimed that a further advantage of the exhibition would be to encourage the development of the poultry and livestock industries in Mexico, much of which had been destroyed during the Revolution. See AGN, ramo Obregón/Calles, vol. 312, leg. 816, exp. C-65.

27. William Beezley, in describing the typical celebrations of El Grito in the nineteenth century, lists most of these same patriotic rituals. See his "Amending Memories."

28. Public homage to the Mexican flag was nothing new in 1921; such ceremonies were typical of national commemorations. The scale of this event, however, overshadowed even the 1910 children's homage to the flag. On that occasion, only boys from the official primary schools held a big children's parade in honor of the flag.

The more pro-government newspapers in Mexico City, in particular *El Universal* and *El Heraldo*, tended to look for signs of national unity and harmony during the 1921 centennial observance. Of the children's homage to the flag, the *El Heraldo* reporter remarked that the event brought together children from a variety of socio-economic backgrounds to celebrate their common past. The participants ranged, said the reporter, from wealthy children "hasta los humildes indigenas de las escuelas de Xochimilco con sus trajecitos de manta y sus huaraches de rojas correas." *El Heraldo*, September 16, 1921.

Flags for the *jura de la bandera* were distributed by the Executive Committee to local schools, but apparently some saw this effort as a money-making scheme. *El Heraldo* reported on September 13 that some schools in the capital were charging the children 50 *centavos* per flag. The paper brought the matter to the attention of the president of the Commission of Public Instruction, who asked the national parents' organization, Padres de Familia, to report any such abuses to the commission. *El Heraldo*, September 13, 1921.

29. Most of these allegories were not new. Based on correspondence related to the Centennial, it appears that these and other public performances that acted as part of the official program were selected by or had to be approved by the Executive Committee. See AGN, ramo Obregón/Calles, vol. 312, leg. 816.

30. Again, information regarding public performances and accounts of attendance may be found in newspapers of the capital during the month of September 1921.

31. Reflecting the fact that, despite the Revolution, some people in the capital continued to revere things Spanish, an editorial in *El Demócrata* on September 16, 1921, commented on the mood at El Grito. On p. 3 the editor said, "the *grito* has changed. No longer are rocks thrown at the homes of Spaniards, nor do voices shout, 'Die!' " He continued: "¡Viva España! ¡Viva España hermana! ¡Viva la América libre!"

32. In the 1910 centennial observance, various social groups participating in a parade placed flowers in front of the urn containing the ashes of Hidalgo and Morelos. The urn had been moved to the Cathedral for that occasion as well.

Underscoring the secular tone of the Obregón administration (and unlike 1910), the Catholic Church had no official role in the 1921 commemoration in the capital. The Catholic hierarchy objected strenuously to their exclusion from official celebrations. Mexico's archbishop José Mora y del Rio wrote in a pastoral letter of September that it was a travesty that God was left out of the commemoration of Independence, especially given His displeasure with the Mexican people over the violence of 1910–1920. To ensure that proper thanks was given to God, the Church held a special Mass on September 27. See *El Universal*, September 5, September 16, 1921. Church officials also issued circulars criticizing some of the festivities associated with the Centennial, in particular public dances because they led to sinful actions. *El Demócrata*, September 14, 1921.

The Vatican had made efforts to patch up differences with the postrevolutionary governments by sending the Bishop of Toronto, Monsignor Burke, to Mexico in 1919 to secure the repatriation of several prelates whom Carranza had repressed. Interim president De la Huerta was somewhat conciliatory toward the Church, reopening churches, repatriating clergy, and holding the October 1920 celebration of the anniversary of Columbus's voyages to America at the Basilica. Bishop Burke reported to the Pope that he had met with Obregón while in Mexico, and Obregón had "promised to respect the Church." The clergy's expectations were thus dashed during the Centennial. See De los Reyes, *Cine y sociedad*.

33. Capital newspapers reported early in the month that the Executive Committee planned to provide daily meals to the poor. A biting editorial in *El Heraldo* on September 4 opined that while officials said that the government would feed about 500 people at each site, the fact that so many beggars had been put into *asilos* (asylums) would greatly reduce that figure. See September 4, 1921. During the 1910 centennial observance, as in many prior national celebrations, the Díaz government had provided free meals and inaugurated new schools, hospitals, and public buildings.

34. Several times during September, newspapers reported instances of corruption associated with these efforts at helping the poor. For example, employees at police stations in two districts made the poor pay for the tickets with which to claim "free" clothing. In another episode, a federal employee was found charging poor families for birth certificates for their children, when the government intended that the service be free of charge during the month of September. See *El Heraldo*, September 12 and 13, 1921.

35. *El Heraldo* stated on September 27, 1921, that the Ley de Indulto resulted in 800 people being released from prisons during the month to date. For those remaining in prison in the capital, the Executive Committee organized special events

such as the showing of films, music, dances, special meals, and patriotic speeches, all of which were open to their family members as well.

36. The intentions of the Centennial Committee to make the 1921 celebrations populist may be found in the minutes of the April Cabinet Meeting: ACT, fondo Calles, gav. 16, exp. 74, inv. 1090. In an *informe* to legislators in early summer 1921, Obregón stated that the fiestas would have "a fully popular character"; Obregón, "Informe Presidencial," n.d., ACT, fondo Obregón, 11040200, leg. 2, exp. 11/19, inv. 4796, p. 25. Executive Committee president López de Figueroa announced that the celebration would not commemorate the political triumph of a privileged class, but the triumph of the people. *El Universal*, Edición Conmemorativo del Primer Centenario de la Consumación de la Independencia, vol. I, no. 4. Despite officials' claims that the 1921 celebration was for "the people" while that of 1910 was for elites, during the 1910 centennial celebration President Díaz's Centennial Commission had planned free plays, concerts, and dances for the general public on several occasions.

37. John Hart, *Revolutionary Mexico* (Berkeley, 1987), 337.

38. De los Reyes, *Cine y sociedad*, 100.

39. Alan Knight, "Revolutionary Project, Recalcitrant People: Mexico, 1910–1940," in Jaime Rodríguez O., ed., *The Revolutionary Process in Mexico: Essays on Political and Social Change, 1880–1940* (Los Angeles, 1990), 231.

40. ACT, fondo Obregón, 11040200, leg. 2, exp. 2/19, inv. 4796.

41. A history of the working classes in Mexico City during and after the Revolution is provided in Donald C. Hodges, *Mexican Anarchism after the Revolution* (Austin, 1995); John Hart, "The Urban Working Class and the Mexican Revolution: The Case of the Casa del Obrero Mundial," *Hispanic American Historical Review* 58, no. 1 (1978): 1–20; and idem, *Anarchism and the Mexican Working Class, 1860–1931* (Austin, 1978), among other sources. The newspaper *El Universal* claims that the Executive Committee requested the help of the syndicate, but *El Heraldo* and *El Demócrata* report that members of the syndicate volunteered their services for these purposes. Regardless, the workers participated in the Centennial in this manner.

Officials expressed a desire to celebrate the Centennial in a "dignified" way numerous times in the planning stage, including in statements in the press and in the cabinet meeting of April 1921. David E. Lorey addresses the issue of public disorder in commemorative events in Chapter Ten, this volume. The celebrations of El Grito in which a number of people were killed and injured, both before and after 1921, were common. See National Archives of the United States, Record Group 59, 812.415/35 and 812.415/38, for example.

42. Information regarding working-class participation in official commemorations was taken from Mexico City newspapers, particularly *El Demócrata* and *El Heraldo*, and from Casasola, *Historia Gráfica*, 2:1560.

43. See, for example, Alan Knight, "Popular Culture and the Revolutionary State in Mexico"; and Lorey, Chapter Ten, this volume.

44. Alvaro Obregón, "Informe Presidencial," n.d., ACT, fondo Obregón, 11040200, leg. 2, exp. 11/19, inv. 4796, p. 25.

45. Officials at times even asked private groups sponsoring centennial events to make their activities essentially "Mexican." When Mexico City's School for the Blind was organizing one of the many musical reviews that took place during September, Obregón persuaded Juan Cervantes, the school's director, to include as many Mexican artists as possible. Cervantes had been planning to hire a number of show people who were in Mexico City with Jack Mason's New York Review for his own

production, but Obregón intervened. The president had nothing against foreign artists, he said, but since foreign dignitaries were there for the festivities, the country should put on exhibit only Mexican artists. See correspondence between Obregón and Cervantes, September 16 and 17, 1921, AGN, ramo Obregón/Calles, vol. 312, leg. 816, exp. C-65.

46. Such events were apparently very well attended. A newspaper review of September 17 reported that the Teatro Iris was filled and "a great multitude of all our social classes struggled . . . to enter. It was necessary to close the doors." *El Heraldo*, September 17, 1921.

47. *El Universal*, September 14, 1921.

48. Ibid., September 26, 1921.

49. *El Heraldo* reported on September 28, 1921, that 300,000 people were in attendance; *El Demócrata* reported on the same day that 500,000 were present.

50. *El Heraldo*, September 29, 1921.

51. Dr. Atl is generally recognized as a leader in the nationalistic muralist movement in Mexico during the 1920s, in which José Clemente Orozco, David Siqueiros, Diego Rivera, and others participated. Beginning in the 1920s, these artists regularly incorporated indigenous themes into their art. Dr. Atl, a Marxist and at one time an anarchist, had worked with Obregón on various occasions. For example, he acted as the government's emissary to the Casa del Obrero Mundial in 1920. See John Hart, *Anarchism and the Mexican Working Class*, 132; Leopoldo Castedo, *A History of Latin American Art and Architecture from Pre-Columbian Times to the Present* (New York, 1969), 224ff.

52. The governor, Librado Abitía, responded that he would send teachers in the following year: "As you know, these Maya Indians are completely degenerate since they almost never work, eat poorly, and abuse alcohol." If they continued in that behavior, he predicted, the race would disappear. ACT, fondo Calles, gav. 1, exp. 9, inv. 9.

53. ACT, fondo Obregón, 11040200, exp. 2, leg. 5/19, inv. 4796.

54. In early 1921 the Ministry of Agriculture hired anthropologist Manuel Gamio to conduct a national study of *las razas indígenas* to determine their needs and to create legislation aimed at "redeeming" them.

55. See Elaine C. Lacy, "Literacy Policies and Programs in Mexico, 1920–1958" (Ph.D. diss., Arizona State University, 1991), chapter two.

56. Information on the Semana del Niño may be found in the majority of *capitaleño* newspapers of September 1921.The government's educational efforts generally resulted in favorable comments in the press. One editorial praised the government, saying: "We have permitted each family to act as an isolated tribe, . . . without the state or society working toward the unification of their efforts in the sense of the general betterment of all. The true creation of the Mexican nation lies with the current generation. We must put on each child the stamp of the new race." The Obregón government had taken steps in that direction with the Semana del Niño, according to *The Mexican Herald*, September 13, 1921.

57. Bodnar, *Remaking America*, 16.

58. Ing. Federico Cervantes, identified in the press as an official of the Federal Army and a Villista, spoke in opposition to Iturbide's rehabilitation at the event sponsored by the Asociación del Colegio Militar, arguing in support of Guerrero as the real hero of Independence. See *El Heraldo*, September 5, 1921. His remarks brought a storm of protest from many persons in attendance. See *El Universal* and *Excelsior* on the following days.

59. See letters pertaining to Guerrero's place in the centennial observance in AGN, ramo Obregón/Calles, vol. 312, leg. 711, exp. C-41.

60. *El Demócrata*, September 12, 1921.

61. Letter from Obregón to López Figueroa, AGN, ramo Obregón/Calles, vol. 312, leg. 711, exp. C-41.

62. *El Demócrata*, September 28, 1921.

63. Ibid., October 2, 1921.

64. *El Heraldo*, October 4, 1921.

65. Information on the actions of the Chamber of Deputies related to the Centennial was taken from the *Diario de los Debates de la Camara de Diputados del Congreso de los E.U. Mexicanos*, Año II–Periodo Ordinario XXIX Legislatura, vol. 3 (September and October 1921), and from Mexico City newspapers of the same period.

66. A factor that increased tensions was that the deputies, after attempting and failing to receive additional funds from Obregón for expenditures on the centennial festivities, in a secret session voted 750,000 pesos in extraordinary expenses for their own use during the celebrations. The public, incited by criticism of the *diputados* by several Mexico City newspapers, was outraged. Deputies argued that the funds were necessary, given that they, too, planned to honor visiting dignitaries and had been excluded from official functions.

67. *El Universal*, September 14, 1921. During the debates over the national heroes, Liberal deputies accused their Conservative opponents of not knowing their own history. Conservatives labeled Liberal deputies "Jacobins."

In response to criticism over holding the recognition of the Independence heroes in the Cathedral, government officials made it clear that in the future such ceremonies would take place at a new Pantheon of the Independence Heroes, the first stone of which would be laid during the centennial observance. The government allocated 1 million pesos for the structure. Apparently it was never constructed, however. See *El Universal*, Centennial Edition, September 1, 1921.

68. *El Demócrata*, October 8, 1921.

69. For a discussion of elite society in the capital in the 1920s, see Larissa Adler Lomnitz and Marisol Pérez-Lizaur, *A Mexican Elite Family, 1820–1980: Kinship, Class, and Culture* (Princeton, 1988); Alan Knight, "The Mexican Revolution: Bourgeois? Nationalist? Or Just a 'Great Rebellion'?" *Bulletin of Latin American Research* 4 (1985): 1–37; idem, *The Mexican Revolution: Counter Revolution and Reconstruction* (New York, 1986); Leone B. Moats, *Thunder in Their Veins* (New York, 1932); and John Hart, *Revolutionary Mexico*.

70. The crown was loaned for the event by one of the "damas antiguas" of the court of Maximilian. De los Reyes, *Cine y sociedad*, 122.

71. The president himself was swept up in the admiration of all things Spanish. In an *Excelsior* article of September 4, 1921, in which the newspaper reported that Mexico had renewed close ties with Spain, Obregón responded to a reporter's query as to whether Mexico should erect a monument to Hernán Cortés. Ever the politician, the president said that he would first prefer to test public opinion on the topic, but he claimed to be "an admirer of the feats" of Cortés and thought that the cruelties committed by the conquistadors were "of the times and not of Spain." In the same interview, Obregón expressed his desire to meet the members of a Spanish opera company that was performing in Mexico City, in order to express to them his admiration of Spain, and he indicated his intention to invite King Alfonso XIII to visit Mexico.

72. The role played by newspapers in defining national culture should not be minimized. Benedict Anderson argues that the novel and the newspaper "provided the technical means for 're-presenting' the *kind* of imagined community that is the nation." See *Imagined Communities: Reflections on the Origin and Spread of Nationalism* (London, 1983), 23–25.

73. *El Universal*, September 21, 1921. A monument to Queen Isabella was begun during the 1910 centennial observance, but because of the chaos of the Revolution, no one could recall where the monument had been started. Editor Félix Palavicini opined in an editorial that Isabella was not the best figure to represent ties between Mexico and Spain, given that any Latin American country could erect a statue in her honor for the same reason. Instead, the person who most represented the link between Mexico and Spain was Hernán Cortés, the "racial father of Mexico."

74. Information regarding the various currents of Liberal intellectual ideas in the early twentieth century was taken from Henry C. Schmidt, *The Roots of Lo Mexicano: Self and Society in Mexican Thought, 1900–1934* (College Station, TX, 1978); Enrique Krauze, *Caudillos culturales en la Revolución Mexicana*, 6th ed. (Mexico, 1990); Enrique Florescano, *El patrimonio cultural de México* (Mexico, 1993); Roger Bartra, *The Cage of Melancholy: Identity and Metamorphosis in the Mexican Character* (New Brunswick, NJ, 1992); and Alan Knight, *The Mexican Revolution: Counter Revolution and Reconstruction*, among others.

For a discussion of nationalism and *mestizaje* after the Revolution, see Alan Knight, "Racism, Revolution, and *Indigenismo*: Mexico, 1910–1940," in Richard Graham, ed., *The Idea of Race in Latin America, 1870–1940* (Austin, 1990). The effort to articulate Mexican identity and culture was not new in the postrevolutionary period; it had occupied Mexican thinkers and writers since the eighteenth century. In the nineteenth century, literary societies, newspapers, and journals "boosted interest in Mexicanism." See Schmidt, *The Roots of Lo Mexicano*, 28.

75. See Schmidt, *The Roots of Lo Mexicano*, 88–89. The influential intellectual Alfonso Reyes no doubt contributed to this mindset. Reyes had left Mexico for Spain in 1913 after the political fall of his father Bernardo and returned to Mexico City after the Revolution. Reyes's essays, which emphasized the Spanish component of Mexican identity, had great impact in the capital.

76. See Alan Knight, *The Mexican Revolution: Porfirians, Liberals, and Peasants* (Cambridge, 1986), 62, 66–67. *El Universal* first appeared on the scene in 1916, and it regularly published the ideas of Mexico's intellectuals, especially the "seven wise men," remnants of the Ateneo de la Juventud. See Krauze, *Caudillos culturales*.

77. For example, *El Universal* sponsored a number of contests related to the Centennial, including the aforementioned *juegos florales*; and one of them, a literary contest, rewarded the best essay on the topic of whether Iturbide "should be rehabilitated in the hearts and minds" of Mexicans. Another required a synthesis of the "civilizing work of the Spanish conquerors." Palavicini also played a key role in convincing the Ayuntamiento of Veracruz to rename one of its major thoroughfares "Avenida Hernán Cortés" as part of the centennial observances.

78. For a discussion of *indigenismo* in the postrevolutionary era see Alan Knight, "Racism, Revolution, and *Indigenismo*," 82–83, 86. As Knight explains, a strain of *indigenismo*, mostly rhetorical in nature, had surfaced toward the end of the Porfiriato, and more strident "Indianism" gained strength during the 1920s. Ideas regarding the place of the Indian in Mexican society were in flux in 1921.

79. David A. Brading, "Manuel Gamio and Official Indigenismo in Mexico," *Bulletin of Latin American Research* 7 (1988): 76.

80. Schmidt, *The Roots of Lo Mexicano*, 78; De los Reyes, *Cine y sociedad*, 108ff. Gamio published a number of books on Mexico's indigenous populations, including *Forjando Patria*, *Ethos*, and a five-volume work entitled *La población del Valle de Teotihuacán*.

81. *El Universal*, September 25, 1921. María Bibiana Uribe was from San Andrés Tenango in Puebla. See *El Universal*, August 2, 1921. Information regarding her *padrino* may be found in *El Universal*, August 24, 1921.

82. *El Universal* reported that at a social gathering in honor of Uribe, she was "the object of stares of all the elegant men and women gathered there. What curiosity was in the delicate faces of the female guests! It was as though they looked at a rare flower." María was not intimidated by the fine tapestries and rich furnishings, the paper reported, for "she had known the riches of Moctezuma and Netzahualcoyotl." Her coarse long cotton dress and bare feet were "charming" alongside the fashionable short silk skirts and "very fine" shoes of the society women. See *El Universal*, August 4, 1921.

83. Ibid., August 17, 1921.

84. Ibid., September 25, 1921.

85. *El Heraldo*, September 25, 1921.

86. De los Reyes, *Cine y sociedad*, 123.

87. In describing nineteenth-century celebrations, William Beezley says that "flowery wars" emerged in the Porfirian era as part of high society's efforts to re-create the glorious indigenous past. The flowery war, "a mock re-creation of the Aztec ritual, [was] a parade of coaches decorated with flowers from which passengers hurled blossoms at each other." See *Judas at the Jockey Club*, 16–17. Beezley also describes the Porfirian elite practice of adding lavish private affairs to religious and civic holidays, which were then reported in great detail in the newspapers' society pages, in "The Porfirian Smart Set Anticipates Thorstein Veblen in Guadalajara." See Beezley, Martin, and French, *Rituals of Rule*, 173–90.

The notion of elite celebratory practices acting as examples of virtuous behavior was common during the Porfiriato as well. Beezley describes a handbill from that era that encouraged holiday traditions in which the rich would act as examples for the poor. See "Porfirian Smart Set," 186. In 1896 elites in Mazatlán staged a type of "flower war" in order to "wean the natives from coarser sports." *Judas at the Jockey Club*, 129. In the early 1920s, Mexico City newspapers gushed over elite social practices, praising their fine examples as they attended events such as symphony concerts.

Mexico City elites recognized the need for and their role in improving the social and cultural level of the masses in 1921. Early that year Municipal President Herminio Pérez Abreu asked Miguel Lerdo de Tejada to look for means of elevating the morality, culture, and "artistic level of entertainment" of the common people, "since the Ayuntamiento was like a father that should care for the moral health of the children." De los Reyes, *Cine y sociedad*, 104.

The Porfirian past continued its hold on many of the *capitaleño* elite throughout the Obregón years. In 1922 a number of films appeared about Díaz, which, together with those exhibiting the Porfirian-style lavishness of the 1921 Centennial, created a public controversy over the Díaz years. The newspaper *Excelsior* in 1922 published the dictator's memoirs in part in response to the debate. See De los Reyes, *Cine y sociedad*, 126.

88. Beezley, "Porfirian Smart Set," 186; idem, "Amending Memories," 7.

89. De los Reyes, *Cine y sociedad*, 104.

90. *El Heraldo*, September 26, 1921.

91. Information regarding neighborhood activities may be found in several Mexico City newspapers in September 1921. Those with more information on this topic include *El Heraldo* and *El Demócrata*. Information may also be found in the AGN, fondo Obregón/Calles, vol. 312, leg. 816, exp. C-65.

92. *El Demócrata*, September 23, 1921.

93. *El Heraldo*, September 11, 1921.

94. *El Universal*, September 24, 1921.

95. *El Demócrata*, September 23, 1921.

96. *Omega*, September 15, 1921.

97. Comparisons between the Mexican and French Revolutions were not uncommon in the capital during that time. An editorial in *El Demócrata* upon the occasion of Obregón's assumption of the presidency likened the recent Revolution to the French conflict and said that the Mexican Revolution was now over. ACT, fondo Obregón, 110402, exp. 2, leg. 1/19, inv. 4796.

98. The Obregón government's progress in the area of land reform worked its way into the centennial observance as well. Obregón considered a gradual redistribution of land best, and his government slowly returned or created new ejidal lands. To collect political capital from these efforts, the government organized a *fiesta del ejido* as an official component of the centennial celebration. *El Universal* reported that in each of the *mil poblaciones* that had received ejidal lands, residents would come together and celebrate by planting a tree on September 16, and the oldest local citizen would pronounce the "Oración del Ejido" which the government distributed. See September 15, 1921.

CHAPTER TEN

Postrevolutionary Contexts for Independence Day
The "Problem" of Order and the Invention of Revolution Day, 1920s–1940s

DAVID E. LOREY

After the most violent phase of the Mexican Revolution (1910–1920) was over, Independence Day came to be celebrated in a new context—the very vibrant ritual context molded by the recent experience of civil war and popular mobilization. While September 16 continued to draw massive crowds and much comment in the Mexico City press, it ceded an important measure of its symbolic value to new, "revolutionary" festivals. Such revolutionary festivals provide a unique window through which to view the role of public ritual in the process of political consolidation and in social change after the Revolution.

The most important public ritual to arise from the Revolution came to be held on November 20, "Revolution Day." The date commemorates Francisco I. Madero's famous call to arms in 1910: on November 20 all towns in Mexico were to rise up against the thirty-four-year rule of Porfirio Díaz. Although Madero was forced to take action before the appointed date and the Revolution got off to a premature start, November 20 has generally been accepted as the beginning of the violent phase of the revolutionary struggle.

Starting as a scattered series of informally organized events in the late 1910s and early 1920s, the Revolution Day holiday developed in the mid- and late 1920s into an officially sanctioned event of massive proportions. By the early 1930s, November 20 had become the most important date on the postrevolutionary calendar of secular holidays, even without official status as a national holiday. Public events on November 20 were extremely well attended, attracting tens of thousands of participants and spectators: in 1931, 20,000 athletes took part in the parade; in 1932, 30,000; in 1934, 50,000.[1] The number of persons marching in the parade may have been matched by five times as many spectators.[2]

Featured events on Revolution Day were a military parade, sports displays, speeches, dedications, and various other public spectacles involving at times the highest officials. By the late 1930s the parades on Revolution Day included a wide array of actors representing important social sectors and corporate groups: the army, the states, public and private schools, private clubs and social groups, professional and philanthropic organizations, labor unions, women's groups, indigenous groups, and regional and folkloric characters such as *charros* (cowboys). The date of November 20 was used for many simultaneous symbolic acts. In 1936, for example, a new 100-peso note bearing the picture of Madero was issued on November 20.

Throughout the 1920s and 1930s, Mexican policymakers debated whether to designate November 20 as a national holiday, a festival day without work. Although the date was proposed as a national holiday to commemorate the reformist impulse represented by Madero's challenge to the *ancien régime* as early as 1917, it was not until 1936 that November 20 was officially approved as Revolution Day. By that time, the date had come to signify much more than the reformist beginnings of Madero's revolution; it had expanded to encompass a revolution of myriad meanings.

The "Problem" of Order and Traditional Popular Festivals

Perhaps the central image or leitmotif of the November 20 events was order in all things: orderly conduct in the public sphere served as a symbolic foundation for order in political and social life. The order of the parade route, the ordering of marchers, and orderly individual and group behavior on Revolution Day all contrasted with other contemporary celebrations.[3] This concern with order on November 20, I suggest, was a reaction to the historical pattern of celebrations of Independence Day on September 16 and the Day of the Virgin of Guadalupe, Mexico's patron saint, on December 12.[4] Prior to the emergence of the November 20 holiday, celebrations of these dates were the favorite annual public festivities for large sectors of the population. Both commemorations bore the markings of traditional popular festivals in which "feasts and disturbances were one."[5]

The disorderly celebration of traditional festivals took many forms. Individuals acted in disorderly fashion, of course, but there was also an encompassing social or collective disorder that characterized traditional commemorations of patriotic dates. Additionally, there were occasions of community—or corporate—disorder, moments when disorder was organized to accomplish a specific political purpose.[6] It was common for newspaper accounts of both the Independence Day and December 12 revels to distinguish between popular and elite celebrations, noting the overwhelmingly popular character of the dates. In 1922 one wit noted that while the rich celebrated September 16 with more respectability, the rest had a better time.[7] In general, popular festivities overshadowed the official remembrance of these dates.[8]

Celebrations of Independence Day had long been characterized by the individual and community display of high spirits (frequently fueled by alcohol), violence, and massive street parties distinguished by "music and noise in all quarters." In the 1930s, Independence Day crowds in the streets of Mexico City were estimated to number in the hundreds of thousands (at a time when residents of the city numbered no more than two million).[9] Along with everyday rowdiness, individuals in these crowds committed assaults, burglaries, shootings, robberies, thefts, and other acts of delinquency.[10] Automobile drivers, many of them drunk, hit pedestrians, after which they usually fled the scene.[11] The patriotic enthusiasm of popular celebrants was frequently used as an excuse for high jinks of various kinds. In 1926 a man was roughed up for not yelling "¡Viva México!" A cartoon of 1923 has a man who has killed another man and wounded others explaining his acts by saying that he was carried away by patriotism. The stealing of Mexican flags was also a part of the disorder of September 16.[12]

The expression of high spirits by Independence Day revelers was aided by the protective cover of night, as festivities usually reached a peak late in the night of September 15 in recognition of Father Miguel Hidalgo's early-morning call to arms on September 16, 1810. Continuing the trend established during the Porfiriato, this nighttime climax was reached after three days of preparatory festivities, including the Day of the Charro on September 14 and special events such as the Festival of Light of 1924, in which merchants of the Tacoma area of

Mexico City heralded the arrival of electricity.[13] Probably because the activities took place largely at night and because they generally involved drinking and mayhem, September 16 celebrants were pre-

La Gritería (The uproar) by Ric y Ric. From *Excelsior*, September 16, 1945.

dominantly male, as indicated in photographs and cartoons.[14] High spirits frequently had their sequel in disorder and violence of various sorts:

> During the afternoon, the crowds in the taverns grew larger; they grew even more during the evening. When the running around of the multitudes through the streets of the central areas began, there was a shocking number of drunken persons who appeared to have been vomited up by Hell, such was their badness and so horrendous their blasphemies.
>
> And since no one obeyed the government decrees (and the police did not have the courage to make people comply), these knaves used pistols or daggers, depending on their category; and because the savagery among the rabble is always colored by a bloody and cowardly hue, aggressions and attacks became frequent. A terrifying number of shameful acts were committed, which shows the criminal influence of alcohol on the fierce instincts of the riffraff.

Automobiles, driven by crazed drivers, collaborated with the terrible drunks in the carnage. With their thoughtless speed, without paying any attention to traffic signals or even to pedestrians, they careened all over the place, running into one another, killing anyone who got in their way, and knocking down an infinity of persons.[15]

Minutes before the *grito*, the drunkenness of Miguel Sánchez made him crazy and, armed with a pistol, he entered the patio of his *vecindad* [a type of dwelling] shooting all around, obliging his peaceful neighbors to barricade themselves in their apartments. But Dolores Salas Gómez did not realize the dangerous mood of her neighbor and left her apartment door open. Sánchez was able to enter and fired three shots that fortunately did not find their mark. The drunken man, probably thinking that he had killed Dolores (who, frightened, had thrown herself on the bed), left her apartment running, jumped in a car in the street, and fled.[16]

Like September 16, December 12 was characterized by huge crowds of people in the streets and a myriad of popular entertainments. On the Day of the Virgin, pilgrims from all over the country, numbering in the hundreds of thousands, flocked to Guadalupe's Basilica north of Mexico City to make offerings and take part in the festivities.[17] The streets leading to the Villa de Guadalupe were choked with pedestrian and motor traffic, the latter providing transportation from the center of the city to the site. At times the streets became so crowded that traffic ground to a standstill for hours.[18]

Although on December 12 the "carriages of the aristocratic classes" made their way through the crowded streets "mixing with the dirty buses" of the poor, the Day of the Virgin had been the preeminent popular celebration in Mexico ever since Mary's supposed appearance to the humble mestizo, Juan Diego, in the sixteenth century. On December 12 the popular classes dominated the scene at the Basilica and in the surrounding streets, even if rich Mexicans too made their devotions.[19] There were balloon ascensions, bullfights, lotteries, shooting galleries, "Indian" dances, a blessing of roses, feasts of traditional foods, and the imbibing of traditional drinks in front of the flower-bedecked church. After nightfall, celebrants were dazzled by great fireworks displays representing the four apparitions of the Dark Virgin.

Popular groups took advantage of the occasion of December 12 to disport themselves in drinking, fighting, the protesting of price increases, and other secular activities.[20] As was the case with Independence Day, the most exciting occurrences on December 12 seem to have taken place after dark. Typical of the annual mayhem are the following two notices:

> José de la Cruz and his lover, María Villarreal, both drunk, began to fight because [José] paid a compliment to a passing girl and [María], in revenge, smiled at a man she did not know. The jealousy sparked in both of them goaded them into a bloody fight, and, as both of them were persons *de pelo en pecho*, having among their clothes knives, they drew them and attacked each other furiously. Both were gravely injured.
>
> Another of the wounded was Moisés Nieto, who, being completely drunk and seeing a train approaching, took it into his head to play bullfighter with it. He stood in the middle of the tracks, trying to wave it on with his jacket. . . . Although the engineer tried to stop the train, he was unable to do so in time and the unfortunate [Nieto] was struck and thrown on the rails, the wheels of the locomotive amputating his leg.[21]

There were official attempts to control such disorderly outbursts of popular patriotic enthusiasm on September 16 and December 12. The most general were the moving of the principal Independence Day festival to a stadium (the Mexico City racetrack), where onlookers were seated rather than were able to mill about in the open. Enclosed spaces such as stadiums lent themselves to more ordered shows commemorating the anniversary. To limit public drunkenness and violence, drinking in bars, liquor sales after noon, and the carrying of firearms in the street were prohibited on September 16.[22]

Various attempts were also made to replace boisterous street festivals with private parties, which often took the form of European-style entertainment: "These kermesses will not be like so many popular fiestas, but rather will be subject to appealing programs and to the strictest morality. Gambling or diversions that might be scandalous or disagreeable will not be permitted."[23] In accord with these initiatives, wealthier celebrants increasingly took their Independence partying indoors. Beginning in the early 1930s, Mexico City restaurants hosted special Independence Day dinners and competed with one another to attract middle-class patrons.[24]

Similar measures also developed for December 12. In 1926 the Basilica was closed at seven o'clock in order to discourage late-night rowdiness. Attempts were made to stagger the arrival of groups of pilgrims at the Virgin's shrine in order to prevent the gatherings from taking on the "character of a public protest."[25] Special police details, including mounted gendarmes, encircled the area with checkpoints where they attempted to see that no alcoholic beverages, knives, or firearms passed through.[26] Concern with order on December 12 seems to have increased over the course of the 1930s. Headlines begin to trumpet the "scandals," fights, and numbers of dead and wounded or, alternately, and gradually increasing over the decade, the achievement of "complete order."[27]

Such attempts to reform the "popular and unstructured" nature of the rituals with order were generally unsuccessful, however.[28] One example suffices to illustrate the difficulty. On Independence Day in 1922, three persons were reported killed and twenty-eight wounded from pistol shots fired on the night of the 15th. When authorities intervened the following year to limit the celebratory shooting of pistols, the outcome was nevertheless strikingly similar: three persons were reported killed and twenty-eight wounded—but this time all concerned were hurt with knives rather than guns.[29] Despite all efforts to establish order, the usual problems continued as before—burn victims from fireworks and bystanders hurt by drunken revelers on September 16,[30] illicit sales of beer and pulque on December 12.[31]

The popular sectors made it clear that they liked their celebrations this way and that they would (literally) fight to keep them. An item in *Excelsior*, for example, expressed sadness, with perhaps an undercurrent of disbelief, at reports that order had prevailed on Independence Day: "A certain newspaper has stated that in the September 16 celebrations, there were no dagger thrusts, and no shots fired. If this is true, then this is not my city, for they have changed it!"[32] The message to authorities, in word and in deed, appears to have been clear: attempts to introduce order on September 16 or December 12, to change the traditional meanings of the dates, would be resisted.[33] Popular groups jealously protected their right to enjoy themselves on their own terms,[34] and Independence Day continued to be violent into the postwar period. In 1947, for example, six people were killed and forty-seven more were hurt, although in 1949 there was apparently less violent crime and fewer injuries, but thirty-four thefts were reported.

Order in the Revolutionary Festival

The new Revolution Day celebrations that developed in the 1920s and 1930s established a marked contrast to the disorderly conduct typical of Independence Day and of the Day of the Virgin. The new

"revolutionary" festival achieved this distinction through an orchestrated combination of self-discipline and social discipline. Displays
of sports prowess in particular distinguished November 20 from traditional popular revelry and provided a way to incorporate popular
groups into patriotic celebrations in an orderly—and thoroughly ordered—manner. Order was much commended by observers; even
minor disruptions during the parade were discussed at length.[35]
Whereas the celebrations of September 16 remained rowdy and violent into the 1940s, as noted above, Revolution Day began and remained a festival of and about order.[36]

The most significant of the themes that became associated with
the orderly commemoration of November 20 were the control, reform, and modernization of the Mexican military. The military in the
immediate postrevolutionary period was a national institution only
in name. In fact, it was made up of many armies characterized by
regional and personalistic, rather than national, loyalties.[37] By 1916
the Constitutionalist Army had grown to over 200,000 troops commanded by 50,000 officers, over 500 of whom claimed the rank of
general.[38] Beginning in 1916, Venustiano Carranza entrusted to his
closest lieutenants the crucial task of breaking local loyalties within
the military and forging a truly national institution, loyal above all to
the president.

The single most pressing political task faced by Mexican presidents as they established the postrevolutionary order in the 1920s
and 1930s was keeping the army (or armies) out of politics. Again
and again in the 1920s rebellious military units threatened the government. This conflict was acknowledged in the political rhetoric of
the day. In the presidential campaign of 1929, for example, José
Vasconcelos (the candidate for the Anti-Reelectionist Party), charging that the army was much too large for Mexico's real needs, called
for a sharp reduction in military expenditures.[39] Civil authorities regularly exhorted soldiers and their leaders to serve the nation and its
humble classes.[40]

Revolution Day parades after the mid-1920s became a public focal point for the attempts by Presidents Alvaro Obregón (1920–1924)
and Plutarco Elías Calles (1924–1928; de facto 1928–1934) to bring
the revolutionary armies under the control of the government and to
turn them into a modern, professional institution. By the late 1920s
an extensive military parade began to be the most important featured
event on November 20. Ever more extravagant ceremonies were held
annually at Balbuena, the military sports complex on the eastern edge

of the capital. At the center of these activities were rituals that symbolically established the preeminence of civilian authority and drew professions of loyalty to the new regime from military commanders and common soldiers alike.

The November 20 ceremonies frequently highlighted the new military order through the display of competitive sports and athletic events. Military readiness was linked with orderly physical training and discipline: "the military sports field is a place where commanders, officers, and troops . . . will continue to educate themselves physically."[41] Prominently featured in the parades were floats depicting the sports practiced by the army: polo, fencing, swimming, soccer, and baseball, among others.[42] American football was introduced into the celebrations with much fanfare in 1930,[43] and sports that were perceived as modern and Western thus led the way.[44] Expressions of enthusiasm for sports reinforced their growing influence in military life in the 1920s in which fields, gymnasiums, and nationwide army programs provided troops with physical exercise and recreation.[45]

In an intriguing evolution, traditional military exercises and sports events were increasingly mixed on November 20. In 1929, for example, the celebrations at Balbuena featured gymnastics performed by armed troops from the First and Second Regiments of the Presidential Guard followed by more gymnastics by seven hundred female workers from the military munitions factories.[46] In the center of the stadium, directly in front of the presidential platform, stood various companies of the army in sports uniforms, "giving a note of color and a harmonious teamsmanship" to the event.[47]

In such cases, the substitution of sports counterparts for uniforms and traditional military drills is striking. In its English-language pages, *Excélsior* noted: "Instead of bright uniforms and flashing bayonets, the paraders were composed almost in their entirety by men and women representing almost every branch of sport and were dressed in the costume of the sport in question. . . . The demonstration included several thousand members of the police force, soldiers, and firemen, but all wearing the clothes of some branch of sport."[48] Cavorting military sportsmen were important enough to be reviewed by the Mexican president. In the sports ceremonies at Balbuena, the president commemorated the achievements of high-ranking military officers. In 1929 he also judged the November 20 floats. In 1935 displays of athleticism were used to honor generals, commanders, and soldiers for twenty years' service by President Lázaro Cárdenas. The November 20 sports ceremonies united military and civilian entities in the name of the Revolution, emphasizing the military's readiness to defend the postrevolutionary order as symbolized by the president.[49]

Due to the overwhelming popularity of the sports and athletic events, these official displays and competitions became the major draw of the November 20 celebrations. Athletes entered from all walks of life, and, as one observer noted wryly, "of the athletic parades, we must say that the participants are athletes in name only, including as they do the lanky, the short, and the fat, in fact, anyone who judges himself sufficiently agile."[50] After the 1920s, sports were the principal features of both military and civilian events. Trends in military and civilian ceremonies reinforced one another and underlined the importance of youth: the military was a school to thousands of Mexican young people; as in the schools, sports were a method of inculcating the new values of work, hygiene, punctuality, and the like.[51]

An orderly commemoration of November 20, the Zócalo, Mexico City. *Archivo General de la Nación*

Annual "revolutionary games" to begin on November 20 were established in 1930. Lázaro Cárdenas, then president of the Partido Nacional Revolucionario (PNR), announced this new element of the November 20 celebrations in an advertisement in *Excélsior*: "The president of the PNR invites the residents of the Federal District to attend the parade of the athletes who will participate in the First Games of the Revolution, organized by this party to commemorate the glorious date of the initiation of the Liberating Movement." The parade was to start by the statue of Carlos IV and proceed to the central Zócalo, where athletes competing in the games would swear an oath combining a pledge of allegiance and a pledge of sporting creed; the president of Mexico would preside.[52] After 1930 and the initiation of the revolutionary games, the PNR became an increasingly visible host of the November 20 festivities. In 1932, for example, two huge flags of the PNR followed the squadrons of motorcycles in the parade.[53] The party's official paper, *El Nacional,* devoted much of its coverage on November 20 to PNR-sponsored events and published commemorative editions. At the same time that party involvement increased, the parades remained a popular draw: *La Palabra* noted in 1934 that the 60,000 athletes marching in the parade were both "official" and "spontaneous" participants.[54]

What was the meaning of the increasing presence of sports in the official celebration of Revolution Day? I suggest that sports events were adopted primarily because they helped to impose order on Revolution Day celebrations. Sports rituals accomplished this end through their recognized capacity to mimic, model, and mediate real violence, perhaps releasing potential urges to violence in the process.[55] As Mona Ozouf has argued for the French case, "The enactment of mimed violence . . . is a way of bringing to an end violence that is acted out."[56]

Symbolically, and practically too in some cases, sports competitions channeled conflict at the community, regional, and national levels into activities that were both orderly and constructive. The sports parades reinforced notions of the impropriety of real violence in public places: sports events on November 20 provided for both marchers and spectators the liberty of physical movement in open space but also established an atmosphere of control, constraint, and discipline.[57]

At the national level too, sports activities on the occasion of November 20 constituted a theater of power in which order was established. The Revolution Day sports parade, for example, reduced the likelihood of what most Mexican elites, policymakers included, saw as the largest social threat to the new regime: the resurgence of popular rebellion. As Marjorie Becker notes, "the specter of the popular armies was to haunt the Constitutionalist victors for two decades."[58] Even if not a popular host, the revolutionary armies did contain within their ranks by far the largest organized groups of persons from the popular classes in Mexico.

Given the recent experience of a civil war that had been colored at times by class and ethnic resentments, organized sports parades in commemoration of the Revolution—violence under firm control and subservient to the new state—removed in symbolic terms the threat of another uprising of a disorganized mass of soldiers, most of whom came from humble social backgrounds.[59] Part of their ability to play this role stemmed from the urban nature of the parade grounds; the urban arena of the main celebratory events in Mexico City seemed to exclude the sort of agrarian tensions and movements that had fueled the Revolution in certain regions.

In various ways, then, sports events on November 20 constituted well-regulated violence, one of the aims of which was to prevent social violence. As in Revolutionary France, "the festival play[ed] at violence in order to contain it all the better."[60] In addition to the various functions outlined above, sports provided a way to incorporate popular groups in patriotic celebrations in a thoroughly orderly—in fact, thoroughly ordered—manner.

Other practices served to strengthen the orderliness of the Revolution Day events imposed by the new sports activities.[61] Effective attempts were made at crowd control: in 1932, for example, soldiers were assigned to line the parade route from the Plaza de Carlos IV to the Zócalo to "keep people out of the street and from bringing disorder to the athletic parade."[62] The November 20 celebrations took place during daytime hours, a sure way to reduce the incidence of drinking and the rowdiness associated with the cover of night. And the Revolution Day events prominently featured women and children, which imposed a very effective, if indirect, form of social control. All of these characteristics facilitated order and underlined its importance.

In contrast to their central place on Revolution Day, sports never came to dominate the commemoration of September 16. On Independence Day, the official parade remained a formal military affair. The focus of the September 16 parade was increasingly on the modernization and "Westernization" of the Mexican military's training and its newly acquired hardware.[63] There was order, certainly; but this parade was not designed to incorporate the orderly celebration of popular groups.

Conclusion

Revolution Day's focus on order—with displays of sports prowess at its center—set it apart from the traditional popular revelry of September 16 and December 12. Order served many important purposes, reinforcing a particular type of political consolidation and promoting a certain direction for social change. In fact, one of the most important accomplishments of the November 20 celebrations was to present the two themes of postrevolutionary political consolidation and "revolutionary" social change as mutually reinforcing pathways.

Why was Revolution Day so successful in attracting celebrants young and old, middle-class and poor? In a significant departure from the general nineteenth-century trend toward separate celebrations for popular and elite social groups, Revolution Day brought people together across class lines—perhaps the most telling characteristic of this revolutionary festival. Herein lay a new vision of Mexican development directly related to the experience of the recent civil war, with its popular mobilization, that had so thoroughly shaken notions of Mexican reality.

Whereas on September 16 and December 12 popular merrymaking had taken place alongside or, more frequently, at some distance from official observances, on November 20 the popular festival was part and parcel of the official recognition of the anniversary. And the way in which these groups were brought together was very significant. For on Revolution Day, social groups attended the parades and rubbed shoulders not as classes but as corporate groups—soldiers, women, and youth. In this incorporation, sports activities proved particularly useful in symbolically leveling the social playing field and establishing new grounds for constructive competition.

This novel use of public space to symbolically transcend class (and other divisive issues such as region and ethnicity) on Revolution Day was both a product of order and actively promoted orderly conduct.[64] The erasing of the distinction between "high" and "popular" forms of celebration encouraged conformity by all participants to new behavioral conventions. Orderly behavior in the public arena could in turn serve as a basis for the resolution of conflicts that had earlier made political consolidation impossible during a decade of civil war after 1910.

Notes

1. Various newspapers made estimates. On November 19, 1934, for example, *La Palabra* estimated 60,000.

2. This ratio is drawn from the U.S. case. See Mary Ryan, "The American Parade: Representations of the Nineteenth-Century Social Order," in Lynn Hunt, ed., *The New Cultural History* (Berkeley: University of California Press, 1989), 133.

3. Organized parades, and particularly parade routes, must not in all cases be orderly. See Ryan, "The American Parade," 134.

4. That December 12 was a "patriotic" celebration as well as a religious and ethnic one is clear from newspaper accounts: see, for example, *Excélsior*, December 12, 1921, December 12, 1926 ("Catholics have received instructions to adorn the facades of their houses with the national colors so that all the city will appear festive as on the national holidays"), and December 13, 1940 (the Virgin is "a symbol, now not only religious, but also patriotic").

5. Eugen Weber, *Peasants into Frenchmen: The Modernization of Rural France, 1870–1914* (Stanford, CA: Stanford University Press, 1976), 383. See Charles Rearick, "Festivals in Modern France: The Experience of the Third Republic," *Journal of Contemporary History* 12, no. 1 (January 1977): 437.

6. See my comments on conflict among rival labor organizations in 1935 in David E. Lorey, "The Revolutionary Festival in Mexico: November 20 Celebrations in the 1920s and 1930s," *The Americas* (July 1997). I owe the notion of collective disorder to a student, Maythé Rueda.

7. *Excélsior*, September 17, 1922. Elites also had a good time, however. A cartoon from 1926 has an upper-class woman confronting her husband the morning after: "Last night you didn't get home until early in the morning, and you were falling-down drunk." The man replies: "I suffered a lapse: I couldn't remember whether you said 'Have three drinks and come home at 10, or have 10 drinks and come home at three.' " *Excélsior*, November 17, 1926.

8. See typical photographs in *El Demócrata*, September 17, 1924.

9. *Excélsior* on September 18 reported 500,000 for 1938.

10. Quote is from *Excélsior*, September 16, 1932. Notices of disorder abound. See, for example, *Excélsior*, September 16, 1921 (assault, burglaries), September 17, 1921 (shooting), September 15, 1926 (activities of Red Cross), September 16, 1926 (people hurt), September 17, 1927, September 16, 1935, and September 18, 1935 (robberies, flags stolen, thefts, delinquency), September 16, 1928 (list of robberies, victims of patriotic acts).

11. *El Demócrata*, September 17, 1923.

12. *Excélsior*, September 17, 1926, September 17, 1923, September 17, 1927.

13. See photographs in *Excélsior*, September 15, 1934. On the Feria de la Luz, see *El Demócrata*, September 16, 1924. On the Porfirian celebration, see William H. Beezley, "Amending Memories: The Nimble Mnemonics of Nineteenth-Century Celebrations of Independence," unpublished paper presented to the seminar at the Latin American Centre, Cambridge University, 1995.

14. See cartoons and jokes about Independence Day celebrations (fights, police, pinching of women, "metropolis as insane asylum," and alcohol use) in *Excélsior*, September 16, 1921, September 17, 1922, and September 16, 1923. For a parallel nighttime influence, see Roy Rosenzweig, *Eight Hours for What We Will: Workers and Leisure in an Industrial City, 1870–1920* (New York: Cambridge University Press, 1985), 72. For women in parades in the United States, see Ryan, "The American Parade," 147–48.

15. *El Demócrata*, September 17, 1924.

16. *Excélsior*, September 18, 1936.

17. *Excélsior*, December 13, 1925, and December 13, 1933, report 200,000.

18. Ibid., December 12, 1921.

19. Ibid., December 13, 1923. Many accounts emphasize the mixing of "all social classes" in the December 12 celebrations: see, for example, ibid., December 13, 1926.

20. Ibid., December 13, 1924 (protest of food and oil prices).

21. Ibid., December 13, 1933.

22. See, for example, ibid., September 15, 1931, September 15, 1932, and September 17, 1927; and *El Demócrata*, September 15, 1924.

23. *Excélsior*, September 15, 1927. On controlling disorder during the 1921 centennial celebrations, see Chapter Nine, this volume.

24. Typical examples are *Excélsior,* September 15, 1934, September 15, 1935, September 15, 1936, and September 15, 1937. From cartoons, it appears that women expected to be included in these evening outings.

25. *Excélsior*, December 12, 1926.

26. Ibid., December 13, 1926.

27. Ibid., December 13, 1933, December 13, 1935 (wounded with rocks, knives, and guns, robberies); December 13, 1930, December 13, 1936, December 13, 1937, December 13, 1938 (order, less drunkenness).

28. See Rosenzweig, *Eight Hours for What We Will*, 71.

29. *Excélsior*, September 17, 1922, September 17, 1923. In Worcester, bonfires replaced fireworks; accidents decreased, but fires increased. See Rosenzweig, *Eight Hours for What We Will*, 163.

30. *Excélsior*, September 17, 1923.

31. Ibid., December 13, 1930.

32. Ibid., September 19, 1935.

33. For notices of attempts to bring celebrants under control and introduce order to the celebrations, see, for example, *Excélsior*, September 16, 1926 (police inspector general outlaws firearms from September 15 through September 17), and September 15, 1928 (cantinas closed, firearms prohibited, fireworks banned).

34. See Rosenzweig, *Eight Hours for What We Will*, 5.

35. *La Palabra*, November 19, 1934.

36. For rowdiness on September 16 into the 1940s, see, for example, *Excélsior*, September 18, 1940, September 18, 1945, September 18, 1947, and September 18, 1949. For an early comment about order on November 20, see Letter to Secretary of State from the Guadalajara consulate in 1917 (National Archives, Washington, DC, Record Group 59: 812.415).

37. See Dudley Ankerson, *Agrarian Warlord: Saturnino Cedillo and the Mexican Revolution in San Luis Potosí* (DeKalb: Northern Illinois University Press, 1984), 195.

38. Edwin Liewen, *Mexican Militarism: The Political Rise and Fall of the Revolutionary Army, 1910–1940* (Westport, CT: Greenwood Press, 1968), 45.

39. Ibid., 106.

40. Ibid., 95, 120, and passim.

41. *Excélsior*, November 21, 1929.

42. *La Prensa*, November 20, 1929.

43. *Excélsior*, November 15, 1930.

44. On the changing relative prestige of sports, see John W. Loy, Barry D. McPherson, and Gerald Kenyon, *Sport and Social Systems: A Guide to the Analysis, Problems, and Literature* (Reading, MA: Addison-Wesley, 1978), 365.

45. Liewen, *Mexican Militarism*, 95.

46. *La Prensa,* November 20, 1929.

47. Ibid., November 21, 1929.

48. *Excélsior*, November 21, 1931.

49. It was not only on November 20 that the role of the military in Mexican society was recast in ritual events. A fascinating example of the theme of military

action in constructive service to the new state is apparent in the celebration of Arbor Day (February 20), which by the early 1930s featured military leaders planting trees in national antideforestation campaigns. See, for example, *Excélsior*, February 14, 1932; in this year the secretary of war ordered commanders of military operations throughout the country to "organize festivals in homage to trees and the planting of as many trees as possible." On February 15, 1935, *Excélsior* reported that "troops will be responsible for the care of the trees, thus fulfilling the intentions of the President of the Republic."

50. In a similar vein, the same commentator also opined that the athletic parades benefited only the sellers of "character costumes": *La Palabra*, November 19, 1933.

51. For this connection between military and modern values and practices in the French case, see Weber, *Peasants into Frenchmen*, 299ff.

52. *Excélsior*, November 20, 1930.

53. *La Prensa*, November 20, 1932.

54. *La Palabra*, November 19, 1934.

55. On sports and violence, see Loy et al., *Sport and Social Systems*, 287, 288, 387; and Paul Connerton, *How Societies Remember* (New York: Cambridge University Press, 1989), 49. See also Thomas G. Sanders, "The Social Functions of *Futebol*," in *Brazilian Mosaic: Portraits of a Diverse People and Culture,* ed. G. Harvey Summ (Wilmington, DE: Scholarly Resources, 1995), 159–62.

56. Mona Ozouf, *Festivals and the French Revolution*, trans. Alan Sheridan (Cambridge, MA: Harvard University Press, 1988), 103.

57. See ibid., 27–28.

58. Marjorie Becker, *Setting the Virgin on Fire: Lázaro Cárdenas, Michoacán Peasants, and the Redemption of the Mexican Revolution* (Berkeley: University of California Press, 1995), 5.

59. See Kevin J. Middlebrook, *The Paradox of Revolution: Labor, the State, and Authoritarianism in Mexico* (Baltimore: Johns Hopkins University Press, 1995), 154–55; and George L. Mosse, *The Nationalization of the Masses: Political Symbolism and Mass Movements in Germany from the Napoleonic Wars through the Third Reich* (New York: Howard Fertig, 1975), 82.

60. Ozouf, *Festivals*, 103.

61. On contrasts between "respectable" and "rowdy" parades in the United States, see Susan G. Davis, *Parades and Power: Street Theater in Nineteenth-Century Philadelphia* (Philadelphia: Temple University Press, 1986), 159–61; and David Glassberg, *American Historical Pageantry: The Uses of Tradition in the Early Twentieth Century* (Chapel Hill: University of North Carolina Press, 1990), 25, 30. See Ryan, "The American Parade," 152. There is a parallel with the Safe and Sane July Fourth movement in the United States: see Rosenzweig, *Eight Hours for What We Will*, chapter 6; and Davis, *Parades and Power*, 169. On replacements of traditional with official fests, see Weber, *Peasants into Frenchmen*, chapter 21, esp. 387.

62. *La Prensa*, November 20, 1932.

63. See, for example, *Excélsior*, September 18, 1943, and September 16, 1944. On the importance of the modernity of the armed forces, see ibid., September 18, 1944.

64. See Rosenzweig, *Eight Hours for What We Will*, 66.

Suggested Readings

Anderson, Benedict. *Imagined Communities: Reflections on the Origin and Spread of Nationalism*. New York: Verso, 1991. Rev. ed.

Beezley, William H., Cheryl English Martin, and William E. French, eds. *Rituals of Rule, Rituals of Resistance: Public Celebrations and Popular Culture in Mexico*. Wilmington, DE: Scholarly Resources, 1994.

Bodnar, John. *Remaking America: Public Memory, Commemoration, and Patriotism in the Twentieth Century*. Princeton: Princeton University Press, 1991.

Bryson, Lucy, and Clem McCartney. *Clashing Symbols?: A Report on the Use of Flags, Anthems, and Other National Symbols in Northern Ireland*. Belfast: The Queen's University of Belfast, 1994.

Duncan, Robert H. "Political Legitimation and Maximilian's Second Empire in Mexico, 1864–1867." *Mexican Studies/Estudios Mexicanos* 12, no. 1 (Winter 1996): 27–66.

Hobsbawm, Eric, and Terence Ranger, eds. *The Invention of Tradition*. New York: Cambridge University Press, 1983.

Ozouf, Mona. *Festivals and the French Revolution*. Trans. by Alan Sheridan. Cambridge, MA: Harvard University Press, 1988.

Pani, Erika. "El proyecto de Estado de Maximiliano a través de la vida cortesana y del ceremonial público." *Historia Mexicana* 45, no. 2 (October–December 1995): 423–61.

Rearick, Charles. "Festivals in Modern France: The Experience of the Third Republic." *Journal of Contemporary History* 12, no. 1 (January 1977).

Ryan, Mary. "The American Parade: Representations of the Nineteenth-Century Social Order," in Lynn Hunt, ed., *The New Cultural History*. Berkeley: University of California Press, 1989.

Salazar Mendoza, Flor de María. *La Junta Patriótica de la Capital Potosina: Un espacio político de los Liberales (1873–1882)*. San Luis Potosí, Mexico: Instituto de Cultura de San Luis Potosí, 1999.

Waldstreicher, David. *In the Midst of Perpetual Fetes: The Making of American Nationalism, 1776–1820*. Chapel Hill: University of North Carolina Press, 1991.

About the Editors and Contributors

Editors

WILLIAM H. BEEZLEY, one of the pioneers in the United States of the cultural history of Mexico, wrote essays in the early 1980s that examined Mexican popular culture and political humor. In 1987, Beezley published *Judas at the Jockey Club*, which examined the efforts at modernization during the regime of Porfirio Díaz. A professor of history at the University of Arizona, he received his Ph.D. from the University of Nebraska. With Colin MacLachlan, Beezley has written *El Gran Pueblo: A History of Greater Mexico* (1994) and *Latin America: The Peoples and Their History* (2000). He and Michael C. Meyer have just completed *The Oxford History of Mexico* (2000).

DAVID E. LOREY received his B.A. in history from Wesleyan University and his M.A. and Ph.D. in Latin American history from UCLA. From 1990 to 1997, he was Coordinator of the Program on Mexico and Visiting Professor of History at UCLA. Since 1997, Lorey has served as Program Officer for U.S.-Latin American Relations at the William and Flora Hewlett Foundation in Menlo Park, California. His publications include *The University System and Economic Development in Mexico since 1929* (1993); and *The U.S.-Mexican Border in the Twentieth Century* (1999).

Contributors

ISABEL FERNÁNDEZ TEJEDO is an independent scholar in Mexico City, where she is a member of the Area de Investigaciones Históricas y Sociales.

CARMEN NAVA NAVA is teaching at the Universidad Autónoma Metropolitana-Xochimilco. Well known for her research on the Calles era, she is a member of the Area de Investigaciones Históricas y Sociales.

MICHAEL COSTELOE, professor of history at the University of Bristol, England, is a member of the Academia Mexicana de la Historia.

SERGIO ALEJANDRO CAÑEDO GAMBOA completed the study included in this volume as part of his Master's thesis at the Universidad Iberoamericana, Mexico City. He is currently a Ph.D. candidate at the University of California-San Diego.

VERÓNICA ZÁRATE TOSCANO teaches at the Instituto Mora and is a researcher in the Consejo Nacional de Ciencia y Tecnología.

JAVIER RODRÍGUEZ PIÑA is a professor of sociology at the Universidad Autónoma Metropolitana-Azcapotzalco.

NORA PÉREZ-RAYÓN E. is a member of the Department of Sociology at the Universidad Autónoma Metropolitana-Azcapotzalco.

MAURICIO TENORIO TRILLO teaches history at the University of Texas.

ELAINE C. LACY is an associate professor of Latin American history at the University of South Carolina, Aiken. Her research has focused on Mexican literacy campaigns between the 1920s and 1940s, Mexican popular culture in the 1920s, and Hispanics in the southeastern United States. Currently she is completing a volume on the 1921 commemoration of Mexico's Independence.

Index

Latin American Silhouettes
Studies in History and Culture

William H. Beezley and
Judith Ewell
Editors

Volumes Published

Silvia Marina Arrom and Servando Ortoll, eds., *Riots in the Cities: Popular Politics and the Urban Poor in Latin America, 1765–1910* (1996). Cloth ISBN 0-8420-2580-4   Paper ISBN 0-8420-2581-2

Roderic Ai Camp, ed., *Polling for Democracy: Public Opinion and Political Liberalization in Mexico* (1996). ISBN 0-8420-2583-9

Brian Loveman and Thomas M. Davies, Jr., eds., *The Politics of Antipolitics: The Military in Latin America*, 3d ed., revised and updated (1996). Cloth ISBN 0-8420-2609-6   Paper ISBN 0-8420-2611-8

Joseph S. Tulchin, Andrés Serbín, and Rafael Hernández, eds., *Cuba and the Caribbean: Regional Issues and Trends in the Post-Cold War Era* (1997). ISBN 0-8420-2652-5

Thomas W. Walker, ed., *Nicaragua without Illusions: Regime Transition and Structural Adjustment in the 1990s* (1997). Cloth ISBN 0-8420-2578-2   Paper ISBN 0-8420-2579-0

Dianne Walta Hart, *Undocumented in L.A.: An Immigrant's Story* (1997). Cloth ISBN 0-8420-2648-7   Paper ISBN 0-8420-2649-5

Jaime E. Rodríguez O. and Kathryn Vincent, eds., *Myths, Misdeeds, and Misunderstandings: The Roots of Conflict in U.S.-Mexican Relations* (1997). ISBN 0-8420-2662-2

Jaime E. Rodríguez O. and Kathryn Vincent, eds., *Common Border, Uncommon Paths: Race, Culture, and National Identity in U.S.-Mexican Relations* (1997). ISBN 0-8420-2673-8

William H. Beezley and Judith Ewell, eds., *The Human Tradition in Modern Latin America* (1997). Cloth ISBN 0-8420-2612-6   Paper ISBN 0-8420-2613-4

Donald F. Stevens, ed., *Based on a True Story: Latin American History at the Movies* (1997). Cloth ISBN 0-8420-2582-0   Paper ISBN 0-8420-2781-5

Jaime E. Rodríguez O., ed., *The Origins of Mexican National Politics, 1808–1847* (1997). Paper ISBN 0-8420-2723-8

Che Guevara, *Guerrilla Warfare*, with revised and updated introduction and case studies by Brian Loveman and Thomas M. Davies, Jr., 3d ed. (1997). Cloth ISBN 0-8420-2677-0   Paper ISBN 0-8420-2678-9

Adrian A. Bantjes, *As If Jesus Walked on Earth: Cardenismo, Sonora, and the Mexican Revolution* (1998; rev. ed., 2000). Cloth ISBN 0-8420-2653-3   Paper ISBN 0-8420-2751-3

Henry A. Dietz and Gil Shidlo, eds., *Urban Elections in Democratic Latin America* (1998). Cloth ISBN 0-8420-2627-4   Paper ISBN 0-8420-2628-2

A. Kim Clark, *The Redemptive Work: Railway and Nation in Ecuador, 1895–1930* (1998). ISBN 0-8420-2674-6

Joseph S. Tulchin, ed., with Allison M. Garland, *Argentina: The Challenges of Modernization* (1998). ISBN 0-8420-2721-1

Louis A. Pérez, Jr., ed., *Impressions of Cuba in the Nineteenth Century: The Travel Diary of Joseph J. Dimock* (1998). Cloth ISBN 0-8420-2657-6   Paper ISBN 0-8420-2658-4

June E. Hahner, ed., *Women through Women's Eyes: Latin American Women in Nineteenth-Century Travel Accounts* (1998). Cloth ISBN 0-8420-2633-9   Paper ISBN 0-8420-2634-7

James P. Brennan, ed., *Peronism and Argentina* (1998). ISBN 0-8420-2706-8

John Mason Hart, ed., *Border Crossings: Mexican and Mexican-American Workers*

(1998). Cloth ISBN 0-8420-2716-5
Paper ISBN 0-8420-2717-3

Brian Loveman, *For* la Patria: *Politics and the Armed Forces in Latin America* (1999). Cloth ISBN 0-8420-2772-6
Paper ISBN 0-8420-2773-4

Guy P. C. Thomson, with David G. LaFrance, *Patriotism, Politics, and Popular Liberalism in Nineteenth-Century Mexico: Juan Francisco Lucas and the Puebla Sierra* (1999).
ISBN 0-8420-2683-5

Robert Woodmansee Herr, in collaboration with Richard Herr, *An American Family in the Mexican Revolution* (1999).
ISBN 0-8420-2724-6

Juan Pedro Viqueira Albán, trans. Sonya Lipsett-Rivera and Sergio Rivera Ayala, *Propriety and Permissiveness in Bourbon Mexico* (1999).
Cloth ISBN 0-8420-2466-2
Paper ISBN 0-8420-2467-0

Stephen R. Niblo, *Mexico in the 1940s: Modernity, Politics, and Corruption* (1999).
Cloth ISBN 0-8420-2794-7
Paper (2001) ISBN 0-8420-2795-5

David E. Lorey, *The U.S.-Mexican Border in the Twentieth Century* (1999).
Cloth ISBN 0-8420-2755-6
Paper ISBN 0-8420-2756-4

Joanne Hershfield and David R. Maciel, eds., *Mexico's Cinema: A Century of Films and Filmmakers* (2000). Cloth ISBN 0-8420-2681-9 Paper ISBN 0-8420-2682-7

Peter V. N. Henderson, *In the Absence of Don Porfirio: Francisco León de la Barra and the Mexican Revolution* (2000).
ISBN 0-8420-2774-2

Mark T. Gilderhus, *The Second Century: U.S.-Latin American Relations since 1889* (2000). Cloth ISBN 0-8420-2413-1
Paper ISBN 0-8420-2414-X

Catherine Moses, *Real Life in Castro's Cuba* (2000). Cloth ISBN 0-8420-2836-6
Paper ISBN 0-8420-2837-4

K. Lynn Stoner, ed./comp., with Luis Hipólito Serrano Pérez, *Cuban and Cuban-American Women: An Annotated Bibliography* (2000).
ISBN 0-8420-2643-6

Thomas D. Schoonover, *The French in Central America: Culture and Commerce, 1820–1930* (2000).
ISBN 0-8420-2792-0

Enrique C. Ochoa, *Feeding Mexico: The Political Uses of Food since 1910* (2000). ISBN 0-8420-2812-9

Thomas W. Walker and Ariel C. Armony, eds., *Repression, Resistance, and Democratic Transition in Central America* (2000). Cloth ISBN 0-8420-2766-1   Paper ISBN 0-8420-2768-8

William H. Beezley and David E. Lorey, eds., *¡Viva México! ¡Viva la Independencia! Celebrations of September 16* (2001).
Cloth ISBN 0-8420-2914-1
Paper ISBN 0-8420-2915-X

Jeffrey M. Pilcher, *Cantinflas and the Chaos of Mexican Modernity* (2001).
Cloth ISBN 0-8420-2769-6
Paper ISBN 0-8420-2771-8

Victor M. Uribe-Uran, ed., *State and Society in Spanish America during the Age of Revolution* (2001). Cloth ISBN 0-8420-2873-0   Paper ISBN 0-8420-2874-9

Andrew Grant Wood, *Revolution in the Street: Women, Workers, and Urban Protest in Veracruz, 1870–1927* (2001).
ISBN 0-8420-2879-X

Charles Bergquist, Ricardo Peñaranda, and Gonzalo Sánchez G., eds., *Violence in Colombia, 1990–2000: Waging War and Negotiating Peace* (2001).
Cloth ISBN 0-8420-2869-2
Paper ISBN 0-8420-2870-6

William Schell, Jr., *Integral Outsiders: The American Colony in Mexico City, 1876–1911* (2001). ISBN 0-8420-2838-2

John Lynch, *Argentine Caudillo: Juan Manuel de Rosas* (2001).
Cloth ISBN 0-8420-2897-8
Paper ISBN 0-8420-2828-6

Samuel Basch, M.D., ed. and trans. Fred D. Ullman, *Recollections of Mexico: The Last Ten Months of Maximilian's Empire* (2001). ISBN 0-8420-2962-1